A STUDY OF THE USSR AND COMMUNISM: AN HISTORICAL APPROACH

"American youth must examine the framework of its freedom,
look around the world it has inherited,
become acquainted with conflicting ideologies
and then make knowledgeable comparisons....
Our loyalties must be rooted in knowledge and understanding,
not in ignorance and prejudice.... The more
American citizens know about communistic doctrine and purposes,
as well as the advantages
offered by our own democratic government,
the deeper will be the loyalties to our government
and to its traditions and ideals."

—Joint Committee of the National Education Association
and The American Legion

"We encourage and support schools and colleges
in the presentation of adequate instruction
in the history, doctrines, objectives, and techniques of communism,
thereby helping to instill
a greater appreciation of democracy and freedom under law,
and the will to preserve that freedom."

—Resolution of the House of Delegates,
American Bar Association

A STUDY OF THE USSR AND COMMUNISM:

AN HISTORICAL APPROACH

by

Alfred J. Rieber
Associate Professor of History,
Northwestern University

and

Robert C. Nelson
Staff Correspondent,
The Christian Science Monitor

Classroom Advisers,
Norman J. Kirby, John Huizinga, and Ronald Miller
Maine Township High School
Park Ridge, Illinois

SCOTT, FORESMAN AND COMPANY
Chicago · Atlanta · Dallas · Palo Alto · Fair Lawn, N.J.

AUTHORS' INTRODUCTION

A full understanding of the challenge of communism to the free world can best be gained through a study of history. The Communist threat must be assessed in the light of the Soviet power supporting it, which in turn requires an examination of the U.S.S.R. of today as derived from Russian history.

Because this problem is the most formidable one facing us, it is imperative that we have more than a superficial knowledge of the subject. Only through an analysis of past events in their historical context can the full measure of the present be taken.

Winston Churchill once labeled the Soviet Union "an enigma," but that is no longer true. More than a decade of Western scholarship has made available a wealth of relevant data and interpretative material. Based upon the most important of these studies, this book seeks to present an objective analysis of the origins, growth, and present state of the U.S.S.R. and communism.

A.J.R., R.C.N.

Alfred J. Rieber
is associate professor of history at Northwestern University;
Ph.D., Columbia University; Certificate, Russian Institute, Columbia University;
author of
Stalin and the French Communist Party, 1941-47;
United States exchange student, Moscow University, 1958-1959.

Robert C. Nelson
is a staff correspondent of *The Christian Science Monitor;*
winner of the Sigma Delta Chi national prize for reporting in 1961;
graduate of Northwestern University and Columbia University,
where he majored in international affairs.

design:
Mary Ann Dorr

maps and charts:
Paul Hazelrigg

TO THE TEACHER

The structure of this book enables it to be used in a variety of ways. Taken as a whole it may serve as a resource unit for a concentrated four- to six-weeks' study. It may also be used in whole or in part to supplement courses in U.S. history, world history, geography, civics, economics, or problems of democracy.

A geographic background and the history of Russia to 1917 is presented in the first two chapters, and the development of Communist ideology from the Russian Revolution to the present day is treated in chapter three. This part of the book is important to the fullest understanding of the topical chapters that follow.

These chapters deal first with communism within the U.S.S.R. — in politics and government, economics, and cultural and intellectual life, respectively. The final two chapters focus on international communism, including the response of the United States.

Each of the last five topical chapters is also organized chronologically, thus providing considerable flexibility in use, yet constituting an organic whole.

TABLE OF CONTENTS

Elliott Erwitt: MAGNUM

CHAPTER 1

THE USSR: LAND AND PEOPLE

*The accidents of geography —
a vast land with rich
but widely scattered resources,
a harsh climate, few warm-water outlets
or natural barriers —
have helped shape Russian history.*

The natural and human resources of a country — in sum, its geography — constitute a powerful factor in the history of a people and their land. Although geography alone does not determine everything in the historical development of a country, it does pose certain problems to be overcome if a people are to survive and flourish. To a certain extent, the choice of means to overcome these obstacles remains with the people. But no matter what political institutions or economic way of life they choose or may be forced to choose, the challenge of their environment changes little.

THE VAST EURASIAN PLAIN

The first thing to keep in mind is the enormous size of the Soviet Union, which covers one sixth of the earth's surface. The vast Eurasian plain covers most of the land area of the country. It forms

Brian Brake: MAGNUM

More than 5 million people live in Moscow, the capital and political center of the
U.S.S.R. All battle a common enemy — severe winter weather. On the opposite page:
A part of the vast taiga, the most extensive evergreen forest in the world.

the stage for the unfinished play of Russian history. Stretching
from Poland on the west to the Yenisei River on the east, this great
Eurasian plain is the largest single plain in the world.

Only the Ural Mountains, which have conveniently served
geographers as a natural dividing line between European and
Asiatic Russia, bisect this immense flatness, but these mountains
have never served as a barrier to trade, colonization, or conquest,
nor have they ever been a significant factor in climatic changes.

The Eurasian plain looks very much like a vast amphitheater
facing north, ringed as it is on the south, southwest, and east by
chains of mountains. Only on the west, facing Europe, is there no
natural frontier. This has always caused serious problems of defense for the people in the western part of the plain. It also has
offered them the possibility of expanding in that direction against
weaker neighbors. In either case, the open way to the west has
always posed, and poses even today, a strategic as well as a geographic problem for the people of western Russia.

Rarely have the frontiers in this region been stabilized for long
periods of time. Even within the last half century, the western
frontiers of Russia have been altered at least five times.

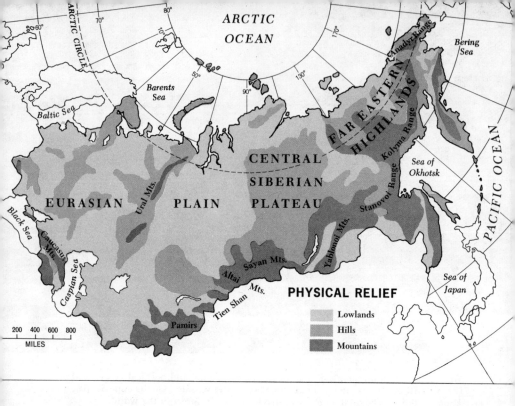

For certain periods of time, such as the war years 1914-1921 and 1939-1945, the frontier lines were in a state of flux and the area was the scene of large-scale fighting. It appears natural, then, that any government which controls western Russia will keep a wary eye cocked on the western frontier. To most Russians, the enemy has always come from the west. When a young Soviet student recently took a visiting American scholar to the still visible trenches outside Moscow and pointed west saying, "They came as usual from there," the problem became vividly clear.

Because the great plain constitutes a natural geographic unit, the tendency in the past has been for a single government to seek control of the entire area. Such governments have attempted to subject all other powers in the area to one absolute authority. Therefore, the entire history of the plain can be summarized as a struggle for political supremacy. A record of strife and war has been the result. Thus it is not surprising that one of the first important short-range aims of the Communist party in 1917, after it had taken power (in the western part of the plain), was to subdue the rest of the plain before it moved to spread its power elsewhere.

CLIMATE

The size of the Eurasian plain, together with its location, also influences its climate. Climate, in turn affects the entire life cycle of the people, their customs, the raising of food, and their industrial growth.

The climate of the plain is mostly continental. That is, the climate is characterized by great extremes of temperature in summer and winter, by short spring and fall seasons, and by relatively small rainfall and low humidity.

The immense east-west stretch of Russia lies far from any body of water which might moderate the climate. Most of the country is in more northerly latitudes than the United States. The city of Leningrad is situated on the 60th parallel, the line which also touches the southern tip of Greenland. The Russian city of Archangel is less than two hundred miles south of the Arctic Circle.

Russian winters are severe and long, but they are somewhat less severe in western Russia than in bleak Siberia deep in the hinterland. Russian winters also are majestically serene. A strange stillness and a dry crispness fill the clear atmosphere, helping to make the low temperatures endurable.

These winters, however, can suddenly become savage. For example, temporary thaws, especially in the west, can unleash surging floods which have the volume to inundate whole cities. Russians still warn foreigners not to wander too far on foot into the countryside in winter, even on the clearest day, because, without warning, a destructive ground blizzard — often fatal to men and animals — may sweep across the plain, and fierce arctic winds, blowing unimpeded from the North Pole across the breadth of Russia, can drive all but the hardiest from the streets.

Russians fortify themselves against the winter with as much determination as though they were preparing for a military campaign. Heavy double doors and windows with thick drapes are the rule, even in railroad cars. In fact, houses and hotels are frequently overheated.

The great Russian stove has played an almost legendary role in these cruel winter seasons. Tall as a man and four feet wide, these mammoth heaters can still be seen in country houses and huts. On the coldest of winter nights they may even be slept upon.

Such weather slows the pace of the countryside. Nearly all work slows to a standstill. A near stifling confinement is forced upon the peasant, who seems almost to hibernate. Long winters bring other hardships for the Russian peasant. The growing season in the Eurasian plain is short, compared with most parts of the United States, and sudden changes in the weather often cause severe damage to crops.

Vast areas of soil are frozen for many months each year, and other large zones are permanently frozen below a depth of about one foot. This *permafrost* zone covers nearly one half of the U.S.S.R. and poses serious difficulties. During the First Five-Year Plan, the Soviet government tried to use steel converters in the permafrost zone. But, as the great heat produced by the furnaces began to penetrate the icy soil, the converter buildings settled unevenly into the softening earth and the converters themselves were rendered useless. The severe winters of the plains have occasionally thwarted foreign invaders. In 1812 Napoleon's Grande Armée, over 600,000 strong, suffered terribly from the Russian winter. Heavy snows, severe cold, and Russian attacks reduced that seemingly unconquerable force to a ragged band of perhaps 100,000 men in less than two months.

The Russian winter, often called "General Winter," also devastated the Nazi war machine at a critical moment in its drive on Moscow in 1941. The Russians suffered too, but fuller knowledge and consequently better preparations, plus greater stamina, enabled them to weather the worst of the punishing weather.

It is still astonishing to a foreigner to observe Russian peasant women drawing water from outside wells and carrying on other chores outdoors without gloves when the thermometer is 30 or 40 degrees below zero.

The spring thaws come upon Russia with startling suddenness. The great ice packs on the rivers groan loudly as they break up and roads become seas of mud. Some Russians claim even to have seen cows sink out of sight on village streets during the thaw. Nature and humans seem to rouse themselves to shake off the numbness of the long cold.

These pleasant days are short-lived, however. Soon the hot, dry winds of central Asia bring summer weather, summer that is as hot as the winter was cold. Even in some areas of northern Siberia, inhabitants complain that the bare ground is almost burning hot beneath their feet.

Summer also is the wet season. The moisture races across the land in torrents as swift and sudden as were the blizzards of winter,

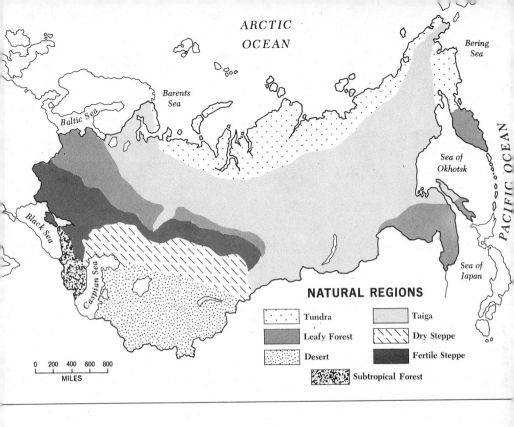

NATURAL REGIONS

but the rains rarely free the earth for long from its dusty dryness.

It is almost as if the peasant of western Russia conserves his energy for these two or three summer months when he hurls himself into a frenzy of activity, only to lapse again into inactivity when once the first flurries of snow whirl from the gray October skies.

This alternation of rush and rest has led some students of Russia to conclude that the climate is responsible for the great and sudden extremes of the Russian character. We shall see that it is not entirely valid to attribute either the history or the character of a people solely to geographic factors. Yet the power of these forces is not to be denied.

SOILS AND VEGETATION

Climate is not the only menace to agricultural development in Russia. Although it is larger than the United States and Canada, the Soviet Union has less arable land. This is due as much to infertile soils and poor drainage as to the short growing season.

Homer Smith

Paul's Photos

The Soviet Union may be divided into seven natural regions: the tundra, the taiga, the leafy forest, the fertile steppe, the dry steppe, the desert, and the subtropical forest.

The most northerly of these regions is the *tundra,* a bleak, frozen, nearly level plain of the arctic. It is an area where little can be grown and where few people live.

To the south of the tundra is the world's greatest forest. The northern section of it, the *taiga* as the Russians call it, is a dense coniferous forest, a dark and dreary country where the sun rarely penetrates the forest depths. Wolf, fox, and bear still roam the uninhabited parts.

Taken together, the tundra and the taiga cover two thirds of the Soviet Union. Along the southern edge of the taiga, slim white birches begin to appear amid the dark-green mass. The dark-green conifers and the white birches give a dramatic and beautiful contrast to the forest. Most of this wooded land covers infertile soil called podzol. When dry it is powdery, and when wet, like plastic clay. Two thirds of the Soviet Union is covered with these podzol soils.

The podzols extend into the next region to the south, the *leafy forest.* There you can find a variety of trees such as oak, maple, linden, and elm, mixed with birch, pine, and spruce.

Cutting down vast tracts of forest to make way for planting has long proved a great challenge to the Russian farmers. Agriculture has never flourished in northern Russia. Life there must be wrested from a stubborn and unyielding land. Yet, for all its poverty, the forest lands afforded protection in early Russian history against nomadic raiders from the south.

Homer Smith

Within the U.S.S.R. are great contrasts in topography and climate. The vast, flat, fertile steppe land and the even vaster taiga provide different living standards and different cultural environment than the desert, mountain, and tundra regions.

Homer Smith

Forest products such as honey, wax, timber, and, later, pitch and other naval stores were important means of livelihood for the peasant population. Even today, the great forest lands of the Soviet Union are a valuable natural resource.

As the leafy forest thins out to the south, it gives way first to the wooded steppe, where clumps of trees alternate with large clearings, and then to the famous *fertile steppe,* the next natural region of the U.S.S.R. The rolling, treeless plain stretches off in all directions, seemingly endless. A hundred years ago large parts of the steppe were covered with tall, feathery grass.

In the very center of the treeless steppe lies a narrow band of the most fertile soil in the Soviet Union. It is called the black-earth region. Its soils are heavy with humus. Like a wedge, it narrows as it moves east, outlining the traditional invasion path along which nomads moved to eastern and central Europe from the Altai Mountains and the deserts of Mongolia. With its rich soil, the open steppe land was admirably suited to the earliest agricultural populations.

Gradually the black-earth region yields to a *dry steppe* or semidesert. Unlike the fertile steppe, this area can support only short grass and scattered scrubby bushes because of the meager rainfall.

In turn, the dry steppe merges with the *desert.* In clay or sandy areas of the desert, vegetation is scanty; in stony desert areas, vegetation is nonexistent.

In ancient times cities flourished even in this seemingly infertile desert. The oases of Samarkand, Bukhara, and Kokand, for example, served as way stations on the caravan routes to China. Aside from these occasional oases, however, the area is unsuitable for agriculture. Only through immense and costly irrigation projects can crops be grown on this land. At the southern edge of the desert lie the grasslands of Kazakhstan, where the soil is good but the rainfall scanty and unpredictable.

It was here, in the early 1960's, that Soviet Premier Nikita S. Khrushchev launched a vast experiment to plow up the grass and plant wheat. His own advisers, as well as foreign specialists, warned that two or three years of insufficient rain would dry up the topsoil and that the fierce central Asian winds might then blow it away. However, Khrushchev launched the program as a gamble. Soon a gigantic dust bowl began to form, and it became clear that the experiment had failed.

The last of the major natural regions is the *subtropical forest*. This small area receives heavy rainfall and enjoys a mild climate favorable for growing fruit, tea, grapes, and a variety of broadleaf evergreen trees.

RIVERS AND PORTS

Helping to unify this enormous country is a complex river system. The rivers of Russia have always provided routes for trade and national growth. They form one of the most important natural commercial and communication systems in the world. They are long rivers, with many tributaries and large drainage basins.

Each of the early centers of population commanded one of the river systems: Kiev, the Dnieper River; Vladimir and Suzdal, the Volga; and Moscow, the upper Volga system.

The rivers of western Russia flow from north to south. The Dvina-Dnieper route links the Baltic Sea to the Black Sea; the Volga route links the Baltic to the Caspian Sea. It is important to note that the Dnieper route established communication between northern Europe and the Byzantine Empire, and that the Volga route linked Europe with the Middle East.

Three of the four main rivers in Siberia—the Ob, the Yenisei, and the Lena—flow from south to north. Although some freight is carried on these rivers, their usefulness would be far greater if they did not flow northward to the icebound arctic in contrast to the generally east-west direction of trade. The fourth great river, the Amur, flows generally northeast and forms the boundary between Siberia and Manchuria.

Beginning under tsarist regimes, extensive canal construction was undertaken to complement the river routes. Canals between the Volga River and the Baltic Sea, for example, took the place of roads and even of railroads. The Soviet Union has continued this construction with systems that link the Baltic, White, Caspian, Azov, and Black seas in European Russia. The major canals in this system are the Baltic-White Sea Canal, a project made infamous by the use of slave labor in 1933, the Moscow-Volga Canal, and the Volga-Don Canal.

Since 1940, however, with refinements in railroad and air transportation, the development of river transport in the Soviet Union has slowed substantially. Even river use for hydroelectric power has had little practical appeal. The most useful rivers for power development are in the highlands of eastern Siberia, far from population centers and subject to great seasonal variations in flow. It is clear that the rivers of Russia have enjoyed their greatest importance in the years past.

Just as navigable rivers are positive factors in internal trade and communication, a country's coastline figures importantly in contacts with the outside world. Russia has benefited from its river system, but it has suffered because of its dearth of warm-water seaports. Although it has the longest coastline of any country in the world, Russia's access to the world's sea lanes is limited by natural conditions.

Russia's coastline is surprisingly short when compared to the greatness of its land mass: 27,000 miles of seacoast to 8,650,000 square miles of land. In contrast, Great Britain has more than 4000 miles of coastline to 94,279 square miles of land.

Most of Russia's coastline lies far from the centers of life in the country. In fact most of the Russian coast borders the frozen arctic north. For the most part, its other coasts are low and marshy; what few inlets there are, are choked with sand and gravel. There are very few deep, safe harbors; still fewer are ice-free all year.

The best harbors are at Riga, on the Gulf of Riga, an arm of the Baltic Sea; at Odessa, on the Black Sea; and at Murmansk, on the Kola Peninsula near northern Finland. Before 1940, however, Riga was Russian only intermittently. The city was so highly prized by the Russians that they fought a twenty-year war in the 16th century and another of similar duration in the 18th century to try to annex it. Again, in 1940, the Soviet Army invaded and conquered independent Latvia, partly at least, because of Riga.

Ice blocks the northern seas and harbors of the U.S.S.R. during much of the year.

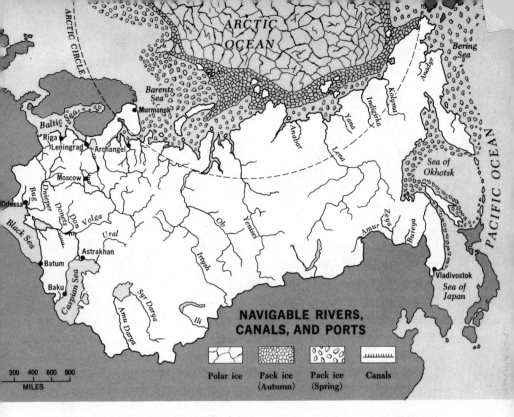

NAVIGABLE RIVERS,
CANALS, AND PORTS

| Polar ice | Pack ice (Autumn) | Pack ice (Spring) | Canals |

200 400 600 800
MILES

Yet, with all of Riga's value as a port, overall access to the Baltic Sea is largely contingent upon Denmark's and Sweden's control of the narrow straits between the Baltic and the open sea.

Warmed by the Gulf Stream, the harbor at Murmansk is ice-free, despite the nearness of the ice-studded Barents Sea. But Murmansk is relatively new as a port and is far from Russia's major cities.

Far to the south, Odessa, on the Black Sea, is almost always ice-free and has a deep harbor. Like Riga, it came under Russian control only in the 18th century. Also like Riga, it is situated on a "bottled" sea. In this case the crucial neck of the bottle is the fabled narrow straits between the Black Sea and the Mediterranean, which are controlled by Turkey.

Historic Russian efforts to play a preponderant role in the Baltic and Black Sea areas have been aimed at protecting these harbors and guaranteeing economic links with the rest of Europe.

Ports on the Caspian are useful only for trade with Iran. Those on the Pacific, principally Vladivostok, are clogged with ice during winter, and lanes to the open sea can easily be controlled by Japan.

It is not surprising, then, that Russia has no great naval tradition nor, until recently, much of a merchant marine. Historically, the thrust of Russian expansion has been over land, not water.

MINERAL RESOURCES

Russia's vastness embraces an impressive catalogue of mineral riches. Yet, because vastness can also mean remoteness, much of this natural wealth is frustratingly inaccessible. Most all of this wealth of mineral resources, however, is of the best quality.

The total energy reserves of the Soviet Union, fuel and water power, make up 23 per cent of the world's energy resources. The United States has 29 per cent. These two giant countries together control more than half of the energy resources of the world.

Russia's coal reserves are located far from the centers of population. Ninety-four per cent of Russia's fuel reserves are coal, a quantity sufficient to meet foreseeable needs for many centuries.

The major fields of coal are the Donets basin in western Russia, the largest single producer in the country; the Kuznetsk basin in Siberia, with the highest quality coal; and the Karaganda field, which produces good coking coal for the nearby steel industries of the Urals.

The cost of mining and transporting coal from each of these fields is astronomical. To ship coal from Kuznetsk to the industrial centers of central Asia and the Urals, for example, costs approximately 40 per cent of the total worth of the coal itself.

In particular the Russian metallurgical industry has suffered from this transportation problem. In addition it has had to cope

Rivers and canals have played an important part in the history of Russia. Today they play a secondary role to rail, air, and motor transportation, but today rivers are important sources of hydro-electric power. This power dam and canal locks are on the Dnieper River at Zaporozhye.

Paul's Photos

with shipments of coking coal in which no more than 50 per cent of the tonnage was of the required high quality.

Petroleum is declining in importance as a fuel in the Soviet Union, in contrast with its increased use in the United States. In part, this phenomenon is due to the lack of new oil strikes in the Soviet Union. From producing one half of the world's petroleum in 1901, the Soviet Union had slipped to producing only 7 per cent in 1960. The chief oil fields are at Baku, at the eastern tip of the Caucasus Mountains on the Caspian Sea, and along the western approach to the Ural Mountains, near the city of Kuibyshev.

As in the United States, reserves of high-grade iron ore in the U.S.S.R. are rapidly dwindling. The three major deposits are at Krivoi Rog, in the Ukraine; at Kerch, in the Crimea; and at Magnitogorsk, in the Urals. The Soviet Union has only moderate reserves of copper, but the Russian deposits are far distant from production centers and are low-grade ores.

Modest deposits of bauxite for aluminum production force the Russians to import heavily from the high-grade fields of Hungary. Lead and zinc supplies come in part from Polish mines. The world's largest deposits of manganese—a key ingredient in steel— are found in the Soviet Union.

Apparently there are few uranium deposits in the Soviet Union. The main sources of fissionable raw materials are East Germany (Saxony) and Czechoslovakia.

Great and often drastic effort is expended by the Soviet Union to overcome geographical handicaps and to achieve an increasingly self-sufficient economy. By asserting its absolute authority over the nation, the Soviet government has tried to shift entire segments of the population into semiwilderness areas to develop resources and regions into industrial or agricultural complexes. But frequently this resettlement has been done with alarming disregard for human well-being.

NATIONALITIES

The Soviet Union is one of the few truly multinational countries left in the world. An old peasant proverb claims: "Russia is not a country, it is a world."

Estimates vary on the number of national and tribal groups in the Soviet Union, but there are over 170 separate peoples and about 200 languages or dialects (most of these are fractional distinctions).

The Slavs comprise the largest ethnic group and include Great Russians (more than half), Ukrainians, and Byelorussians (White Russians, a major segment of the Slavic people, not to be confused with the political group called White Russians, anti-Communist opponents of the Soviet regime).

These groups formed the core of the old Russia (before 1917) and were the driving force in the conquest and colonization of the rest of the Eurasian plain. Originally dwelling in western Russia (and still largely concentrated there), they can now be found everywhere in the country.

The languages of the three groups, especially Russian and Byelorussian, are very similar, though there is still a disagreement

Jim Blair: photographs

as to whether Ukrainian is a dialect of Russian or a language of its own.

These nationality groups are Russian or Eastern Orthodox Christians, a fact which led to serious religious difficulties with Roman Catholic Poles and Lithuanians to the west, especially when one religious group held political control over the other.

The second largest ethnic group is the Turko-Tartar, a predominantly Moslem religious group which inhabits parts of the Volga basin, the Caucasus (the Azerbaidzhanians), the Crimea, and much of central Asia. Remnants of the great migrations from the East, they have maintained their separate social and religious customs against the russifying attempts of the tsarist monarchy and, though much less successfully, against contemporary Soviet power.

The peoples of the Caucasus include Christian Armenians and Georgians as well as a number of primitive and colorful smaller tribes which until the 1930's held on to ancient tribal ways deep in the fastness of the Caucasus.

Though few in numbers, the Jewish, Baltic, and German groups in the Soviet Union have played important roles. Absorbed when Russia helped carve up old Poland in the 18th century, the Jewish town population of west Russia suffered from discrimination and persecution under the monarchy and to a lesser extent under Soviet power. Still, a relatively large number of Jews were active in democratic and revolutionary organizations, in the creative arts, and in the sciences.

Up to 1941, the German population was also influential, especially before the revolution when Germans enjoyed great favor at court. But together with some other smaller nationality groups, they were deported to the east by the Soviet government as a

Slavic peoples comprise the greatest part of the population of the U.S.S.R. —about 78 per cent.

23

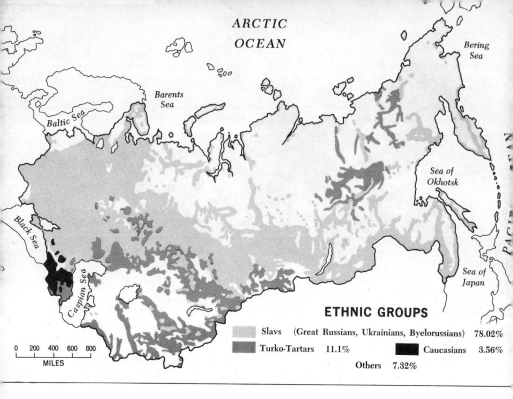

ARCTIC OCEAN

Bering Sea

Barents Sea

Baltic Sea

Black Sea

Caspian Sea

Sea of Okhotsk

Sea of Japan

ETHNIC GROUPS

Slavs (Great Russians, Ukrainians, Byelorussians) 78.02%

Turko-Tartars 11.1%

Caucasians 3.56%

Others 7.32%

0 200 400 600 800
MILES

security measure when World War II approached, and have never been allowed to return to their former homes in the Ukraine and along the Volga.

Under the Russian tsars, especially in the years before 1917, there were systematic attempts by the state (the national government) to assimilate the various ethnic groups and religious minorities by russifying them. These measures often took on a most brutal and discriminatory character.

The official policy of the Soviet regime today is equality of all nationalities. The Soviet constitution proclaims the right to national self-determination, but a closer look at the doctrine shows its hollowness. Any nationality has the right to secede from the state as long as this is the will of the leadership of the working class, that is, the Communist party. But since such a request would be decided to be counter to the interests of the working class, then according to both Lenin and Stalin, such secession is unthinkable.

NATIONAL REPUBLICS

Again in theory only, all the major and several of the smaller ethnic

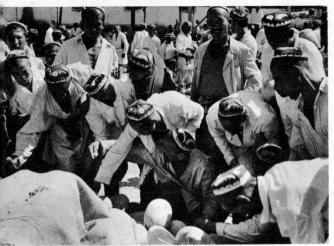

Henri Cartier Bresson: MAGNUM   Homer Smith

"Russia is not a country, it is a world," reads the old peasant proverb. The U.S.S.R. is one of the few multinational countries. National groups have retained, in many cases, their traditions and languages. The men at the left are Uzbeks. The young woman is a Buryat Mongol from northern Siberia.

groups have their own national republic and enjoy legal and political autonomy. The U.S.S.R. is made up of fifteen Soviet republics, in addition to numerous autonomous republics, regions, and national districts, which in theory enjoy certain cultural and political rights. In fact, both the Ukrainian and Byelorussian republics send representatives to the United Nations as sovereign powers.

In fact, however, most of these rights are formal, not real, as later chapters will show. Non-Russians, furthermore, have not held the number of important posts in the state and party which their numbers might warrant. Their local cultures have been allowed to survive, indeed are encouraged, as long as they do not contradict the political, economic, and social aims of the state.

"National in form and socialist [that is, in this context Communist] in content" means little more than freedom to use one's own language and wear one's own costumes, but always in the service of the state. All religions have, of course, suffered severe persecution by the Soviet state.

When these nationalities had an opportunity to leave the Russian state during the brief reign of the democratic provisional government in 1917, most of them, with the exception of the Finns, Baltic peoples, and the Poles, preferred autonomy to independence. They appeared to understand that the economic, strategic, and historical ties which bound them together were strong enough and valuable enough to compensate for the lack of their own nation-state. It is

Typical peasant houses like this one near Moscow are small, built of logs, have lean-to sheds, double windows to keep out the cold. The ornate carving at the right once decorated a peasant house.

difficult to know, however, what effect four and one-half decades of Soviet Communist rule have had on this point of view.

The human resources of the Soviet Union should not be under-estimated as one of the major assets of the country, particularly the low ratio of population to resources.

The population of the Soviet Union in 1962 was an estimated 214.4 million. The growth of this population has been erratic since 1917 due to revolution, war, famine, deportations, and World War II. The huge losses incurred by the Soviet Union in the war, esti-mated at 10 million, slowed up the increase considerably following 1945. Between 1940 and 1957, the natural increase of population in the United States was more rapid than that in the Soviet Union. It also appears true that the Soviet mortality rate is slightly higher than that of the U.S. However, both the death rate and infant mortality rate of the U.S.S.R. have dropped considerably from the last peacetime year of the monarchy in 1913, an indication of Soviet advances in medicine and public health. The average age level of the present Soviet population, compared to that of the United States, is a relatively young one.

Population mobility since World War II reflects two main trends: a movement from west to east and a continuation, en-couraged by the state, of the historic migration from rural terri-tory to the cities. Both reflect the Soviet effort to industrialize and to develop natural resources more fully.

In sum, the Soviet population is vigorous, growing today at a rate slightly above that of the United States and, like the American population, taking advantage of the potential of its country's growth to shift as opportunities shift.

Robert Capa: MAGNUM

A Ukrainian family at home. Ukrainians are Slavs, and comprise about 13 per cent of the population of the U.S.S.R. Some of the most fertile farm land in the Soviet Union is found in the Ukraine.

SUMMARY

Here, then, we have the setting for our study of the Soviet Union and communism. We see an enormous country, dominated by a vast Eurasian plain that is repeatedly swept not only by searing summer winds and sudden and bitter winter blizzards, but by a parade of raiders and invaders, wanderers and revolutionaries, in one of the most dramatic national histories of all time.

Here is a rich assortment of natural resources, but a storehouse whose treasures are often too remote, too costly, or too inferior to tap.

Here is a giant's mass of land with a dwarf's measure of warm-water coastline; an ideal natural system of rivers but one stunted by wrong-way currents and ice-locked outlets.

Here is a conglomeration of nationalities, languages, and customs, widely scattered but rigidly bound by an absolute, tightly knit, monolithic government.

Against this background we now introduce the forces of Russian history. As they are explained, you will see that the roots of Soviet affairs of today trace to political, social, ideological, and economic seeds sown many years ago.

Brian Brake: MAGNUM

TERMS TO KNOW

Eurasian plain	continental climate	tundra
fertile steppe	population mobility	taiga
Slavs	ethnic group	podzol
leafy forest	permafrost	dry steppe

QUESTIONS ON THE CHAPTER

1. How has the lack of a natural frontier affected the western part of the Eurasian plain?

2. Describe the summer and winter climate of the Eurasian plain.

3. Explain why agriculture is limited in the tundra and taiga regions.

4. Where is the best farm land in the Soviet Union? What is this region called?

5. In what ways have the great river systems of Russia contributed to the development of the country?

6. Name the best harbors in the Soviet Union. Give reasons why this country has relatively few good harbors.

7. What is the Soviet Union's biggest problem in the development of mineral resources?

8. Explain what is meant by the old saying "Russia is not a country, it is a world."

9. The Slavs comprise the largest ethnic group in the Soviet Union. What peoples are included in this group?

10. What trends in population mobility have been evident since World War II in the Soviet Union?

QUESTIONS FOR DISCUSSION

1. Geography is a potent influence in the development of a nation as a world power. The United States became the greatest power in the world partly due to its vast, fertile farm lands and its tremendous mineral resources. Evaluate Soviet power today in terms of the strong and weak aspects of Russian geography.

2. The history of the Eurasian plain can be summarized as a struggle for political supremacy. Provide examples from Russian history which tend to justify or contradict this statement.

3. Select one of the seven natural regions of the Soviet Union (tundra, desert, taiga, leafy forest, fertile steppe, dry steppe, subtropical forest) for intensive study. Be prepared to discuss the development of industry in this region, if any, and the development of agriculture, if any, as well as the history of the peoples which have occupied this region.

4. Choose one of the major ethnic groups in the Soviet Union for study in depth from the point of view of customs, characteristics, and language.

BIBLIOGRAPHY

For Reference: ☐ Ginsburg, Norton, ed., *The Pattern of Asia*, Chapter 38: "Russia and Asia." Prentice-Hall, Inc., 1958. ☐ Kish, George, ed., *Economic Atlas of the Soviet Union.* University of Michigan Press, 1960. For Further Reading: ☐ Lengyel, Emil, *The Soviet Union: The Land and Its People.* Oxford Book Company, 1961. ☐ Nazaroff, Alexander, *The Land of the Russian People*, J. B. Lippincott Company, 1960. ☐ Thayer, Charles W., and others, *Russia.* LIFE World Library, 1960.

CHAPTER 2

HISTORY OF RUSSIA TO 1917

*The turbulent history of Russia
prior to 1917 was marked
by aggressive warfare, autocratic rulers,
political stagnation, economic injustices,
and isolation from western Europe.*

Russian history is like a set of variations on four sombre themes.
These themes, occurring and recurring, sometimes muffled, sometimes harsh, sometimes disguised so that they can scarcely be
recognized, make Russian history different from United States
history. These four themes account, in part, for what Russia is
today. As a prelude to the present, they should be understood so
that they may be detected as today's history unfolds.

The first theme is the struggle of the Russian people to conquer
the Eurasian plain and dominate its approaches. Military expansion
and colonization played equally important roles in this process.

The second theme is the powerful role of Russian government.
Almost from the beginning of Russian history, the state has force-
fully dominated the individual Russian, his church, his private
organizations, and even the various social classes of his society.

The third theme of Russian history is Russia's remoteness and
backwardness. Russia always has been separated from the rest of

The church along with the autocratic state was one of the dominating influences in the history or pre-revolutionary Russia.

Europe. The population has seemed to be swallowed up, lost, in the great land mass of the country. This was especially evident in Russia's technological backwardness. Not only geographically but culturally Russia was on a remote edge of the West's burgeoning civilization. It shared only part of the great historic achievements of Western tradition. It accepted a form of Christianity but seemed never to absorb the Greek, Roman, and Judaic traditions of Western civilization. Although Russia enjoyed a flourishing of some arts in the 13th century, it knew nothing of a renaissance such as Europe had experienced.

The Reformation in the 16th century touched Russia only indirectly. The scientific revolution which began in the West in the 17th century arrived in Russia a century and a half later. In numerous ways Russia lagged many years behind the surging Western world in intellectual and technological achievements. True, there were several periods of highly developed cultural life, but few of notable originality until the 19th century.

Thus the 20th century found Russia brilliant and independent in the arts but technologically what today we would call an underdeveloped country.

The fourth theme of Russian history, one which appeared late on the scene, was the developing social consciousness among a small group of intellectuals. These intellectuals were particularly concerned with the political and social problems of their time. They did little to disguise the profound distaste and revulsion with which they viewed the official government and Russian royalty. But toward the peasants, who suffered most from tsarist oppression, they felt deep compassion. It was from this small group, called the intelligentsia, that Russia's many revolutionary doctrines sprang. But in those days Russia was an autocratic state, ruled by heavy-handed monarchs called tsars, the Russian equivalent of caesar. Unable under these circumstances to express their opposition freely, the intellectuals were forced to resort to illegal action.

Now let us notice how these four themes of Russian history repeat themselves and develop up to 1917:

Theme one is international: expansion by conquest.

Theme two is political: the authoritarian state.

Theme three is economic: an isolated, technologically backward country.

Theme four is social and intellectual: a tradition of radical and illegal activity which develops to a revolutionary pitch in 1917.

A Russian prince and his bodyguard exacting tribute from the peasants (early 13th century).

EARLIEST TIMES: KIEVAN RUSSIA

We know very little about the origins of the people who inhabit Russia. From artifacts and early chronicles we learn that probably during the 5th and 6th centuries tribes of Slavic peoples moved from their homes in the foothills of the Carpathian Mountains (between present-day Poland and Czechoslovakia) to the fertile but exposed western part of the great Eurasian plain, where they were open to attacks by barbarous nomads from central Asia.

The hardy Slavs sustained the shock of repeated invasions. By the 8th or 9th century the Slavic peoples had dispersed through the broad valley of the Dnieper River north to the settlement of Novgorod and south to Kiev. Along this trade route — from the Baltic Sea on the north to the Black Sea on the south — they settled down, developing their own culture and customs. In time they united their tribes in a loose federation.

In the late 9th century the Varangians, a band of warrior-traders composed of Scandinavians, Baltic peoples, and possibly some Slavs, moved into control of the Dnieper route. They rapidly imposed their own military-administrative structure upon the existing tribal federation.

The city of Kiev, because of its commanding position on the Dnieper in the midst of the fertile steppe, became the capital and cultural center.

The Varangians were easily absorbed into the local population. Gradually the Kievan federation came to be governed by Slavs, and ultimately Russian princes, for by this time Russia had become the name of their country. (The origin of the name Russia is disputed, but probably came from a local Slavic term.)

In Kievan Russia there was never an autocratic centralized government authority. The princes shared their power with local town councils and a council of the upper nobility (boyars) called the boyar duma. By the early 11th century, the princes began to divide the land among their sons. Although each was subordinate to the chief Kievan prince, these local princes slowly won sovereignty over their lands.

Socially and economically Kievan Russia was the most open society Russia ever experienced. Trade and handicrafts flourished. An urban class served as a buffer between the nobles and the peasants. The peasants even owned their own land, a right their heirs in the 18th, 19th, and 20th centuries would struggle to obtain.

Culturally, Kievan Russia was bound to the civilization of the eastern Mediterranean. Christianity was introduced in the late 10th century. It was Greek Orthodox in form, reflecting the influence of Byzantium (Constantinople, and later Istanbul, Turkey). It took centuries to penetrate the entire country and reach all the people, but from its first introduction into Russia Christianity was a great cultural force.

The Russian alphabet was developed, based on the Greek alphabet. From the great Byzantine cultural center came painting, mosaic work, architecture, and church literature.

In the 12th century Kiev was a large city of 600 churches and immense wealth. Serious problems menaced this grandeur, however. The growing number of sovereign Russian princes became increasingly restive, less and less able to settle conflicting claims peacefully. In 1169 even Kiev was stormed by the prince of Vladimir-Suzdal, sacked, and stripped of its prestige.

At the same time raiding nomads from the East, sometimes migrations of entire tribes across the southern plains of Russia, undermined Kievan agriculture and trade. Commerce declined further when, after the First Crusade, Byzantine trade shifted away from the north. In 1204 the capture and sacking of Constantinople (Byzantium) by the crusaders sapped the remaining strength that once had flowed north to Kiev.

Harried by internal strife and threatened by external attacks, the population (as early as the 12th century) began migrating into the forests of the north. They settled in the basin of the Oka and Volga rivers, dominated by the towns of Vladimir and Suzdal, which together became the new political and cultural center.

THE MONGOLS

Even this new center of power was threatened by a bold new enemy on the east. Following a series of reconnaissance raids, a giant Mongol army under Batu Khan, a descendant of Genghis Khan, invaded Russia. Between 1237 and 1240 Batu Khan conquered all of the great Russian cities except Novgorod.

For the next two centuries—until about 1480—central and northern Russia were under Mongol control. Southeast Russia became the empire of the Mongols, the fabled Golden Horde. The Dnieper area was taken over by the aggressive and expanding

Polish-Lithuanian state. Thus Russia had been divided into three fragments. Only Novgorod in the northwest clung to a precarious independence, gradually becoming an important trading center linked to northern Europe.

Initially the impact of the Mongol onslaught was utterly destructive. Along with many other towns and cities, Kiev was leveled, never to regain its former glory. Town councils lost their influence. It took eight centuries for the Russian city population to recover its strength.

Skilled craftsmen were taken away to the Mongol capital at Sarai on the Volga. Some skills were snuffed out, not to reappear until the 17th century. For 100 years trade dwindled. The Mongols taxed the Russian people heavily, but stationed no troops permanently in the Russian lands.

In many cases the Mongol conquest accelerated trends already under way in Russia. For example, the unruly princes continued to divide the land among their sons until political power was fragmented and Russian national unity was shattered.

The fortunes of the peasant, already dire, worsened. Infertile soils of the forest zone yielded only meager crops. Many peasants fell hopelessly into debt; still others lost their land to greedy princes who turned away from the hazards of trade along the Dnieper and more and more to the land for income. But this trend had begun during the Kievan period.

The society became increasingly agricultural and self-sufficient. No middle class counterbalanced the power of the landlords over the impoverished peasants.

The princes finally realized that if they were to enlarge their property wealth, the division of the land into smaller and smaller parcels had to be reversed. Thus began the long and danger-strewn process of unifying all the Russian lands.

THE RISE OF MUSCOVY

A few princes, including the prince of the city of Moscow, were granted the right to collect taxes for the khan of the Mongol Golden Horde. With this authority the princes put pressure on weak neighbors to pay or suffer fearful consequences at the hands of the Mongols. Eventually the Moscow prince won the privilege of being the sole tax collector for the mighty khan.

Under the Mongol yoke, the church had been the only bond of unity among the subjugated Russians. It now supported the efforts of the Moscow prince to unify the nation. Slowly the Moscow prince gathered strength, attracting more and more nobles anxious to share the spoils of his victories over the other princes.

Moscow, at the very center of the Oka-Volga river system, was astride the main trade and communication routes. Its position also was relatively safe from sudden attack. The Moscow princes managed their affairs cautiously during these transition years (1375-1505), bought and married into ownership of assorted key central Russian lands, and bided their time while the power of the Mongol Golden Horde waned.

By the middle of the 15th century Moscow dominated north central Russia. At length, strength mustered, the prince of Moscow boldly defied the now weak Golden Horde by refusing in 1480 to pay annual tribute, and freed himself from the last vestiges of foreign domination.

Politically and socially the cost of this achievement was high. In uniting the Russian lands, the Moscow prince had seriously encroached on the rights not only of the peasants but of the nobility. The state went on to broaden its powers until, with the approach of the 16th century, it achieved its quest of supreme and unchallenged autocratic power. Even the church had by this time recognized the supremacy of the state. No class or institution could check the power of the prince. The town councils had long since disappeared. The boyar duma was steadily weakening. How different from the early realm of Kiev! And what a clear foreshadowing of the trail of oppressions that would lead to the present!

IVAN IV (THE TERRIBLE)

At this critical moment in 1533, one of the most famous Muscovite princes came to the throne. Ivan IV (1533-1584), who is more familiarly known as Ivan the Terrible, declared himself tsar in 1547, the first Russian ruler to use this title.

Powerful enemies still ringed the Muscovite state, cut off as it was from the sea and unprotected by natural frontiers. As during the struggles against the Mongols, great sacrifices were essential to support the military forces. Complete subservience was demanded of the population.

Left: Ivan the Terrible (1533-1584), a contemporary woodcut. Right: The death of Ivan the Terrible (from a painting by K. E. Makowski).

Ivan proceeded to crush the remaining power of the upper nobility. He terrorized the church. The rights of peasants were further restricted. Under Ivan's autocratic rule everyone served the state: the nobles, as its officials; the peasants, as taxpayers, food producers, and military recruits; the church, as moral and ideological support.

The nobles had lost many of their social privileges, such as the right to transfer their allegiance to another prince. They had become underlings in the officialdom of the state.

The church was powerless to challenge the temporal power of the state; it could only apologize for it.

The rights of the individual had fallen before the demands of the state. Serfdom and autocracy had become the pillars of Russian society. Serfdom was finally abolished officially in 1861 but lasted in varying forms even longer.

As the clamps of state rule tightened around the Russians of Muscovy, so also the ring of enemies of Moscow perpetuated the encirclement of the tsardom.

By land and sea Muscovite Russia was blocked from the outside world. To the north was Sweden. To the west and southwest was Poland-Lithuania. To the east lay the weakened but still formidable remnants of the Golden Horde, organized in the khanates of Siberia, Kazan (on the middle Volga), Astrakhan (on the south Volga), and Crimea.

To smash his enemies, Ivan the Terrible mounted two whirlwind campaigns toward the east. He conquered Kazan (1552) and Astrakhan (1556) and thus opened the way for trade with the Middle East and for further penetration into Siberia.

In 1583-1584 another event widened Muscovy's power in the East. One of the bandit-Cossacks (the warlike horsemen of the Russian steppe), named Yermak, defeated the Siberian khan and claimed all of western Siberia for the Muscovite tsar. The door to the Pacific was open. Within a century Russian explorers, trappers, and runaway peasants had conquered and colonized the great forests all the way to the coast.

In his campaigns against enemies on the west, Ivan was less successful. A tragic and futile twenty-year war against Sweden and Poland-Lithuania, fought by poorly trained and equipped Russian troops, failed to win for Russia "a window on the Baltic Sea" and the prized seaport of Riga.

But even in defeat an important lesson was learned in Moscow: Russia must have military and technological aid from the West. Furthermore, Russia must have loyal and active allies. Alone Russia could not match these enemies on the western flank. No sooner would Russia attack one foe than the others would counterattack. If it could not win allies of its own, Russia then must find a way to divide and then conquer its enemies one by one.

THE TIME OF TROUBLES

Meanwhile, Ivan's suppression of the population, continued by his successors, fomented the Time of Troubles in Russia. One of Ivan's henchmen, Boris Godunov, first as regent under the feeble-minded Tsar Feodor (1584-1598) and then as tsar himself (1598-1605), bound many peasants to the land by harsh decrees and made many enemies among the nobility. Following a terrible famine, the discontented elements—peasants, poor nobles, and Cossacks—revolted. When Boris died a year later in 1605, Russia fell into chaos while a swarm of pretenders claimed the throne. The Swedes and Poles saw their chance to attack once more.

The Polish King Sigismund even tried to put his son on the Russian throne. Only after an arduous struggle were the Russian people able to muster a strong enough army to drive the foreigners from Moscow and central Russia and to restore order.

In the aftermath Russia was an exhausted and still seriously divided nation. In 1613 a feeble effort was made to limit the power of the next tsar and establish some permanent representative assembly. But fear and mistrust overwhelmed reason and resolution.

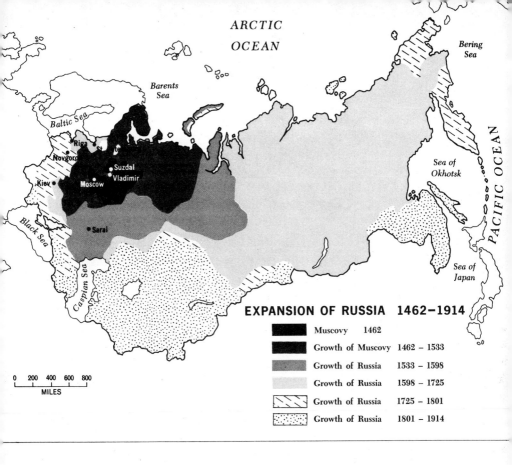

ARCTIC
OCEAN

Bering
Sea

Barents
Sea

Baltic Sea

Riga
Novgorod
Kiev
Moscow
Suzdal
Vladimir

Sarai

Black Sea

Caspian Sea

Sea of
Okhotsk

Sea of
Japan

PACIFIC OCEAN

EXPANSION OF RUSSIA 1462–1914

■	Muscovy 1462
■	Growth of Muscovy 1462 – 1533
■	Growth of Russia 1533 – 1598
░	Growth of Russia 1598 – 1725
▨	Growth of Russia 1725 – 1801
⸬	Growth of Russia 1801 – 1914

0 200 400 600 800
MILES

ROMANOV RULE BEGINS

So numerous were the noble factions vying for authority that they
could agree only to restore the power of the autocrat and hope that,
whoever he might be, he would take the initiative to rise above the
partisan interests. A compromise candidate of middle noble rank,
Mikhail Romanov (1613-1645), was chosen to rule. He and his
descendants ruled from 1613 in an unbroken line until 1917.

The first two Romanovs were new faces in the autocracy, but
their policy of forcing everyone to serve the state was old and
worn. In 1649 under Alexei (1645-1676), a new legal code divided
the people into rigid classes. Under this code most peasants were
bound to the land by law. But this merely made official the serfdom
that had long been a fact. The townspeople also were bound to
their towns. The church and the nobility were declared closed
classes, and both were strictly regulated by the state.

In western Europe serfdom was coming to an end, while in
Russia the power of the autocrat over all classes was being firmly

Moscow as it appeared in the 17th century (drawn by A. M. Vasnetov).

established. Yet, without this autocratic power, Tsar Peter I (the Great) could not have begun to modernize Russia in the next century.

Under the early Romanovs, meanwhile, Russia regained much of the territory it had lost in the Time of Troubles. After the revolt of the Cossack leader Bogdan Khmelnitsky against the Poles, much of the Ukraine (including the city of Kiev) was brought back under Russian control for the first time since the Mongol invasions of the 13th century.

So decisively did Moscow's power mount and Poland's authority wane that after 1667 Russia reversed its foreign policy and treated Poland as its ally. A Polish wedge was driven between Russia's enemies on the west; the common enemy front was broken at last. This, too, would help Peter the Great later in his struggle to seize a port on the Baltic.

The first Romanov tsars, Mikhail and Alexei, worked to reopen contacts with western Europe. They sought not only to strengthen their military establishment but to increase trade and introduce elements of Western culture into Russia. Here also was a foreshadowing of Peter the Great's time.

The 17th century was a time of trial for the Russian Orthodox Church. In order to buttress the church in the Ukraine and along the western frontier against the expansionist pressures of the Roman Catholic Church, the Russian patriarch Nikon (1652-1660) instituted reforms in the liturgy and religious books to bring them into line with the conduct of the other Eastern Orthodox churches. But a group of nationalistic Russian churchmen who violently opposed these reforms divided the Russian church in the 1660's. Those who refused to accept the reforms were called schismatics, or Old Believers. The clergy drove these Old Believers from the church and asked the state to punish them. This gave the state a new measure of power over the church and also prepared the way for Peter's reforms.

PETER I (THE GREAT)

Peter I (the Great) came to the throne in 1682 and ruled until 1725. While his reign was not a complete break with Russia's past, it was, nevertheless, a period of great change. In a haphazard and disorganized way, Peter tried to recast Russia in the mold of the great European powers. In a nation as backward and vast as Russia, this program of reform was a colossal undertaking. With his new and powerful army and Poland as his ally, he fought a twenty-year war with Sweden to win his "window to the West," the Baltic provinces and Riga. In territory conquered from Sweden he built his new capital, St. Petersburg, facing west.

Peter expanded small mills and factories in order to lay the foundations of Russian industrial development in the Urals and central Russia. He summoned a host of foreign technicians, artists, architects, teachers, and engineers to advise and train Russians.

Peter reorganized the church and placed it under direct state control. Its cultural monopoly was destroyed. In place of church domination of social customs, dress, literature, and architecture, Western models appeared among the upper classes.

So rapid was the transformation that it turned out to be merely a surface change in many respects. Those who clung to old fashions, as the Old Believers had clung to their ancient church customs under Tsar Alexei, resisted Peter's changes. But with the ferocity of a bear, Peter brooked no opposition. He mercilessly crushed rebellions. In order to carry out his plans, he imposed still greater burdens upon the people. Everyone owed service to the government, and anyone who resisted faced brutal punishment. Peter

Left: Peter the Great (1672-1725), a death mask.   Above: Peter the Great's soldiers forcing his subjects to shorten their beards and coats to satisfy his personal wishes (from a painting by G. von Urlaub).   Right: Mass execution in Moscow, 1699, of the streltsy (guardists), ordered by Peter the Great, demonstrated the absolute authority of the tsarist rulers (a contemporary drawing).

even had his own son tortured to death because he suspected him of working against his plans.

When Peter died in 1725 many of his innovations died with him. But one thing was certain—Russia would never again return to the ways of its past.

THE LEGACY OF PETER THE GREAT

Peter's legacy was a mixed one. On the one hand Russia was now a great power, stretching from the Baltic to the Pacific, from the arctic to the dry steppes. Industry and trade were growing. Cultural bonds with the West were stronger than ever before.

On the other hand the lot of the serf had worsened. A cultural gap was beginning to open between the peasants and the now partially westernized nobility. This ever-widening split in Russian society was never bridged. Here is at least a partial explanation of the character of the Russian revolutionary movement.

Peter had relied primarily on the nobility for leadership and in doing so he had failed to encourage an independent middle class to promote the economic development of the country. Perhaps this circumstance was unavoidable, because the Russian merchantry was a small and wretched group at this time.

Nevertheless, the continuation of serfdom and the commanding economic position of the nobility were serious obstacles to the progressive westernizing of Russian economy. Here was another factor which had an important bearing on the revolutionary movement.

It would not be accurate to blame Peter the Great for this state of affairs. He could not see the implications for the future in his policies. Nor could he overcome the resistance of the people to his reforms. Would his successors maintain his reforms or would they lose the trail he had begun to blaze across the vast Eurasian plain?

THE YEARS BETWEEN 1725 AND 1762

Peter the Great had made no provisions for the succession to the throne. As a result, for the next thirty-seven years, to 1762, the Russian throne was the center of a struggle for power. There were palace revolutions and widespread political instability. In the confusion of these years, the nobles were able to evade the obligation to serve the state. No longer was there a tsar's firm hand over Russia. In 1762 the nobility won their freedom from obligatory state service and were allowed to keep all their lands and serfs.

But the tsar and the nobility opposed taking the next logical step of freeing the serfs. In fact throughout the years of palace revolts, the nobles tightened their grip upon the serfs until the peasantry was reduced to little more than a tax-paying property.

The nobles had broadened not only the economic and cultural gulf between themselves and the peasants, but the social gulf as well. The nobles became a privileged and leisure class, living freely from the toil of personal serfs whose condition approached that of slavery. So unjust was this situation that the serfs were convinced that the nobles had, in fact, prevented the tsar from freeing them, too. This legend was not true but it persisted and created lasting bitterness between the two classes. It even gave rise to a violent peasant rebellion under Emelyan Pugachev which set a pattern for later peasant revolts in the 19th and 20th centuries.

THE ENLIGHTENED DESPOTS

Political stability finally returned to Russia in 1762 when Catherine II (the Great) (1762-1796) seized power and began to rule as an enlightened despot. Enlightened despotism was a theory accepted by some 18th-century European kings that the ruler should maintain his autocratic power—that is, be a despot—and at the same time should wield his power reasonably and efficiently—that is, be enlightened.

Although Catherine is traditionally grouped with such other enlightened despots as Frederick the Great of Prussia and Joseph II of Austria, she did not entirely deserve this reputation.

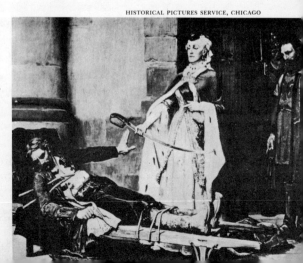

Catherine the Great in a gesture of magnanimity returns his sword to the wounded and defeated Polish patriot, Thaddeus Kosciusko, to show that he is not disgraced. The defeat of the Polish armies under Kosciusko ended Polish independence and Kosciusko was imprisoned until the death of Catherine the Great in 1796. Paul I set him free.

She did nothing to improve the lot of the majority of Russian people. Her administrative and educational reforms remained largely on paper. During her reign, however, Russian cultural and court life achieved new brilliance. Her armies conquered from the Ottoman Turks most of the southern steppes bordering the northern shores of the Black Sea. This conquest opened up the rich, black-earth region to cultivation and gave Russia valuable ports on the Black Sea.

In the west, Catherine failed to maintain the policy of manipulating Poland as a Russian protectorate. She agreed instead to carve up Poland with Prussia and Austria. This agreement proved to be a grave error because it brought into the Russian Empire a large group of Poles culturally advanced but politically hostile. It removed the buffer between the Russian and German states and ended Russian influence in the parts of Poland that had fallen under Prussian and Austrian rule.

Catherine's son, Paul I, succeeded her in 1796. He vaguely pursued a policy that sought to reëstablish the traditional power of the autocrat over the growing privileges of the nobility. Several factors, however—his unbalanced mind, his great hatred of all his mother's work, his short reign, ending with his assassination in 1801—clouded over his few achievements.

His son, Alexander I (1801-1825), who was implicated in Paul's murder, was now the last hope of enlightened despotism. Alexander has been called the "enigmatic tsar" because he could not make up his mind whether or not to introduce the basic social and economic reforms which were so necessary to the stability of the Russian state. He was torn between his father's image of the cruel, military monarch and his grandmother's image of the reasonable, cosmopolitan, enlightened ruler.

Pressures of foreign policy merely served to aggravate Alexander's indecisiveness in domestic matters. He was especially concerned with foreign policy in the wake of Napoleon's invasion of Russia in 1812 and the subsequent Russian counterinvasion of Europe. As a result reforms at home were postponed.

NICHOLAS I AND THE DECEMBRIST INSURRECTION

Meanwhile serious discontent was growing among the young army officers who had served in the Russian army of occupation in France and absorbed some of the revolutionary ideals of freedom and representative government.

When Alexander died suddenly in 1825, one of the small secret societies of these officers attempted to overthrow the autocracy. The so-called Decembrist insurrection was crushed by the new tsar, Nicholas I (1825-1855). This uprising was, in one sense, the last of the palace revolutions. In a more important way it was the beginning of a new revolutionary tradition which sought not merely to replace one tsar by another but to establish a more representative form of government.

Tsar Nicholas was genuinely alarmed by the uprising. Throughout his reign he called for repressive measures in the schools, newspapers, and throughout the army to silence any expressions of opposition or suggestions of reform. The government so separated itself from the people, through its harsh measures and its perpetuation of serfdom, that it seemed at times as though there were actually two Russias, the realm of the tsar and the realm of the peasant masses.

During the reign of Nicholas an attempt was made to arouse the loyalty of the people to the state by applying the slogan "autocracy, orthodoxy, and nationality." It meant (1) continuation of the all-powerful tsar (autocracy), (2) a privileged position for the Russian Orthodox Church and persecution of religious minorities (orthodoxy), and (3) a vague idea of national consciousness or patriotism (nationality). This last idea hardly reached beyond simply applying repressive measures against non-Russian nationalities.

There was nothing in this program that was either new or appealing as far as the masses were concerned. No sense of loyalty to the tsar blossomed among the people. Nicholas assigned several secret committees to study the abolition of serfdom, but he did nothing significant about their findings because he feared that abolition of serfdom would undermine his power.

Surprisingly, during this heavy-handed thirty-year reign of Nicholas I, Russia experienced its first real flourishing of literature. The poet Alexander Pushkin wrote some of his finest works. During this period the Ukrainian writer Nikolai Gogol wrote his masterpieces, *Dead Souls*, a novel, and *The Inspector General*, a play. Both satirized provincial life.

Ivan Turgenev began writing his collection of short stories, *A Sportsman's Sketches*, and novels at this time. The younger Feodor Dostoevsky and Lev Tolstoy had already been recognized.

No one has ever satisfactorily explained this golden age of literature during the cruelly oppressive time of the dictatorial regime of Nicholas I.

In the area of foreign affairs, Nicholas' policies led to defeat and humiliation for Russia in the Crimean War (1854-1856).

Since Catherine the Great's conquest of the fertile southern steppes, the straits between the Black Sea and the Mediterranean had become economically important to Russia as a grain-exporting route to the west. The Russians feared that some strong European power might dominate the decaying Ottoman Empire, throttle Russian trade, and threaten the southern coast of Russia. Therefore, throughout the nineteenth century the Russians tried to exert great influence on Ottoman policy. Four wars and many diplomatic crises with the Ottoman Turks resulted.

In the Crimean War, Great Britain and France supported the Turks, and the Russians were defeated. But defeat cleared the way for much needed reforms.

THE REFORMS OF ALEXANDER II (1855-1881)

In 1855 just one year before the Crimean War ended, Alexander II succeeded to the throne. He realized that one of the reasons for Russia's military defeat was its economic and technological backwardness. He recognized that such backwardness could be traced to serfdom.

In the years after Peter the Great, Russian economic growth had faltered noticeably. For example, at the end of the 18th century, Russia had been mining more iron ore than any other country in the world; but when Alexander II took the throne, Russia produced less even than tiny Belgium.

Alexander II understood that the discontent of the peasant-serfs was fast approaching a climax of mass rebellion. Revolts in the countryside had increased steadily since the beginning of the century. Some landlords and factory owners had even come to agree that serfdom was economically unprofitable, declaring that free labor would be more efficient. For all these reasons, Alexander decided in 1861 to abolish serfdom.

The year 1861 is a critical date in Russian history because it opened the way for the development of modern Russia. But had Alexander's action come too late?

Under the decree, the peasants did not receive all the land. Furthermore, the land was not given to them as private property, but as communal, or village, property.

If the land had always been theirs, as the peasants believed, why then had not the tsar freely given it back to them? Instead of being soothed, peasant discontent smouldered throughout the life of the monarchy, later to flash into a revolutionary flame.

Other major reforms followed Alexander's abolition of serfdom: reform in local government, in the judicial system, in the press, the universities, and the army. All were designed to build Russia from a backward state into one that was powerful and orderly. No reforms were designed to share any power with the people.

Under Alexander the last great wave of expansion brought the Caucasus and most of central Asia under Russian control. But Alexander was hardly a second Peter the Great. At times he was indecisive, apparently overwhelmed by the complexity of his responsibilities, confused by the conflicting advice of his officials, and unable to control the forces he had released or to coördinate the activities of his government.

In the past there had been a few voices of opposition; now there was a chorus of criticism. The groups demanding political liberty and distribution of all land to the peasants were called Populists. Some of the more extreme Populists plotted revolution against the monarchy. By the end of his life, Alexander II became a hunted man in his own country. In 1881 the last active band of Populist terrorists assassinated him, and Russia sank once more into a state of political lethargy.

UNSOLVED PROBLEMS

The new tsar, Alexander III (1881-1894), crushed the revolutionary organizations, halted, and even tried to reverse many of his father's policies, but not even the tsar could hold back the momentum of the social and economic changes set in motion by Alexander II.

By the 1880's industry was forging ahead; peasants began moving into the cities, creating a new industrial working class; even a small middle class took shape. These developments brought new problems. There was not enough farm land to support the growing rural population. Overcrowding, long hours, low wages, and miserable working conditions menaced peasants who moved to the cities.

The needs of the masses were just as pressing as ever, though the character of these needs had changed somewhat. The government did little to satisfy these demands, and the masses had no legal means to make their complaints known. There was no representative assembly. Trade unions and strikes were forbidden. The press was heavily censored.

The embryonic Russian middle class shied away from any reform. In part this attitude was due to the economic weakness of this group. The state had taken the lead in developing industry, just as it had imposed its influence throughout Russian economic and cultural life for centuries. By 1914 the tsarist state owned or operated two thirds of the nation's railroads and the postal, telephone, and telegraph enterprises. It organized state monopolies in some popular commodities like salt and vodka.

The growing middle class wanted to see the government modernized but also feared the rising strength of the masses. Therefore, it turned to the government for protection.

REVOLUTION AND WAR

Meanwhile the intelligentsia—the politically conscious members of the society—found the most appeal in revolutionary doctrines for two reasons: (1) the government continued to balk at reform and (2) other groups in the nation only weakly sought reform. It was during this critical period that the first Marxist revolutionary groups were formed in Russia.

The assassination of Alexander II.

As tension mounted, remnants of the old Populist groups revived and strengthened their organizations. The government grew increasingly fearful of revolution.

A military disaster then further ripened Russia for its first modern revolution. An expansionist Russian policy in Korea and Manchuria angered Japan to the point of attack in 1904. The Russo-Japanese War showed the military weakness of Russia and glaringly spotlighted the incompetency of the regime as it had evolved under Nicholas II (1894-1917).

In 1905 a revolution shook Russia. Elements of every class of the population took part. Peasants seized the land; workers went out on strike. Even the once hesitant middle-class groups backed the strikes and called for political reforms. The revolutionary parties worked hard to overthrow the autocracy.

Under such enormous pressure, Tsar Nicholas was forced to promise a constitution and a representative assembly, to be called the Duma.

But the monarchy recovered its balance. It negotiated a large loan from France, ended the war in the Far East, and recalled the army. Consequently it blatantly revoked many of its promises.

Both the First and Second Duma pushed forward the demand for land reform. Tsar Nicholas dissolved both the First and the Second Duma. Then, in 1907, he changed the electoral law — a violation of the new constitution — in order to obtain a more moderate Duma. In other words Nicholas made concessions only when he was weak and revoked them when he was strong.

Tsar Nicholas II and his family, killed by the Bolsheviks July 18, 1918.

One last effort was made by the tsar to solve the peasant question. From 1906 to 1911 Prime Minister Peter Stolypin introduced legislation which aimed at breaking up the communal ownership of land and creating a class of peasant farmers who would own their own land. He hoped that this new peasant class would become a solid supporter of the tsar in return for this grant of land. No one knows how successful the reform might have been. World War I erupted before the reform measure could be fully carried out.

Russia entered the war to protect its interests in the Balkans on the flank of the strategic straits linking the Black Sea and the Mediterranean. Austria-Hungary was Russia's great rival in this area. Following the Crimean War, Russia had fought the Turks in 1877-1878 and had come to the brink of war several times (in 1878, 1887, 1908), in order to protect its influence and support protégés in the area.

In 1914, when Austria threatened to destroy Serbia, one of Russia's tiny allies, the Russians, believing their national interest was at stake, took up arms again. Thus they set the stage for a new defeat and a new revolution.

Tsar Nicholas conducted the war miserably. The severe strains of heavy losses and lack of munitions and food turned the nation against him. In March 1917, to the great surprise of the nation's revolutionary leaders, a spontaneous, anonymous, almost unanimous uprising in Petrograd (now Leningrad) overthrew the weak monarchy.

A democratically inclined provisional government was established, and in July 1917 Alexander Kerensky was named premier. But the mood of revolt which prevailed made it impossible for him to enforce the authority of the central government. Following a series of defeats, the army disintegrated.

In November 1917 a small band of revolutionary Marxists, demanding an end to the war, land for the peasants, and the establishment of a workers' dictatorship, overthrew the tottering Kerensky government. Their leader was Lenin, whose name and doctrine played the dominant role in the next stage of Russian history.

SUMMARY

We see, then, on the vast geographical stage of Russia that four powerful historical themes early began to influence the character of the people and their state: expansion, authoritarianism, technological backwardness, and a revolutionary tradition.

Through tribal life, a brilliant Kievan civilization, crushing Mongol incursions, and centuries of autocratic tsarism, we observe the shifting fortunes of peasants, nobles, the church, the military, a meager middle class, intellectuals, and the rulers of the state themselves.

We note the massive struggle to reform politically, socially, and economically a country whose progress had for centuries lagged far behind that of the Western world.

We see the Russian monarchy fail to carry on the initiative of Peter the Great in modernizing the land, by refusing to allow the people to share in political power in order to carry on the modernization themselves. We see tsars engage in a series of foreign wars which deplete their nation's strength to resist internal opposition. Finally we see the masses of the nation begin to rise against the regime, pointing toward the moment when it can be overthrown. That moment comes in 1917. At the same time communism enters Russia's story and Lenin's seizure of power signals a turbulent new era.

Charles Kay

TERMS TO KNOW

Cossacks	Golden Horde	Decembrist insurrection
buffer	westernizing	Populists
boyar duma	schismatics	Duma

QUESTIONS ON THE CHAPTER

1. What four themes pervade Russian history?
2. List several ways in which Kievan Russia was influenced by Byzantium.

3. Tell what effects the Mongol invasion had on Russian trade and city life.

4. In what ways did Ivan the Terrible increase the authority of the state at the expense of individual rights?

5. When was the Romanov dynasty established? How long did this dynasty remain in power?

6. Describe what happened to the social class structure of Russian society during the reign of Peter the Great.

7. Why was the partition of Poland among Russia, Austria, and Prussia a grave error on Russia's part?

8. How did Tsar Nicholas I react to the Decembrist insurrection?

9. Why did Alexander II decide to abolish serfdom in 1861?

10. As a result of increased industrialization in Russia during the late 1800's, what new problems were created for the people?

11. What moderate concessions were made by Tsar Nicholas II as a result of the Revolution of 1905?

12. Give one reason why Russia entered World War I.

QUESTIONS FOR DISCUSSION

1. Compare life in Kievan Russia with life in Tsarist Russia. Include among your comparisons the following: (a) political organization; (b) classes of society; (c) economic structure.

2. It has been suggested that the Communist dictatorship in the Soviet Union today is merely an extension of the way of life that the Russian people were used to under the tsars. Examine the history of Russian society under the tsars and discuss the validity of this statement.

3. Communist imperialism represents a decided menace to world peace today. It should be remembered, however, that the desire to acquire territory has existed throughout Russian history and that it is not a new development. Point out examples of this from Russian history, and explain the various reasons behind the continual drive to expand the boundaries of Russia.

BIBLIOGRAPHY

For Reference: ☐ Harcave, Sidney, *Russia: A History.* J. B. Lippincott Company, 1959. ☐ Lawrence, John, *A History of Russia.* New American Library, 1962. ☐ Pares, Bernard, *Russia.* New American Library, 1953. ☐ Vernadsky, George, *A History of Russia.* Yale University Press, 1961. ☐ Walsh, Warren B., *Russia and the Soviet Union: A Modern History.* University of Michigan Press, 1958. For Further Reading: ☐ Dostoevsky, Fyodor, *Best Short Stories.* Modern Library. ☐ Gogol, Nikolai, *The Inspector General.* 2nd edition. Pitman Publishing Corporation, 1945. ☐ Pushkin, Alexander, *Poems, Prose and Plays.* Modern Library. ☐ Thomas, Henry, *Catherine the Great.* Blue Ribbon Books, 1946. ☐ Tolstoy, Leo, *War and Peace.* Abridged edition, edited by Edmund Fuller. Dell Publishing Company, 1955. ☐ Turgenev, Ivan, *A Sportsman's Notebook* (A Sportsman's Sketches). Translated by Charles and Natasha Hepburn. Viking Press, 1957.

CHAPTER **3**

THEORY AND DEVELOPMENT
OF COMMUNIST IDEOLOGY

Karl Marx's theory of communism
has been supplemented or contradicted
but never ignored
by the leaders of the Soviet state:
Lenin, Trotsky, Stalin, and Khrushchev.

Communism is called an ideology. By ideology we mean a body of ideas. The ideology of communism is based upon the theory of ownership and operation of the means of production and distribution of goods, not by individuals, but by society. This society is the result of a class struggle leading to a social revolution and the establishment of a party dictatorship.

If it seems a little difficult at times to trace the ideology of communism, to distinguish between its many official forms and definitions, theories and practices, you may be encouraged to know that there are millions, both in Communist and non-Communist countries, who share your confusion.

Present-day communism is based on the ideas of Karl Marx, modified by Nikolai Lenin and his followers to further the domestic and foreign aims of the U.S.S.R.

Karl Marx (1818-1883): "All philosophies have sought to explain the world; our business is to change it." (From a portrait of Marx and his daughter)

Four of the functions of Communist ideology may be briefly summarized in this way:

First, Communist leaders use ideology to inspire, lead, and indoctrinate the population of the country.

Second, communism designates a single condition, capitalism, as the source of all the world's troubles.

Third, it indicates to leaders of the Communist society what action will best achieve Communist goals.

Fourth, Communist ideology singles out the enemies of the dictatorial Communist government. The Communists claim this helps to bind the people in unbending loyalty to the Communist state.

I. KARL MARX—THE ORIGINS OF MARXISM

Karl Marx (1818-1883) was a German social philosopher, a radical leader, and a journalist. He, among other social critics, observed the worst evils of the world's young industrialization process as they began to appear in the 18th and 19th centuries. Industrial cities were then areas of overcrowding, of unsanitary conditions, crime, violence, unsafe and unsavory workshops, child labor, exploitation, antagonism between worker and employer.

Observing these social conditions first-hand, Marx, together with his close friend and collaborator, Friedrich Engels (1820-1895), began to turn his attention more and more to the idea that private property was at the root of the poverty and degradation of the newly arising working class.

Marx based his theories on years of research. These efforts, he believed, showed conclusively the existence of inevitable historical laws which man could discover and understand. He thus claimed that his theories were not utopian, like those of other philosophers of his day, but scientific. They could be investigated, understood, and verified.

Because the mid-19th century marked a shift in emphasis from philosophical thinking to scientific thinking, the scientific basis which Marx claimed for his ideas had wide appeal.

Despite Marx's protests to the contrary, there was in his philosophy a strong moralistic element which lurked behind the "scientific" mask. He passionately protested the dehumanization of the factory worker. He envisioned man's mind and spirit liberated by the coming of communism. These visions were far removed from the cold, rational analysis he preached.

Marxism may be said to have three elements: (1) philosophical, (2) historical, (3) economic.

MARXISM: ITS PHILOSOPHICAL BASIS

The philosophical basis of Marxism is most often referred to as *dialectical materialism*, puzzling words at first, perhaps, but not too difficult to understand as we learn more about their meaning.

Materialism traces all reality to matter. Matter includes everything we perceive or understand by means of seeing, hearing, smelling, tasting, or feeling. A materialist contends that everything derives from matter, even thoughts, conscience, religion, and philosophy. Thus to a materialist, God exists only as a byproduct of the brain, a physical, material part of the body.

Dialectical refers simply to the manner in which matter acts or changes. Change in the universe, for example, occurs because of opposing forces or contradictions in matter. As the struggle between these forces—we might call them positive and negative forces—reaches a peak of violence, a change in the quality of the matter takes place. A new form of matter appears after this revolutionary change. The new form preserves the best qualities of the elements that were battling before and is something different from the sum of both.

In a way it is like a heated conversation in which you state your *thesis*, or point of view. A friend sharply disagrees with you and states his *antithesis*, or counterargument, to support his side. As your arguments clash, a new point of view begins to take shape. The new viewpoint is quite different from the ones you each believe to be correct but also a little similar to what each believed. This new belief or understanding may be called the *synthesis*.

It is important to understand this scheme of thesis, antithesis, and synthesis because these were the philosophical principles that Marx tried to apply to the history of mankind.

He contended that man's life is based on material things, and depends on the production and distribution of goods. Man must eat before he can think, Marx would argue. In order to change the ways of man's life, therefore, the means of production and distribution must first change. Political, intellectual, and even cultural changes would then follow material change, according to Marxian reasoning.

Marx declared that in earliest societies there was no such thing as private property. He said such societies were primitive communistic. Every man had control over the productive forces he needed to make a living. Men worked together in mutual coöperation. In a sense they were equals.

When some men acquired a control over labor, natural resources, or tools, however, their lives were changed. No longer did they work for themselves in order to feed themselves. Instead, they began to live on the labor of others. This, said Marx, constituted exploitation of one man by another. Exploitation, Marx claimed, was the beginning of the division of mankind into classes and the beginning of the struggle between those who were exploited (the laborers) and the exploiters (the property owners).

Here Marx found what he called the inner contradiction in every society. Ultimately this contradiction leads to revolutionary change, he said. The class struggle was thus the dialectic process operating in history. History itself was the study of the class struggle.

MARXISM: ITS HISTORICAL BASIS

Marx traced five historical stages in the evolution of production:

1 Primitive communism: in which the means of production are owned by everyone

2 Slave society: in which the slaveowner controls the means of production

3 Feudal society: in which feudal lords control the means of production

4 Capitalist society: in which the entrepreneur owns the means of production, but not the workers themselves

5 Socialist society: in which workers own the means of production.

Let us now examine Marx's concept of the transition from one stage of society to another—a violent transition, a revolution.

The class struggle sharpens when a new invention or discovery brings about a change in the production process. For example, consider an agricultural country that has just discovered large quantities of coal and iron which it decides to develop. In order to do this, labor forces must be collected, machinery built, property acquired, and investments made. The men who controlled the agricultural economy are hardly qualified to manage these affairs. Therefore, a new type of economic leader comes to the fore. He will be a manufacturer, an industrialist, a capitalist.

But the landowner resists this reorganization of the agricultural economy into an industrial economy. He foresees the decline of his power over labor and natural resources, over the material means of production which Marx claimed to be the basis of life. The landowner's fierce resistance to change and the rising capitalist is one element in Marx's class struggle. When the economic power of the new capitalist class reaches the point where further progress is blocked by the resistance of the landowner, then social revolution comes about.

In the philosophical terms we introduced earlier, the *thesis* of this process is the feudal landowner. The *antithesis* is the capitalist class. The *synthesis* is a new society of capitalists.

Marx explained the English Revolution of 1688, the American Revolution of 1776, and the French Revolution of 1789 as capitalist revolutions.

When the victorious class takes over, it reconstructs society on the basis of its particular class interests. This, said Marx, shows that the control of the means of production and distribution serves as an actual *substructure,* or foundation, of society. The dominant class, made up of capitalists, controls the government, which is part of the *superstructure* of society. Law, religion, the press, schools, entertainment, science, and the arts are also parts of the superstructure. And all serve the productive interests of the capitalists, says Marx.

MARX'S CLASS–STRUCTURED SOCIETY

ART ▪ RELIGION ▪ LAW ▪ SCHOOLS ▪ SCIENCE ▪ THE PRESS ▪ GOVERNMENT ▪ ENTERTAINMENT

Superstructure of society reflects the influence of the substructure.

⬆   ⬆   ⬆

MEANS OF PRODUCTION and DISTRIBUTION OF GOODS (machines, capital, labor)

Substructure of society influences the superstructure.

⬆   ⬆   ⬆

Capitalists	Feudal Aristocracy	Slave Owners

*Any one class that becomes dominant
will control the substructure of society
and through that the superstructure of society.*

Marx contended that religion is an "opiate of the people" because it deludes them into thinking that life on earth is not important, compared to an afterlife. Therefore, Marx continues, the people will not protest exploitation by the capitalists; they will remain apathetic and passive. This suits the goal of the capitalists, he points out, which is to keep the workers from grumbling or organizing against them.

Marx, the materialist, thought religion was preventing people from struggling to obtain a decent life on earth, the only existence they would ever know.

Therefore, a social revolution affects the ownership, the government, the law, the arts, and religion.

MARXISM: ITS ECONOMIC BASIS

The final element of Marxism is economic. It explains how Marx envisaged the final revolution from the capitalist to the socialist stage of society. This is the revolution which Lenin and his Bolsheviks claimed to have accomplished.

The key word in this phase of Marxism is *exploitation.*

Marx explains exploitation of the working class in terms of two economic theories which, he says, can be scientifically proved:

1 The theory of labor value and
2 The theory of surplus value.

According to Marx's theory of labor value, a manufactured product is worth only the amount of labor which has gone into its making. Although Marx did not mean this theory to be taken literally, he did not explain precisely what he did mean, a serious weakness in much of his theorizing. We can assume that he considered labor to be the only creative force in the productive process. Capital and machines were "dead," or noncreative, elements.

Marx argued that under capitalism labor is treated as just another commodity; it is bought and sold by the capitalists.

But what is worse, Marx said, was the fact that the worker is also being cheated out of the fruits of his own labor. Marx said this happens first because the capitalists control the productive forces which include labor, and second, because the worker can produce more than he requires to subsist.

This reasoning led Marx to work out a theory of surplus labor. A worker receives only enough wages to keep him alive. He then receives only what his labor is worth on the labor market, according to supply and demand. But he produces more value in a day than he receives in the form of wages.

Thus, according to Marx's reasoning, if a man works ten hours a day, what he produces in the first five hours is equal in value to the total he is to receive in wages. For the value of his production in the second five hours, he receives nothing. This is the value the capitalist takes as profit, said Marx, denying the worker the value of five hours of labor. This five hours is surplus value stolen from the worker, Marx charged; the worker, therefore, is exploited.

How does this exploited worker turn into a revolutionary? This process involves three more Marxian laws: (1) the law of capitalist accumulation; (2) the law of the concentration of capital; (3) the law of increased misery.

According to Marx, capitalism feeds on competition. In order to outsell competitors, the capitalist introduces labor-saving devices, cuts prices and even profits, and reduces wages. The cost of this fierce competition to accumulate capital, or money, are so high that the less successful capitalists are ruined. This process results in the concentration of capital.

The ruined capitalists are driven into the ranks of the property-less workers. Capitalists thus become fewer and fewer. To defend their interests, they create trusts and monopolies, powerful organizations concentrating enormous wealth. Here Marx's third theory comes into operation.

Because of the introduction of labor-saving devices with no corresponding effort to relocate or retrain the workers displaced by machines, the supply of workers begins to exceed the demand. More workers are competing for fewer jobs. They accept lower wages. An army of unemployment accumulates. In this state of material misery, brought about by the capitalist system, says Marx, man reaches the limits of suffering and degradation. At this point he has, in Marx's famous words, "nothing to lose but his chains."

The moments for the clash of thesis and antithesis has arrived — the mass uprising of the workers in blind outrage against the capitalists who exploit them. This inevitable moment, says Marx, is the socialist revolution.

The victorious workers take control of the means of production and distribution. Private property is abolished. The defeated capitalists resist, but gradually the workers' state crushes them. The new state, the dictatorship of the *proletariat* or laboring people, was to be only a brief period in the final transition to communism. Marx visualized this as a dictatorship of one class, the workers, over another class, the capitalists, a dictatorship of the majority over the minority. Therefore, as he saw it, only the workers were to enjoy democratic rights. The enormous productive capacity inherited from the capitalists would give the working class the means ultimately to satisfy the needs and desires of everyone. With contradictions in the substructure gone, the superstructure of law, religion, the arts, and government is not needed. With the workers owning the means of production, there are no more surplus values, no more exploitation, and no more classes. Then, having no other purpose, the dictatorship, the state, would wither.

At first, under communism, everybody would work according to his abilities, and be paid according to his work. Soon, however, the introduction of technical innovations which, according to Marx, the capitalists had been afraid to develop, would create such an abundance of goods that "everyone works according to his abilities and receives according to his needs." Stage two of communism would thus arrive.

Shortly, money would disappear, everyone would be permitted to take what he or she would want from public storehouses containing the great material abundance of man. Man would lack nothing and would be free to develop his talents and skills to the highest degree. According to Marx, the sheer pleasure of seeing the fruitful results of his work should be enough to induce man to work. Like money, vice and crime will have fled from this society because, Marx reasoned, these were merely symptoms of a class society where men were exploited by the capitalists.

Marx's vision of the future may have been vague in many respects, but it was optimistic and attractive to those who were miserable and disillusioned.

MARXISM CHALLENGED

Though Marxism was and is a powerful social theory, it is open to serious challenge.

The class struggle is based on an extremely debatable method of analysis. Marx attributes class ideas, or class consciousness, as he calls it, to all the workers. Actually, in all countries, including Russia, these ideas have been confined to small groups of revolutionaries. The histories of international socialist movements, furthermore, show how little sense of solidarity has ever existed between the laborers of different countries.

Marx maintains that scientific invention causes change in the substructure of society. Yet, Marx placed science itself in the superstructure. In fact, Marx never explained adequately the relationship between the substructure and the superstructure. Soviet Communists today juggle elements in both, with complete disregard for the original scheme. This oversimplified forecast of the continuation of the concentration of capital, the increased poverty of the working class, and the elimination of small producers in capitalist countries has not taken place anywhere.

The conflict between labor and capital, worker and manager, has diminished considerably and given way to conciliation and even collusion! The growth of trade unions, the spread of representative government, the increase in social legislation, these elements in the world's progress have solved many of the problems which Marx described.

Actions by governments (in Marx's superstructure) have radically altered the productive process (substructure) without revolution, in many cases without socializing the means of production. Many workers today even own part of the company for which they work through the purchase of stocks and bonds. This is a capitalist, not a socialist, innovation.

By giving such importance to the control of the means of production and distribution as the motivating force in history, Marx ignores or deëmphasizes other basic reasons for the actions of men and groups of men.

One forceful motive is the love of power, as shown in the grasping for dictatorial authority. As the history of the Soviet Union itself so graphically shows, this lust for power can be a fundamental motivation.

Marx ignores another forceful motive, the desire for national unity. Even in the face of economic dislocation and suffering, people strive to create a national state.

Few motives are more powerful among men than the search for truth. What better proof of this than Marx himself? Here was a man who claimed that knowledge, ideas, arose from a material condition. Yet his own ideology arose from the mind of a man who knew nothing from first-hand experience about physical labor.

To sum up: Marx's analysis is not scientific, consistent, or accurate. His disciples have selected facts to fit his theory. They agree that the revolution is inevitable, yet they do everything possible to hasten it, even in the face of conditions which Marx described as adverse to revolutionary success.

MARXISM FINDS ROOT IN RUSSIA

Russians were slower to react to Marx's theories than other peoples in Europe. Marx was partly to blame. He believed that revolution would come first in the industrialized countries of western Europe. But he thought that because of the communal ownership of property in the Russian countryside, Russia might not have to experience the capitalist stage. Perhaps, he reasoned, a Russian agrarian revolution would be successful if it coincided with a genuine proletarian revolution in western Europe. Thus he hardly encouraged the development of Marxist groups in Russia.

Yet, beginning in the 1880's, small numbers of Russian intellectuals turned from Populism to Marxism as an answer to their hope for social revolution. Even then they began to alter certain tenets of Marxism to suit their purposes. These modifications arose from the peculiar Russian revolutionary tradition.

II. RUSSIA'S REVOLUTIONARY TRADITION:
PEASANT DISCONTENT

There were two revolutionary traditions in Russia. One was rooted in the mass discontent of the peasantry. The other can be traced to intellectual protests against the economic backwardness and political authoritarianism of the Russian state.

The tradition of peasant uprisings goes back to the 16th century, when economic burdens and state regulations began to bind the peasant to the land. Often these sporadic insurrections blossomed into large-scale rebellions involving hundreds of thousands of peasants and Cossack horsemen. Such were the uprisings during the Time of Troubles (1604-1613), the rebellion of Stenka Razin (1670-1671), the Bulavin uprising (1707) under Peter the Great, and the great uprising led by Emelyan Pugachev (1773-1774).

In the forty years before the abolition of serfdom in 1861, there were more than one thousand officially recorded disorders. Even after serfdom was abolished, the peasants rose up to protest the terms of the liberation. In 1905-1906 the countryside was in open revolt against both the landlords and the tsar. In most cases these uprisings were spontaneous, leaderless, and highly disorganized. The aims of the rebels were vague and confused. Usually they could be summed up under the slogan "Land and freedom."

Only after the revolution of 1905 did the government begin to meet these peasant demands. But it was much too late then to turn the peasants from violence. Thus in 1917, with the breakdown of military and administrative order in Russia, the peasants in the army and in the countryside moved to carry out their own revolution. They swept aside every form of legal and territorial authority in the countryside, took over the land, and distributed it in a rough sort of equalitarian fashion.

RUSSIA'S REVOLUTIONARY TRADITION: INTELLECTUAL DISCONTENT

In the early years of the 19th century, a more articulate intellectual opposition arose. It was centered in the cities and in the manor houses of rural Russia. Intellectuals who were alert to the shortcomings of the government shared a hostility toward the tsars and tsarinas that can be traced back to the reign of Catherine the Great.

Nobles who had served as officers in the Allied army that occupied France returned home filled with admiration for French doctrines of liberty, equality, and fraternity. A few tried to overthrow the tsarist autocracy in the 1825 Decembrist insurrection.

In the 1830's and 1840's small groups of disillusioned nobles formed intellectual circles to discuss Russia's future in terms of the newest political and social ideas from the West.

These intellectuals soon separated into two groups. One called itself the Westernizers, the other, the Slavophiles.

The Westernizers favored political reform, the introduction of a constitution, and a representative assembly which would help carry on the work of modernizing Russia begun by Peter the Great.

The Slavophiles favored moral regeneration of Russia based on the Orthodox Church. They condemned Peter the Great and all Western ideas (though they themselves borrowed heavily from this source). Actually they did not oppose the principle of autocracy but wanted to bring the tsar into closer contact with the people by means of a consultative assembly and the introduction of free speech.

The tsar persecuted both groups and forced them toward more radical programs. Disappointed by the reforms of the 1860's and spurred to illegal action by the government's clampdown on legal criticism, they drifted closer toward revolutionary action.

By the 1870's revolutionary activity coalesced into the Populist movement. Populism in Russia stood for the overthrow of the autocratic monarchy and the socialization of the land based on the traditional Russian peasant communes. But the Populists could not agree on how best to achieve their goals.

One group, led by Peter Lavrov (1823-1900) and Alexander Herzen (1812-1870), believed that the first task was to educate the peasants in socialism and then to map out a revolution.

Others, inspired by the fiery Mikhail Bakunin (1814-1876), supported the idea of encouraging immediate peasant rebellions throughout the countryside in order to paralyze and topple the monarchy.

In the early 1870's several thousand Russian students, aroused by Herzen's encouragement to "go to the people," left their university classes and flocked to the countryside to work among the peasants and preach the cause of revolution. But the suspicious peasants did not understand these young people with their soft hands and strange talk. Many students were turned over to the tsar's police, others were driven out of the villages, a few were murdered.

This tragic movement to the people exposed the great cultural gap which existed between the intelligentsia and the peasantry, between the intellectual revolutionary tradition and the peasant revolutionary tradition. Intellectual principles of socialism were beyond the comprehension of the illiterate peasants. All they wanted was the land.

In 1876, meanwhile, the more aggressive members of the Populist movement organized an underground party, the Land and Freedom party. Their purpose was to spread illegal propaganda and to organize terrorist attacks upon leading officials of the autocracy. Their units were small and secret to avoid arrests and enforce discipline.

The terrorist wing of the party took the name People's Will and despite heavy losses succeeded in killing Tsar Alexander II in 1881.

To their dismay, however, the autocracy did not collapse. The reactionary and tough-minded Alexander III, who succeeded to the throne, swiftly wiped out the small remnants of the terrorist group. Neither Lavrov's peaceful propaganda nor the terrorism of Bakunin's heirs could overturn the monarchy.

PLEKHANOV INTRODUCES MARXISM

In this time of revolutionary failure, one of the leading moderate Populists, Georgi V. Plekhanov (1857-1918), emigrated to Switzerland to ponder new action.

Turning away from Populism, Plekhanov founded the first Russian Marxist organization. Soon he was being called the father of

Russian Marxism, for his books and articles were smuggled into Russia, where they influenced many students of the new generation. These young people saw around them the development of industry, the rise of a working class, and the chance to base the revolution not on the peasantry but on the proletariat.

III. NIKOLAI LENIN

Among these young people was one named Vladimir Ilyich Ulyanov, known as Nikolai Lenin (1870-1924). He had come from a respectable, middle-class, petty-noble background. It is difficult to explain why he and his brother had become revolutionaries except to say that his entire generation was alive with discontent. From the time he was a young man, Lenin had never allowed his revolutionary ardor to slacken. His brother had been executed for participating in an amateur plot against Tsar Alexander III in the 1880's.

Lenin had been expelled from school for participating in a student demonstration. In the mid-1890's he had been arrested for

Nikolai Lenin (1870-1924): "Without a revolutionary theory there can be no revolutionary movement."

taking part in textile mill strikes and had been exiled to Siberia. There he had reconsidered the problems of organizing a Marxist party for all of Russia.

By this time there were many variations of Marxism in Russia. Lenin hoped to found a newspaper and a party which would eliminate factional differences and create one powerful and determined revolutionary group. The newspaper *Iskra* ("The Spark") was founded in 1900, the party permanently organized in 1903, but Lenin never controlled both as he wanted. In his struggle to do so, he revealed his own thinking about Marxism in Russia. His doctrine has become known as Leninism.

LENINISM: THE PARTY

Organization was a prime element in Leninism. Lenin wanted the Russian Social Democratic party to be small, tightly knit, secret, made up of professional revolutionaries. Only this type of party, he felt, could survive in the life-or-death conflict with the tsarist police. Under the Russian autocratic political system, only a party organized as a conspiracy could succeed.

Advanced revolutionary theory developed by revolutionary intellectuals must guide this party, said Lenin. "Our task is to fight against spontaneity," he wrote. In other words he rejected at the outset Marx's view that class consciousness could arise only from the material conditions of the proletariat. If left alone, Lenin warned, the workers would develop what he called a trade-union consciousness. They would struggle only for higher wages, shorter hours, and better working conditions. These goals Lenin placed second to the political struggle against the autocracy. But the workers, caught up in their daily tasks, could not see this. Only intellectuals like himself could see the broad perspectives of history.

The party, therefore, would have to train the masses to respond unquestioningly to the directives of the party core. This the party would accomplish by infiltrating the trade unions and other organizations of the people. Lenin was convinced that the few could manipulate the many.

Lenin substituted the iron will of conscious leadership for the elemental forces of history which Marx described.

So certain was he that this form of revolutionary organization was needed that in 1903 he proceeded to force a split in the Russian

Social Democratic party. Lenin's group, called the *Bolsheviks*, moved away from the *Mensheviks*, who rejected his uncompromising theory and organization. Lenin never hesitated to split again and again with his followers if they refused to accept his ideas. "Better fewer but better," he said.

Democracy within the party, according to Lenin, would be unrealistic, utopian. He insisted that the majority be subordinated to the minority, the central party committee. And within this committee there must be doctrinal purity and utter loyalty to the revolution. Unreliable elements must be eliminated from this core, demanded Lenin, foreshadowing the ruthless purges of later years.

Lenin paid lip service to a few democratic forms, such as the right of any party member to speak his mind. But once a decision had been made by the leaders everyone was obliged to carry it out. This was called democratic centralism. Furthermore, soon after taking power, the Bolsheviks passed a rule outlawing so-called factionalism. That is, opposition or disagreement could no longer be announced by groups within the party. Even if several party members held the same views, they had to express them individually. But who would dare to stand out alone against the leaders? The right to criticize had been severely weakened.

LENIN'S THEORY OF IMPERIALISM

In another variation on Marxian doctrine, Lenin explained the failure of Marx's predictions on the increased misery of the European proletariat. He also rejected the Marxist view that revolution had to come first in the advanced industrial countries of the West. If the Russians had to wait for revolts in the West—and all this time the lot of the workers of the West seemed to be improving rather than worsening—then the prospects for the Russian Revolution were dismal indeed!

In 1916, on the eve of the Russian Revolution, Lenin introduced his theory of imperialism. As practiced by Europe's great colonial powers, imperialism denoted overseas expansion to acquire worldwide empires. However, Lenin saw this expansion as an attempt by the capitalists to avoid the internal contradictions which Marx predicted would destroy them. In order to restore dwindling profits, he explained, the capitalists sought new investments and new markets among the economically underdeveloped areas of the world, where cheap labor, untapped natural resources, and little or no competition were to be found.

Because of the strength of the capitalist nations and the weakness of the colonial people, said Lenin, the capitalists were able to spread their exploitation throughout the world. With the huge profits from these ventures, the capitalists then could raise the wages of the working class at home. This, Lenin declared, was tantamount to buying their own proletariat with the surplus value taken from the colonial proletariat. Lenin thus explained the rising living standards of Europe. But he warned that this was only temporary.

Marx, he explained, simply had not lived long enough to see that imperialism was the last stage of capitalism. The Marxian contradictions were present, but they were harder to recognize when spread out on a global scale. Lenin prophesied that capitalists would inevitably war against each other over colonial areas. Thus, until recently, Leninists have maintained that wars between capitalist countries were inevitable.

All of this theory had widespread implications for the Russian Revolution and, in later days, for the Chinese and Cuban revolutions. In Lenin's eyes, the most exploited class in the world was no longer the working class of the advanced countries, but rather the working class of the backward countries. Consequently, the consciousness of these workers must be more highly developed. These people could then be expected to become the vanguard of the world revolutionary movement.

LENIN'S THEORY OF COMBINED DEVELOPMENT

The complexities of the class struggle in the backward countries gave rise to another Leninist doctrine, his theory of "combined development."

Because these colonized countries had not yet fully experienced capitalism, but had been influenced by certain aspects of Western capitalist societies, they showed a mixture of Western conditions: bits of slaveholding, feudalism, and capitalism, according to Lenin.

With such a complex variety of problems and struggles at hand, the Communist tactician has a field day choosing how to launch his revolution. Though his tactics may change, the grand strategy is rigid—mobilizing the mass of the population behind the tightly knit party as the prelude to seizing power and establishing the Communist dictatorship.

Communist victories in backward countries, said Lenin, would deprive the imperialist powers of the profits they needed to "bribe" their own proletariat. The imperialists would have to cut wages and lay off workers. Depression would result. The misery of the workers would intensify—as Marx had foretold—and the revolution of the proletariat in the advanced countries would come about at last.

Thus Lenin explained how a revolution could come to Russia before it came to the West. But could this be a genuine socialist revolution?

TROTSKY AND "PERMANENT REVOLUTION"

The splintered band of Russian Marxists—Bolsheviks, Mensheviks, and many smaller groups—hardly had strength enough to carry out a Russian revolution alone.

Neither Lenin nor the Mensheviks understood the possibilities within the disorganized 1905 rebellion against the monarchy for driving toward the socialist revolution. An intense young intellectual, named Lev Davidovich Bronstein, however, saw things differently. Already called by a new name—Leon Trotsky—he threw himself into the revolutionary struggle of 1905 on the basis of his own theory of "permanent revolution."

Lenin and the Mensheviks had thought that the only possible goal of the 1905 uprising was to establish liberal democratic rights in Russia. Trotsky argued that the revolution could be pushed far beyond this point. He reasoned that the Russian capitalists were few in number (which was true) and lacked the power to overthrow the autocracy by themselves (also probably true).

Trotsky maintained that the working class should not only seize control of the revolution and overthrow the autocracy but keep power and push forward to the socialist revolution. By making two revolutions in one, the Russian Marxists could avoid the long period of capitalist development. Karl Marx would hardly have approved, but revolutionaries are impatient people.

Trotsky added that he did not expect the Russian proletariat to reach its goal of socialism alone. It was too small a group and too isolated. Furthermore, the peasants would not tolerate socialism. But Trotsky did expect that the Russian revolution would also

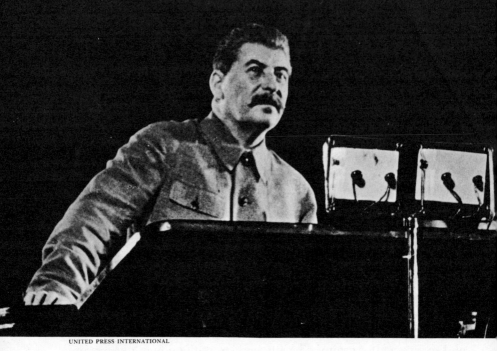

Joseph Stalin (1879-1953): "Iron discipline in the party is inconceivable without unity of will."

touch off a genuine European proletarian revolution. Then the victorious European working class could come to the aid of its class comrades in Russia, help subject the peasantry and, as the climax of "permanent revolution," establish socialism across the vast Eurasian plain.

LENIN AND TROTSKY JOIN FORCES

Few Marxists accepted Trotsky's view in 1905. By 1917, though, Lenin had come round to accepting part of Trotsky's theory and together they moved to implement the theory of "permanent revolution." They transformed the democratic insurrection of March 1917 into the socialist revolution of October 1917.

At the same time, Trotsky—after many years of opposition—accepted Lenin's idea of the small, hard-core, conspiratorial party. By joining forces on these two crucial matters, Lenin and Trotsky rode to power. After they took power, however, the eagerly awaited revolution in the west did not materialize.

What then should the Russian revolutionaries do? Should they direct their energies primarily to encouraging other revolutions?

Or should they first build up their own industrial power in order to help backward countries in their struggle against imperialism?

LENIN'S DEATH STARTS A STRUGGLE FOR POWER

Before these questions could be answered, Lenin died. Both Lenin and Marx were gone. Lenin's band of followers was weakened by dissension. Who would chart the rest of the way along the road to world revolution?

Because theory had become such a complex but vital dimension in the life of the Russian revolutionaries, the struggle for Lenin's mantle of political leadership was both ideological and personal.

Trotsky maintained that the real problem before the Bolsheviks was the increased opposition and hostility of the peasantry. With so much land in their hands, he argued, they were turning into petty capitalists. As they became stronger, he warned, they would begin to resist attempts to socialize the country. Trotsky viewed the threat of peasant hostility as a serious danger for the future of the Communist state. Again Trotsky declared the difficulty, perhaps impossibility, of building socialism in Russia without revolutionary pace-setting in the advanced countries. Thus he reasserted his doctrine of "permanent revolution."

IV. STALIN'S "SOCIALISM IN ONE COUNTRY"

The history of communism in the U.S.S.R. now becomes the story of Joseph Stalin's rise to power.

Stalin (1879-1953) had become Bolshevik party general secretary in 1922, following a long career of party service. He became Trotsky's main rival in the struggle for power in Russia.

In 1925 Stalin offered Russia a more attractive solution than Trotsky's "permanent revolution." The bulk of the peasantry, he declared, was not capitalistically minded. According to Stalin, many peasants were landless and would therefore be eager to join forces with the workers. He called for the party to encourage such an alliance in order to provide the state with a dictatorship combining the proletariat and the poor peasantry. On the basis of this coalition, Stalin predicted the possibility of "building socialism in one country" — Russia.

Stalin did not anticipate an early revolution in the West and pointedly asked Trotsky if Russians should be expected to sit on their hands waiting for a revolution which might not come for decades.

Trotsky did not propose that Russians sit on their hands. In fact his program for the economic development of Russia at this stage was much more radical and tough-minded than Stalin's. But his theoretical analysis exposed him to Stalin's rough ridicule.

Stalin's doctrine of socialism in one country did not mean that he was giving up the idea of world revolution. By building socialism in Russia first, he wrote, the party would be constructing a basis from which world revolution could later spread. In fact, the final victory of socialism in one country hinged on the successful completion of world revolution.

The difference between the Stalin and Trotsky approaches was one of emphasis. But in the heat of the conflict between them, this was difficult for many to realize. Further blurring the differences was Stalin's tactic, after he had won the battle with Trotsky, of branding as "Trotskyite" many ideas which Trotsky in fact had never supported.

Even after Trotsky was driven from Russia into exile (1927) and hunted and finally murdered by a Stalinist agent (1940), Stalin, the Soviet dictator, feared the reappearance of Trotsky's ideas in his own party and among the world's Communists. Stalin, even more than Lenin, would not tolerate factionalism in theory or in practice. Unlike Lenin, Stalin ruthlessly destroyed those who held opposing opinions within the party. Monopoly of ideology was one of the keys to Stalin's absolute power in the Soviet state.

STALIN'S NEW THEORY OF THE STATE

Stalin's theoretical pronouncements did not contribute as many original and important ideas to the Communist movement as did Lenin's. As Lenin had altered Marxism, Stalin adjusted Leninism to cope with and explain the many new situations that continued to arise unexpectedly in Russia. One of these adjustments in theory was Stalin's reëvaluation of the Marxist-Leninist theory of the state.

Both Marx and Lenin had maintained that the dictatorship of the proletariat would be only a brief transitional stage en route to communism. But by 1930, the Russian state was showing no signs of withering away. It was rapidly acquiring more and more power over the lives of the people.

Stalin brought Marx's handy dialectic into play again. He argued that the strongest and mightiest form of the state had to be achieved before anything withered away. That his argument was contradictory did not bother Stalin, who explained simply that the dialectic was a process of progress through contradiction. The state, he claimed, had to create the conditions for socialism, because Russia did not develop those conditions before the socialist revolution.

One change in the Marxist scheme brought others. Like a line of toppling dominoes, one alteration overturned another on and on down the revolutionary trail.

STALIN'S DOCTRINE OF PARTY SUPREMACY

Stalin's next modification of Marxism was to enshrine the party above the state. Now that the state was a dictatorship of the proletariat, there was no further need for the conspiratorial party organization. The small, secret party had been Lenin's answer to the harassment by tsarist police. It had been Lenin's organizational design for seizing state power. Now that these aims had been fulfilled, there could be no further justification of the party's continued existence along these lines.

Stalin rejected any democratization of the party. Only the party could see the long-range goals. Therefore, the party had to continue to lead, guide, and direct the masses. Stalin further argued that the class struggle under socialism, like the state itself, would grow to enormous proportions before it withered away.

Stalin followed Lenin's belief, of course, that the party had to keep in touch with the masses, training and controlling them through organizations such as trade unions and youth groups.

"In this sense," he concluded, "it would be said that the dictatorship of the proletariat is in essence the 'dictatorship' of its vanguard, the 'dictatorship' of its party."

STALIN'S PERSONAL DICTATORSHIP

As the final step in Stalin's rise to power, he placed himself above the party. His theoretical justification for this step was this: While socialism was being built in a single country (Russia), the dangers of "capitalist encirclement," were very great. The party had to be converted into "an impregnable fortress into which not a single double-dealer could penetrate." Stalin set himself over all as the steward of this conversion. He accused his critics in the party of weakening the state and thus playing into the hands of capitalist powers coalescing to overthrow the Soviet state. The critics were then purged as capitalist agents.

After 1939 no more dissenting votes were reported at party discussions. Trotsky's prophetic warning to Lenin in 1903 had come to pass: "The organization of the party takes the place of the party itself, the Central Committee takes the place of the organization; and finally the dictator takes the place of the Central Committee."

STALIN AND THE MARXIST DREAM

Yet, for all this manipulation of doctrine, Stalin was not content merely to establish a personal dictatorship. He was still enough of a Marxist to insist upon the ultimate goal of world socialist revolution. Here was the familiar Messianic dream which we found rooted early in the theoretical foundations of Marx and Lenin.

Stalin saw how Lenin used theory to analyze a political situation and then to act. He successfully employed Lenin's method him-

Nikita Khrushchev: "Revolutionary theory is not a collection of petrified dogmas, but a militant guide to action in transforming the world and building Communism."

Homer Smith

self. There is no question that both men analyzed their environments in Marxist terms. Their opportunism, their flexibility, was in the means, or tactics, which they employed, never in the ends or strategy which guided them.

Throughout this book we see Soviet leaders, when faced with economic, political, or cultural problems, discussing only those alternative solutions which will maintain the socialist dictatorship in the short run and further world revolution in the long run. Stalin's successors have not yet strayed from this path.

V. THE USSR TODAY: THE KHRUSHCHEV STAGE OF MARXISM

Under the present leadership of the Soviet Union, the fourth stage in the development of Russian Marxism is being worked out. Plekhanov transplanted Marxism to Russia. Lenin adapted it. Stalin implemented it. Nikita S. Khrushchev claims to have achieved it. That is, Khrushchev says the Soviet Union is at last building a Communist society. Therefore, since Stalin's death and Khrushchev's rise to power, there have been doctrinal changes to describe this new stage in Russian history.

It is important to remember that socialism means something quite different to Khrushchev than it does to Western socialists. To him, it means the first stage in the establishment of a Commu-

nist dictatorship. To them, it means any variety of democratic but state-owned and operated services.

Although socialism, the final stage before real communism, has already been achieved in Russia, according to Khrushchev, the transition from socialism to communism will come gradually. To-day each person in the Soviet Union supposedly works according to his abilities and receives according to his work. Soon, the party claims, everyone will receive according to his needs.

KHRUSHCHEV'S PREDICTIONS ABOUT COMMUNISM

Khrushchev has pointed out, however, that certain Communist features already exist in present-day Soviet society. There are boarding schools, day nurseries, and other institutions operating at public expense.

"In the near future," he further claims, "all the Soviet people's requirements for food, housing, and clothing will be satisfied, free food for school children and accommodation of all children at nurs-eries and boarding schools will be provided."

This will not mean, says Khrushchev, that the state will do away with regulations of working time. A longer time will be necessary for people to acquire "the inner need" to work according to their abilities. This, in turn, means that the basic task of the country remains: to increase the country's productive forces. Ideal com-munism can be achieved only if the Soviet Union surpasses the level of production in the advanced capitalist countries, especially the United States.

Khrushchev also predicts that the distinction between physical and mental labor will begin to disappear as the techniques of pro-duction are developed. Automation, for example, will free men from hard physical labor and thus erase the differences between skilled and unskilled labor.

In the rural areas the building of communism requires the merger of private garden plots and collective farm property with state properties in order to eliminate all privately owned land. Farm villages will develop into urban-type communities. The differ-ences between town and countryside will fade. Peasants will live in apartments, work on the land for wages. Their lives will resemble as closely as possible those of the workers in the cities.

The coming of communism will mean that certain functions

performed by state agencies will gradually be taken over by local people's organizations. The state will at last begin to "wither away." So far, only health services, resort facilities, sports activities, and, to a very limited extent, the militia or police, have been mentioned by Khrushchev as areas where this shift in responsibility can be carried out.

HOW KHRUSHCHEV SEES THE WORLD

Khrushchev sees a changed and changing capitalist world. He claims that the capitalist powers which once surrounded the Soviet Union with superior economic and military force have lost their advantage. "Capitalist encirclement" no longer exists for the Soviet Union, in Khrushchev's judgment. Thus he does not think that there is any danger of a restoration of capitalism in the U.S.S.R. He also claims that political opposition no longer exists within the Soviet Union.

He contends that the enormous power of the Communist camp is such an important factor in the minds of the capitalist leaders that they will no longer dare risk wars among themselves. Thus Khrushchev seems to modify the Leninist-Stalinist doctrine of the inevitability of war under capitalism. Communist strength strikes a balance of power with the capitalists that allows for peaceful coexistence between communism and capitalism. By these words Khrushchev means that the Communist bloc has no need to go to war. Instead, by peaceful competition communism will convince the masses of the world of its superiority as an economic system, Khrushchev boasts, and communism will inevitably triumph.

But what has happened to the social revolutions which Marx predicted? Have the Soviet leaders abandoned the idea of world revolution, of achieving their goals by violent means? Khrushchev himself gives the answer somewhat as follows: The dictatorship of the proletariat need not be established through a civil war, but there must be a revolutionary change. According to him, the degree of violence will depend upon the will of the capitalists to resist, not upon the working class. As examples of the peaceful road to socialism, Khrushchev and other Soviet leaders cite the Communist take-over in the Baltic States in 1940 and in Czechoslovakia in 1948. In both cases the Communists hesitate to note that the threat of overwhelming Soviet armed intervention forced the democratic forces to surrender to Communist minorities.

Khrushchev has concluded that in countries where there are strong military forces and where capitalism is firmly established (presumably the United States is included here), the transition to socialism will take place "amidst sharp revolutionary class struggle."

Other people say that there are different ways to socialism-communism, but Khrushchev indicates that "one cannot reach socialism by some other road that lies to the side of the common path indicated by Marxism-Leninism." The only apparent exception to this law can be found in his assurance that backward countries in which Communists have seized power can skip the stage of capitalism in building their economies, if the Soviet Union helps them.

LENIN'S TRADITION OF REVOLUTION PERSISTS

Khrushchev continues the Leninist tradition of encouraging revolutions in backward countries with promises of economic and military aid from the Soviet Union.

Stalin's policies have borne fruit. The economic and military power of the Soviet Union—"the construction of socialism in one country"—has indeed become a base for world revolution. A recent practical application of this doctrine was the Soviet threat to rain rockets upon any country which interfered with the dictatorship of Fidel Castro in Cuba. The power of the Soviet Union has become an umbrella over countries in which Communist forces have set up minority dictatorships.

Many careful students of Soviet affairs conclude that Khrushchev's theory of peaceful coexistence is a tactical shift, rather than a basic change in Soviet ideology. It is a flexible doctrine which opens up many possibilities for putting pressures on the Western world at every vulnerable point.

Although Khrushchev is less of a theorist than Lenin or Stalin, he too considers ideology an important aspect of Soviet strength. He insists upon unity of ideas within the Soviet Union and even within the Soviet bloc. He sees two main enemies within the Communist camp: *revisionism* and *Stalinism*. His violent attacks upon both indicate that, for him, ideology is no mere Communist frill.

VI. REVISIONISM

Revisionism is the epithet used by the Soviet leaders since Lenin's time to indicate any interpretation of Marxism which differs from their own on party organization and the need for revolution.

Many groups of Marxists in the advanced industrial countries of the West, for example, enjoyed civil and political rights. They regarded socialism as a desirable, indeed, inevitable goal. But they radically changed the means to achieve it from illegal revolutionary, to legal democratic. Since the earliest disputes between Lenin and these revisionists, some of whom were Russian, the democratic socialists and revolutionary Communists have been bitter enemies.

The Communists regard the democratic socialists as their most dangerous antagonists in the ideological struggle, because the socialists offer the same ends but promise success at far less cost to humanity.

Since 1917, democratic socialist parties, such as the British Labour party, the French Socialists, the German Social Democrats, have blunted the edge of Communist propaganda. This is why Khrushchev condemns revisionism.

STALINISM

Stalinism is to Khrushchev no less dangerous because it emphasizes the inevitability of war so long as capitalism survives. It also asserts that the class struggle in the socialist countries must increase in intensity before the coming of communism. Khrushchev rejects both ideas.

Khrushchev denies the need for war, because it arouses the suspicion of non-Communist countries and puts them on guard against Soviet policy.

He attacks Stalin's class-struggle claim, because it gives rise to fear among the Russian people of the return of the unlimited powers of the secret police, of the purges, and of the years of terror.

The Soviet premier, therefore, condemns those within the party who wish to revert to Stalin's theories. He extends this condemnation to those in other countries such as Albania and Communist China, who believe that their stage of historic development requires adherence to these policies in order to crush opposition groups and to frighten the people into working harder.

Khrushchev, at a secret meeting during the 20th Congress of the Communist party of the Soviet Union in 1956, sharply criticized the terrorism of Stalin's reign. At the 22nd Party Congress in 1961, he added to the charges against Stalin. Within weeks the body of Stalin was removed from the mausoleum shrine in Moscow's Red Square, where Lenin is also entombed.

Khrushchev also faces the fact that the Soviet leaders no longer have a monopoly of Communist ideology. Communist regimes outside Russia have developed their own variations on the Marxist-Leninist theme in order to cope with their particular social, political, and economic problems.

Marshal Tito's Yugoslavia and Mao Tse-tung's China are the two most important examples of deviations from the Soviet pattern. Interestingly enough the differences are less over the content of the ideology than over the control of the ideology.

TITOISM

The Yugoslav Communists reject the idea that all Communist states must subordinate their policies to the leading role of the Soviet Union in international affairs. They believe, instead, that each national Communist party should enjoy an equal voice in deciding the policy of the Communist bloc. They also maintain that each country can find its own road to socialism.

The Yugoslavs also maintain that the Soviet dictatorship of the proletariat is too narrowly conceived as a party dictatorship. The Yugoslavs, in theory, favor safeguards against overcentralization of political power. They grant some prerogatives, therefore, to nonparty institutions such as representative legislatures, trade unions, possibly other parties. However, the Yugoslav Communists are reluctant to part with their monopoly of power. Their arrest and imprisonment of Milovan Djilas for protesting (in *The New Class*, a widely read book smuggled out of Yugoslavia) against the Communist dictatorship in Yugoslavia points up the weakness of the Yugoslav theorizing on this point.

The Yugoslavs also favor a gradual approach to collectivization, decentralization of economic authority, and especially the introduction of workers' control in the factories.

Yugoslav Communists, also, have spoken of the need to return to

Marshal Tito: "Communism really exists nowhere, least of all in the Soviet Union. Communism is an ideal that can be achieved only when people cease to be selfish and greedy and when everyone receives according to his needs from communal production. But that is a long way off."

Marxist "humanism," showing concern for the welfare of the individual in the face of arbitrary and ruthless powers wielded by secret police and the party. They would supposedly encourage free expression within the Marxist framework. The real meaning here depends upon who happens to interpret the terms "humanism" and "free expression." It has yet to be shown in Yugoslavia that advocates of real democratization of the Yugoslav Communist party can speak out freely even if they remain socialists. Note the imprisoned Djilas.

COMMUNISM IN CHINA: MAOISM

In Communist China, disagreement over ideology again appears to center on different historical conditions of the two countries (U.S.S.R. and China) and on the problem of leadership.

Moscow and Peiping disagree first on the usefulness of the Chinese experience as opposed to the Russian experience in seizing power and carrying out the construction of socialism. In other words they argue about which country's experience should serve as the model for other countries seeking to launch a revolution. By implication the argument also concerns which country, the U.S.S.R. or China, will lead and control those other revolutions.

The main Chinese argument is that Mao Tse-tung first developed the theories of waging revolution from self-sustaining rural bases and of using guerrilla warfare.

The Chinese argue that every leader of a rural-based revolutionary movement in an underdeveloped area—Castro in Cuba, the Viet Cong in South Viet-Nam—is following the Chinese pattern of revolution and not the Soviet.

Following disasters in Chinese agriculture, a number of other claims about Mao's originality in developing socialism in China were withdrawn or sharply modified in the early 1960's.

The most serious disagreement between the Soviet Union and the Chinese Communists arises from the doctrine of peaceful coexistence. But here again the difference tends to be one of tactics, not of principle. Peiping fears that the doctrine of peaceful coexistence is discouraging and therefore weakening to revolutionary movements in the underdeveloped countries. This means that the Soviet Union, in Mao's eyes, is putting its national interests above those of world communism.

To understand Mao's reasoning, it must be borne in mind that China is going through a revolutionary period roughly similar to that which took place in the Soviet Union in the 1930's.

Today the Soviet Union is convinced that time is on its side. Backed by a strong industrial base, a relatively united and satisfied population, and a powerful military force, the Soviet Union need not fear the danger of internal counterrevolution, intervention from abroad, or any threat from a combination of the two.

But the Chinese Communists are faced by large internal unrest, the ever-present threat, in their eyes, of intervention launched from Nationalist China's offshore island bastion of Formosa (Taiwan) with the support of the United States, or a combination of these dangers. Therefore, the Communist Chinese want to spread the world revolution as quickly as possible to keep the armed forces of the United States committed to many widespread strength-sapping local wars. This tactic diverts American energies from any mass intervention in China.

In order to force its people to work harder, the Chinese Communist leaders invoke the threat of foreign intervention. Thus, as far as the Chinese Communists are concerned, their domestic and foreign policies should be based more upon Stalin's ideas than upon Khrushchev's, because their historical development is more comparable to that of Soviet Russia under Stalin than that under Khrushchev.

SUMMARY

Communism is a social, economic, and political theory based on the ideas of the German social philosopher Karl Marx, modified by Nikolai Lenin and his successors. The body of ideas originally assembled by Marx took the form of a protest against the oppressive conditions of early industrialization. Marx offered the workers the promise of a better life. The laws of history, he said, would lead inevitably to a violent revolution of the workers against their employers. The result would be a workers' state. According to Marx, the workers would then own the means of production and

Mao Tse-tung: "Communism is not love. Communism is a hammer which we use to crush the enemy. We are always revolutionists and never reformers."

Fidel Castro: "There is no half-way between socialism and imperialism ... anyone maintaining a 3rd position is, in fact, helping imperialism."

distribution. Therefore, class differences would disappear; the state would wither away; everyone would work according to his abilities and receive according to his needs.

These ideas were adopted and modified by Lenin as the basis for his drive to seize power in Russia. Because in the early 1900's Russia was economically backward, with a small working class, Lenin foresaw the need to create a small, conspiratorial, revolutionary party to make up for the weakness of the workers. He rejected Marx's idea that the revolution would be spontaneous. It had to be led by the vanguard of the workers, the party.

Lenin further modified Marx's ideas by calling for the revolution in an industrially backward country like Russia. He argued that Marx had not lived to see the new economic conditions which made this possible. According to Lenin's theory of imperialism, the working class of the backward countries suffered more at the hands of the international capitalists or imperialists than the working class of the industrial countries. Therefore they might revolt first.

Marx had maintained that the workers' revolution could only come after the middle class had overthrown the authoritarian monarchy and developed a capitalist economy. But this had never happened in Russia. Lenin accepted Trotsky's idea of "permanent revolution." Once the revolution against the authoritarian monarchy broke out in 1917, Lenin and Trotsky succeeded in pushing ahead quickly to a full-fledged socialist revolution that same year. They did not wait for the middle class to establish its political power and take over the economy. They justified "permanent revolution" by pointing to the weakness of the Russian middle class. Again Marx was ignored. Again Russian conditions were offered as the explanation for the change.

Lenin's successor, Stalin, contributed his own ideas to the Communist ideology. Marx and Lenin had argued that socialism (that is, the first stage of communism) could develop only after a world revolution. But Stalin insisted that socialism could be built in one country—Russia. A Soviet-Socialist Russia would then serve as the leader of world revolution, much as Lenin's party had served as the leader of the Russian Revolution.

Stalin further maintained that even while socialism was being built, class struggle in Russia would grow sharper. The Soviet Union was also threatened by capitalist enemies. Therefore, the party would remain small and dictatorial. Neither Marx nor Lenin had advocated this.

Unlike Marx and Lenin, Stalin gradually assumed complete power over the party. He claimed to be the only interpreter of Communist ideology.

Under the rule of Khrushchev, ideology has undergone further modifications. Khrushchev denounced Stalin's ideas on the class struggle in the U.S.S.R. and the threat of capitalist encirclement. The Soviet Union is strong enough, he claims, to spread the world revolution without a war. However, he reasserted the need for a violent revolution to overthrow the most powerful capitalist government.

Khrushchev now claims that the Soviet Union is building communism. Within the near future, he predicts, most of the material needs of the Russian people will be satisfied.

As Communist governments have been imposed on the eastern European countries, China, and Cuba, modifications of the Soviet brand of communism have developed. In every case these modifications have reflected the practical needs of the men who made the revolutions.

Thus Communist theory has undergone many changes and spawned many variations. However, Communist aims remain constant: the belief in the class struggle under capitalism, violent revolution, the establishment of party dictatorships, the state control of the means of production and distribution, and ultimately world domination.

UNITED PRESS INTERNATIONAL

TERMS TO KNOW

antithesis	synthesis	proletariat
revisionism	Bolsheviks	permanent revolution
Communist ideology	nihilism	dialectical materialism

QUESTIONS ON THE CHAPTER

1. State four of the functions of Communist ideology.
2. Name the five historical stages in the evolution of production, as traced by Karl Marx.
3. Explain what Marx meant by the "dictatorship of the proletariat."
4. What are some of the errors made by Marx in his predictions concerning the future of capitalist countries?
5. There were two revolutionary traditions in Russia. Trace the origin and development of each.
6. Which of the Populist leaders was called the father of Russian Marxism and why?
7. Explain Leon Trotsky's theory of the "permanent revolution."
8. In what ways did Joseph Stalin disagree with Trotsky's theory of the "permanent revolution"?
9. Describe the fourth stage in the development of Russian Marxism. What are Nikita Khrushchev's predictions regarding this stage?
10. In what ways does Khrushchev disagree with Stalinism?
11. Compare Titoism, Maoism, and Soviet Communist doctrine.

QUESTIONS FOR DISCUSSION

1. According to Karl Marx, history itself is the study of class struggle. Historians have criticized Marx's theories on both logical and factual grounds. Prepare examples which disprove Marx's basic assumptions (for example: Marx's error in predicting the spread and deepening of poverty among workers in the capitalist countries).

2. The proposition has been made that human behavior patterns would have to be changed radically before total Marxism could be achieved. Tell why this is true or untrue.

3. Lenin, Stalin, and Khrushchev have presented theories differing in some respects with those held by Karl Marx. Discuss the points which depart from Marx's original teachings.

4. It is recognized that there are ideological differences between the Soviet Union and Communist China. What implications does this have for future world politics?

BIBLIOGRAPHY

For Reference: ☐ Caldwell, John C., *Communism in Our World.* John Day Company, 1956. ☐ Committee on Un-American Activities, House of Representatives, 86th Congress, First Session, *Facts on Communism,* Volume I. United States Government Printing Office, 1960. ☐ Cronyn, George W., *A Primer on Communism: 200 Questions and Answers.* E. P. Dutton & Company, 1960. ☐ Daniels, Robert V., *A Documentary History of Communism,* Volumes 1 and 2. Vintage Books, 1962. ☐ Hunt, R. N. Carew, *The Theory and Practice of Communism: An Introduction.* The Macmillan Company, 1957. ☐ Mayo, Henry B., *Democracy and Marxism.* Oxford University Press, 1955. ☐ Meyer, Alfred G., *Marxism Since the Communist Manifesto.* American Historical Association, Service Center for Teachers of History, 1961. **For Further Reading:** ☐ Djilas, Milovan, *The New Class.* Frederick A. Praeger, Inc., 1957. ☐ Moorehead, Alan, *The Russian Revolution.* Bantam Books, 1959. ☐ Wolfe, Bertram, *Three Who Made a Revolution.* Beacon Press, 1948.

Charles Kay

CHAPTER 4

POLITICS AND GOVERNMENT
IN THE USSR

The USSR is a totalitarian state:
political power is monopolized
by the leaders of the Communist party
who maintain firm control of the people
through propaganda and coercion.

The Soviet Union today is ruled by a single-party dictatorship. The party itself, once synonymous with the Bolsheviks and now called the Communist party of the Soviet Union (CPSU), constitutes a small minority of the population. There are approximately 10,000,000 Communists holding authority over a population of 214,400,000.

Within the party there is very little evidence of free discussion or democratic practices. This apparently is true even in the most powerful organ of the party, the Presidium (known until 1952 as the Political Bureau, or Politburo). However, we do not know for certain how rigid the conduct is within the Presidium because the deliberations of this group are a closely guarded secret. Rank-and-file party members have very little say in major party decisions. Elections to policy-making posts in the party are almost always uncontested. A single individual is nominated by the highest councils of the party and is duly elected.

The revolution of March 1917 broke out in Petrograd (Leningrad) which was the scene of street fighting.

Undesirable members of the party are periodically discharged or purged. While purge originally meant, and again today means, loss of influence and personal disgrace, under the rule of Joseph Stalin it usually meant execution as well. Under communism, the purge takes the place of elections as a means of replacing individuals who have failed to do their work or who threaten the power of high party leaders. With the exception of the highest leaders in the Communist party—and even today many of them have been purged—the turnover in membership is surprisingly high.

It is no less true today than it was under Lenin's hand nearly a half century ago that in the Soviet Union the Communist party still is the state. It is the only organized political force in the country and has complete control over the institutions of government.

By virtue of its monopoly of key posts in the government, economic, social, and cultural organizations, the party controls almost every aspect of Soviet life. Even such powerful groups as the Soviet

Army and the secret police have been unable to free themselves from the strict control of the party. This is an awesome tribute to the highly disciplined nature of the party and to the binding force of its ideology.

I. THE PARTY AND THE STATE

Nikolai Lenin and his Bolsheviks seized power in November 1917 with only vague notions of how to rule an enormous nation. They still expected that revolution was imminent among the workers of western Europe. They counted on this worker revolution to spur Russia along the road to communism. Any governmental apparatus would be needed only briefly, during the dictatorship of the proletariat. And then it could wither away, as Marx had forecast.

The world revolution never came. The Bolsheviks had to take stock of a new situation. They had not only to retain power but to retain it in the face of a hostile world. Practical questions demanded immediate attention. At the same time decisions had to be made on how best to lay the foundations for communism. How could industry be developed to satisfy the material needs of the people? How could cultural values be transformed to prepare the people for life in the Communist society?

These were gigantic undertakings for a band of revolutionaries who found themselves in control of a basically agricultural country with a largely illiterate and poverty-stricken population!

Workers and peasants, men and women, enlisted as volunteers in the Red Army — the army of the Bolsheviks — in 1917.

It was not difficult for the Bolshevik conspirators to choose dictatorial instead of democratic means. The few democratic elements in Leninism, held over from Marx in some instances, were to be sacrificed on the altar of political expediency in the turbulent months of late 1917 and early 1918.

No established traditions of civil rights in individual liberties stood in the path of the Bolshevik drive to enlarge the powers of the state. The Russian people did not submit willingly to the sacrifices and sufferings which were loaded upon them. They resisted, often in violent ways, but there was no body of democratic ideals around which to rally. There was no popular democratic organization to unify any opposition to the Bolsheviks. Opposition was scattered, divided, leaderless, and without a program. In the long run it was no match for the disciplined organization, the tough-minded leadership, and the clearly defined goals of the Bolsheviks.

HOW THE DICTATORSHIP OF THE PARTY CAME ABOUT

The process which led to the dictatorship of one party, and of one man over that party, was well advanced by the time Lenin died in 1924. During the Civil War (1918-1921), the Bolsheviks had crushed most of the other political groups in Russia, including the non-Bolshevik socialists.

The time had now come when the few dissenters among party leaders were silenced. While Lenin was alive, a certain amount of free discussion was permitted within the party. For example, important figures like Grigori Zinoviev (1883-1936) and Lev B. Kamenev (1883-1936) were allowed to hold high party positions after they broke with Lenin on critical matters, such as the timing of the seizure of power.

However, as Lenin lay dying in 1923, the struggle for power within the party intensified. Ever tighter restrictions on democracy within the party were enforced. It became clear that one of the fatal flaws in Lenin's small, secret, conspiratorial organization was his failure to provide for succession to the leadership. No one else in the party, not even Trotsky, commanded the personal allegiance Lenin had won with his iron will, keen intellect, and political skill. The rank-and-file members of the party were unaccustomed to electing a leader. Lenin had stood virtually alone.

STALIN SUCCEEDS TO ABSOLUTE POWER

The struggle for Lenin's position in the party lasted from 1923 to 1927. At the end of this period, there was no doubt who would hold the Bolshevik reins. Joseph Stalin emerged as undisputed dictator. Trotsky, Zinoviev, Kamenev—his principal opponents—had been disgraced, purged, or banished into exile.

Stalin's victory came about largely as a result of the key party position he held. He was general secretary, the same position from which Nikita Khrushchev vaulted to dictatorial control of the party and the U.S.S.R. after Stalin's death.

Stalin used this position to bring the party bureaucracy under his control. This led to control over all the Soviet Union, for the party bureaucracy was the framework of power in the country.

During the struggle against the autocratic tsarist monarchy, the Bolsheviks had developed a widespread net of underground organizations called *local committees.* Some of the exiled policy-making Bolsheviks—Trotsky, Zinoviev, and Kamenev among them—had viewed these committees with some disdain. But Lenin had foreseen the need for organization of committeemen as well as policy men. Stalin had been one of these committeemen. In 1917, in fact, most key posts in the Bolshevik organization were in the hands of just such committeemen as Stalin. When the party seized power, these men fanned out to become its local party secretaries throughout the country.

In 1917 the party organization was relatively simple. The party members periodically elected a congress, which formulated policy. The congress in turn elected a Central Committee, which managed routine party affairs.

Soon, however, it became clear that this structure was unwieldy. The Central Committee was much too large to manage the daily affairs of the party. Therefore, in 1919 and 1920, three new party organs were created: the Political Bureau (Politburo), the Organization Bureau (Orgburo), and the Secretariat. Lenin, Trotsky, Kamenev, and Stalin were all members of the policy-making Politburo.

In 1922 when Stalin became general secretary of the Secretariat, he proceeded to increase the number of people working under him. In this way he spread his influence within the party.

So skillful was Stalin's maneuvering that, by the time the Fourteenth Party Congress met in 1925, only a year after Lenin's passing, Stalin's men represented every local party organization in Russia except that of Leningrad. When new members were elected to the Politburo and Orgburo, it was not surprising that Stalin's backers were in the majority.

This show of strength by Stalin surprised many. He had not been considered a leading contender for Lenin's mantle. He was not popular in the party nor was he an impressive speaker. Brilliant intellectuals like Trotsky and Kamenev had frowned upon Stalin's simple ways. Stalin had not been particularly close to Lenin. He was even denounced by Lenin in his last will and testament to the party. How, then, could this son of a Georgian cobbler, this unimpressive man who spoke Russian with an accent, who seemed capable of little more than the drudgery of keeping party records, but who foreshadowed the future by changing his name from Dzhugashvili to Stalin ("made of steel")—how could he challenge the great men of the party?

Stalin's cunning was underestimated by his brilliant but naïve colleagues, who found themselves divided and, one by one, defeated. Only at the end—and then much too late—did they realize the extent to which Stalin had gained control of the party they had helped build.

"He is the new Genghis Khan. He will strangle us," whispered the frightened Kamenev.

With the party firmly under control, Stalin undertook the dual tasks, mentioned earlier, of industrializing Russia and recasting its cultural values in accord with the new Communist society.

THE STALIN PURGES

In 1934 one of Stalin's closest supporters and one of the most popular men in the party, Sergei Kirov (1886-1934), was mysteriously

The early 1920's brought hardships to Russians. Wives of former bourgeoisie sold their dresses in the open markets of Leningrad.

The Supreme Revolutionary Tribunal in 1917. From left to right: a factory worker, a soldier, a peasant, Georgi Zhukov (president), an artisan, a soldier, a clerk.

murdered (under conditions which have given rise to speculation by Premier Khrushchev that Stalin himself instigated the killing).

Stalin used Kirov's murder as an excuse to unleash an incomparably thorough and brutal purge of the party. The reasons for the purge have never been made clear, for by this time the former opposition had been scattered or crushed—Trotsky was living abroad in exile; Kamenev, Zinoviev, and others now held insignificant party posts. Apparently Stalin sought to consolidate his personal power beyond any question. He perhaps reasoned that if his plans to industrialize the country and revolutionize its cultural values went awry, the former famous names of the party would serve as rallying points for criticism and formidable political opposition. Perhaps, too, fear of approaching war in Europe drove him to destroy any groups which might weaken his foreign policy.

The secret police was the cruel instrument of Stalin's purge. Party members were arrested en masse, were executed or deported, often without a semblance of legal procedure. The Bolshevik veterans in the party were virtually annihilated.

Zinoviev, Kamenev, and many others were tried for plotting against Stalin's life. They were tortured into confessing to these crimes and were executed. The toll of this bloody purge has never been tallied, but estimates place the total arrests in the hundreds of thousands and the total executions in the tens of thousands.

The climax of the purge came in 1937 and 1938. It became so rampant and reckless in its final months that loyal supporters of Stalin, members of the Politburo, the overwhelming majority of the Central Committee, many of the highest ranking officers in the Russian Army, many officials in the foreign ministry, and even in the secret police itself, were executed.

Leading writers, musicians, scholars, scientists, heads of economic enterprises, party members, foreign communists and state officials, many of whom were not even in the party, were also rounded up. Enormous forced-labor camps began to dot Siberia.

At last Stalin realized that the purge was paralyzing the country. He turned upon his chief purger, Nikolai I. Yezhov (1895-1938?), blaming him for murdering innocent people.

STALIN WORSHIP

The purge was accompanied and followed by a campaign that was tantamount to Stalin worship. From this time dates the rise of Stalin to a position of such power that his personal rule replaced party rule. Party organizations seemed almost to waste away. According to party law, the party congress was to meet at least every four years, but between the Seventeenth Congress in 1934 and the Eighteenth in 1939, five years elapsed; thirteen more years passed before the Nineteenth Congress met in 1952.

The same situation befell the Central Committee. With trusted lieutenants in the party, in the government organizations, in the secret police, and in the army, Stalin was able to keep ambitious men under his anxious watch and the reins of command firmly in hand.

In 1956 and again in 1962, Premier Khrushchev and other Soviet leaders, secretly at first and openly later, tried to show that Stalin himself had become abnormally alarmed at any sign of opposition and that it had been impossible to restrain him.

It must be remembered, however, that Khrushchev was Stalin's chief aide in purging the Ukrainian party organization, and in 1938 after the purge, he became a member of the Politburo. Therefore, it is no more possible for Khrushchev to absolve himself and his present colleagues of these crimes than it was for Stalin to blame Yezhov. Few of today's Soviet leaders survived those vicious years without having played some role in them.

WORLD WAR II

When the Nazis invaded the Soviet Union in 1941, Stalin moved quickly to create a state committee of defense. The new committee was given absolute power and authority over all party, government, and military organizations.

For the first time state and party institutions, which had functioned separately, were merged to ensure the most efficient administration possible. Furthermore, the party now was urging the people to fight not so much for the Communist state as for the Russian motherland. Patriotic rather than class propaganda prevailed during the first two years of war, when defeat seemed imminent. The battle of Stalingrad in late 1942 and early 1943 marked the turning point of the war. Only after this victory did the party begin to reassert its ideological role in propaganda.

THE PARTISAN MOVEMENT

The party may have been temporarily willing to modify its ideological controls, but it never conceded its administrative power. Perhaps the most striking example of its determination was the organization of the Russian partisan movement behind the Nazi lines in World War II.

At first, the partisans were poorly armed, leaderless bands of peasants and workers. Their activities recalled the historic Russian peasant revolts. But as in 1918-1919 the party, this time using the secret police, organized the partisans and directed their activities toward disruption of Nazi lines of communication and supply.

At no time did the party entirely trust the partisan movement. It was far too spontaneous and undisciplined for the suspicious Stalin. Some small bands went into hiding to resist the return of Soviet local power. The Soviet victory over the Nazis in the east and the reëstablishment of full party control of the nation under Stalin following the war doomed partisan holdouts. The last remnants of this movement were crushed in the early 1950's.

THE PARTY AFTER WORLD WAR II

Those who hoped for a postwar relaxation of party controls were sharply disappointed. Stalin flatly rejected U.S. offers of economic aid to help the Soviet Union rebuild its shattered economy. The party blatantly stated there would be no end to wars until capitalism was destroyed.

Once again war-weary Russians were forced to shoulder the burdens of reconstruction without U.S. help. Cultural life was

Stalin worship reached its height in the mid-1930's. Huge portraits and statues of Stalin were familiar sights in the larger towns and cities of the U.S.S.R.

brought back under party control. The cult of Stalin grew more fanatical. His birthdays signaled outpourings of poems, paintings, musical compositions, testimonials from every state and local party organization to his "genius" and "all-knowing infallibility." He was glorified as "the son of mankind," "the greatest scientist of Marxism-Leninism," and on and on.

STALIN'S LAST YEARS

During the last years of his life, Stalin sought to prevent his subordinates from building up their own personal power. A dangerous game with high stakes was played by men like Nikita S. Khrushchev (1894-   ), Georgi M. Malenkov (1902-   ), and Lavrenti P. Beria (1899-1953). Working to strengthen their own positions in the party without arousing Stalin's suspicions was no easy task.

Their maneuvering was carried out against a background of increasing political and economic frustration.

Postwar recovery had solved few of the critical problems in the party organization, many of which related to a mushrooming governmental apparatus in a lagging economy. It now appears that Stalin sought to break out of this dilemma by resorting again to a sweeping purge. But in 1953, before any except the first phase of this new wave of terror was out of the planning stage, he died.

The front page of *Komsomolskaya Pravda*, April 10, 1953. "Yesterday the Soviet nation bid farewell for the last time to the greatest world hero, Yosef Vissarionovich Stalin. Farewell our teacher and leader, our dear friend. Forward to a complete victory on the road taken by our great leaders, Lenin and Stalin."

On the platform among the representatives are Walter Ulbricht, Palmiro Tagliatti, Jules Duclos, Klement Gottwald, N. A. Bulganin, V. M. Molotov, K. Y. Voroshilov, G. M. Malenkov, N. S. Khrushchev, L. P. Beria, Chou En-lai.

The party had changed greatly under Stalin. It no longer represented the working class but rather the nation's most important and influential people in all walks of life. Only 3 per cent of the party—the full-time secretaries and officials—had any real authority. So centralized had the party become that the entire country's progress was being slowed. Stalin's personal ascendancy had become so paramount that he rarely summoned all the members of the Politburo to meet at the same time. Often he preferred to work through state or secret police channels rather than the party.

In effect the party had become simply one of many institutional systems which the dictator used to carry out his orders. But with his passing, all this changed.

THE STRUGGLE AMONG STALIN'S PARTY HEIRS

As had been the case after Lenin's death in 1924, so in 1953 no one in the party was considered to be Stalin's obvious successor.

In the struggle for leadership, ideological, economic, and personal motives clashed. Powerful contenders held such potential springboard posts as chief of the secret police, leader of the army, and leader of the state government. But the key post—as it had been for Stalin years before—was that of the first (formerly general) secretary of the party. By the end of 1953, this key post was securely in the grip of the experienced and skillful politician Nikita S. Khrushchev. Not all of the facts about the weeks following Stalin's death are clear, but the following is the outline of events.

The first casualty in this struggle for power was Lavrenti P. Beria, the head of the secret police. He was arrested and executed a few months after Stalin's death.

Under Beria, successor to Yezhov (who carried out the purges for Stalin), the secret police had become almost a state within a state.

The police had full control over all forced-labor camps and even over Soviet atomic development. They even maintained their own armed forces with heavy tanks and aircraft, provided all border guards, and maintained agents in every sector of Soviet society, including party organizations, factories, and collective farms.

Beria's arrest, despite his network of agents, must have come as a surprise to him, because neither he nor his supporters resisted openly. The party had lost none of its conspiratorial skill.

Following Beria's downfall, the secret police lost much power and influence. Party people took over key positions. Unreliable officers were purged.

Georgi M. Malenkov, who from 1953 to 1955 based his power on the state apparatus, was the next victim of the post-Stalin struggle for control of the U.S.S.R. Apparently backed by strong support within the party, Khrushchev went on to eliminate other prominent old-line Stalinists, among them Vyacheslav M. Molotov (1890-   ), former foreign minister, and Lazar M. Kaganovich (1893-   ), former member of the Stalin Presidium. Like Stalin, Khrushchev played his rivals against one another and downgraded them one by one.

KHRUSHCHEV'S SUCCESS

In 1957 Nikita S. Khrushchev accused the old-line Stalinists of having formed what he called an antiparty group. He charged them with opposing his views on agricultural and foreign policy matters.

The Presidium and the Central Committee expelled them. Actually, Khrushchev himself had narrowly escaped a similar fate because, on one occasion, he was actually outvoted in the Presidium by these very antiparty men. In that crisis he apparently relied heavily on the support of the army, which by that time had been returned to the command of Marshal Georgi Zhukov (1895?-   ), who had been banished by Stalin to obscurity.

However, Khrushchev apparently saw in the popular Marshal Zhukov a potential rival. In 1957 he forced him out of the Central Committee and relieved him of his post as defense minister. Khrushchev's supporters now controlled the party and all key posts in the secret police, the governmental machinery, and the army. To further consolidate his position, Khrushchev retained for himself the post of first secretary of the party and added the post of chairman of the Council of Ministers, a governmental position comparable to the head of the national cabinet, or premier.

Now Khrushchev was ready to proceed with the attack on those two nagging problems which Stalin had left unsolved: (1) industrializing the Soviet Union and (2) recasting its cultural values along strict Communist lines.

DECLINE OF TERROR

The party under Khrushchev was to lose none of its Stalinist power. Indeed, it probably became more efficient than ever before. What is the party like today?

Terror is no longer the linchpin of Soviet totalitarianism. There is still a rapid turnover in the branches of party membership, especially in relatively high posts such as local and regional secretaries. It is likely that demotion or exclusion from the party no longer means arrest or execution. On the other hand these possibilities are never to be ruled out. New party rules in 1961 provided for periodic turnover in the make-up of the party congress, the Central Committee, and at regional and local levels. In effect these rules constitute a legalized "permanent purge." On the one hand they guarantee removal from important posts of party members who fail to carry out their responsibilities. On the other hand they reject the idea of periodic examination of all party members to check on their Communist loyalty.

PARTY STRUCTURE ADJUSTED

The organs of the party have been given back some of their former importance by Khrushchev. In strict accord with rules, the party congresses since 1956 have been held within the prescribed four-year periods. The most recent was the Twenty-second Party Congress in Moscow in 1961.

The Central Committee has met much more regularly and frequently under Khrushchev than it did under Stalin. But we should note that neither the party congress nor the Central Committee has regained the powers which were lost under Stalin. In this respect, Khrushchev's rein on the party is as tight as was Stalin's. The most important party decisions still are made in the Presidium and in the Secretariat.

The Secretariat retains the organizational power and divides its functions into such departments as Party Organizations (Communist Youth League, trade unions, etc.); Agitation and Propaganda; Culture and Science; Higher Education and Schools; Agriculture; Transport and Communications; Industry, Trade, and Finance; and Foreign Affairs and Planning.

SOME CRITICISM ALLOWED

Khrushchev has welcomed criticism and debate among party members in hopes of exposing administrative wrongdoing, incompetence, and corruption. In almost the same breath, however, party leaders warn against criticism of the foundations of the party and against criticism simply for its own sake.

The party rules of 1961 explicitly condemn factional activity of any kind so that, in the words of one leader, no group of "muddle-headed or immature people can draw the party into a fruitless discussion. . . ." However, these guidelines are so vague and the memories of Stalinist terror so vivid that party members show a marked reluctance to exercise their new "freedom of criticism."

PARTY AUTHORITY GROWS

On the whole the authority of the Communist party has grown significantly since Stalin's death. The methods of the party have become more regular and less violent, but there are no legal or institutional guarantees to check its enormous power. The party is responsible only to itself. Much depends upon the personalities and views of its leaders as to the methods considered most effective.

It is apparent, therefore, that the successful functioning of any institution in Soviet society today depends upon its relationship with the party. We have studied the structure of the Communist party first in this chapter on Soviet government and politics precisely because the party is such a dominant factor. We now turn to the evolution of the apparatus of the state, to see how it is hinged to the Communist party.

II. THE STATE AND THE SYSTEM OF SOVIETS

The state in the Soviet Union today is based upon a system of soviets. In Russian the word *soviet* means "council." *Soviet* is an old Russian word, but until the 20th century it had no particular political meaning. Thus it is not what we might call a Communist word. Karl Marx, for example, never heard of the word *soviet*. Nor did Lenin until the revolution of 1905.

During the general strike that year, when the workers of St. Petersburg rioted against the tsar's oppressive rule, some of the factory workers formed a council to coördinate the strike. The council was called a "soviet" of workers' deputies, and it performed several quasi-governmental functions in order to oversee food supplies, print newspapers, and formulate strike policy.

In Moscow, Kharkov, and in some Siberian cities, similar organizations were formed, all rather spontaneously. Elections of representatives to the soviets were very haphazard. The powers of the soviets were not very well defined. The existing government at that time considered them illegal.

At that time Lenin was suspicious of the soviets. He feared that they would replace his party as the principal force of the later revolution he was plotting. On the other hand Trotsky and the Mensheviks (Marxist revolutionaries opposed to Lenin) saw the soviets as a valuable means of organizing the workers for the great revolution. Not until after the revolution had been crushed and the leaders of the soviets arrested did Lenin realize that, if the party controlled the soviets, the soviets could in turn be used to manipulate the workers. In 1917 when the March revolution broke out and

Every national area of the U.S.S.R. sends delegates to the Supreme Soviet. These delegates are from the sparsely populated Yakutsk A.S.S.R. in northern Siberia.

the workers' soviets were established as revolutionary organizations, Lenin viewed them as ready-made for the new revolutionary government.

When Lenin's view was rejected by other socialists, he set about planning to overthrow the democratic provisional government that had emerged following the March revolution. In November 1917 the Bolsheviks under Lenin toppled the provisional government. They then announced to representatives of the soviets gathered in St. Petersburg that a congress of soviets henceforth would be the foundation of the new government organization.

The 1917 Congress of Soviets was hardly representative of Russia as a whole, for it drew delegates only from among the most revolutionary groups of the time. To make this organization the chief legislative body of the new state was, in effect, to create a dictatorship of revolutionaries.

Lenin hastened to take power after the November revolution, even before the first meeting of the Congress of Soviets. Thus he made clear that it was his revolutionary initiative and not an election that had catapulted him to supremacy in Russia. Lenin named an executive branch of the soviets — the Council of People's Commissars, a kind of cabinet — in which all but three minor posts were held by Bolsheviks.

Practically from the moment tsarism was overthrown in Russia, the Bolshevik party (later to become the Communist party) controlled the state. From the outset the party made clear that the official government would be subordinate to the party.

THE CONSTITUENT ASSEMBLY

The Constituent Assembly was one attempt to provide an alternative government to that of the soviets. The first meeting was in January 1918. Despite the turbulence of the times, elections to this body had been held in 1917, before, during, and immediately after the Bolshevik seizure of power. The balloting had been secret and all adults had freedom to vote. Consequently, the Constituent Assembly was the most freely elected and representative body in Russian history.

The Bolsheviks had permitted the elections to the Constituent Assembly in hopes of gathering strong popular support. When it was discovered that Bolshevik strength in the assembly was definitely in the minority, they dispersed the assembly at gunpoint after its first meeting. The Constituent Assembly was never convened another time, and government at gunpoint had prevailed once again.

Nevertheless, many groups within Russia were spurred to rally against the Bolshevik dictatorship. The Civil War (1918-1921) ensued. Democratic Socialists, national groups such as the Ukrainians and the Turko-Tartars, plus former tsarist officers and nobles, made up the bulk of the anti-Bolshevik armies.

The Whites, as these groups were called to distinguish them politically from the Bolshevik Reds, were seriously split on basic economic and political questions.

Gradually the leadership of the White forces fell into the hands of authoritarian tsarist officers who appeared to offer the people very little. They alienated the nationalities by refusing to promise them local rights if the Bolsheviks were overthrown. They enraged the peasants by talking about compensation for land seizures or reconsideration of the land question. (The peasants, after all, considered the land theirs in the first place and not subject to negotiation.) Without the active support of the majority of the population, the Whites could not muster enough strength to overthrow the Bolsheviks.

Strife among the Whites, added to the strategically central position of the Bolsheviks in and around Moscow, secured for the Reds control of the country's inner lines of communication and transportation. Meanwhile a Red Army had been created with the same iron military discipline that fortified the party. Also contributing to Bolshevik success was the organizational genius of Trotsky and his ruthless conduct of the war.

Realizing that the Bolsheviks, even though highly organized, were not strong enough in numbers to impose all of their policies on the population, especially the peasantry, Lenin shrewdly promised to leave the land in peasant hands. This guaranteed at least their neutrality in the war. And this is really all he needed.

THE FIRST CONSTITUTION

Before the first battles of the Civil War were fought, the Bolsheviks pushed ahead with their plans for a constitution for the new Soviet state. Because of limited Bolshevik control over Russia, the Constitution of 1918 was drawn up only for the portion of the country called the Russian Soviet Federated Socialist Republic (R.S.F.S.R.). In their draft, the Bolsheviks kept carefully in mind the necessity of appealing to those people who had not yet accepted Bolshevik rule. The 1918 Constitution would serve as a model for later revisions in 1924 and 1936 and for the one proposed by Premier Khrushchev in 1962.

The first Soviet Constitution was based on two main principles: (1) concentration of power in one body (the Congress of Soviets) and (2) the revolutionary class nature of the electoral system.

Unlike the United States, where there is separation of executive, legislative, and judicial powers in government, the Soviet system concentrated these powers in the Congress of Soviets. The leaders explained to the Russian people that separation of powers was a product of the class struggle, but that under the Soviet system of the dictatorship of the proletariat, rule by one class required unification of state authority into a single group.

The Congress of Soviets was to elect a central executive committee. This committee would be given full power to act when the congress was not in session. It was also empowered even to appoint members to the Council of People's Commissars (the cabinet), the policy-making arm of the government.

The administration of the country was put into the hands of eighteen commissars, later called ministers as is the practice in western Europe.

The system of soviets extended to the remotest rural villages. The power of these local soviets was not clearly defined despite the vigorous contention of some party members that the Bolshevik slogan "All power to the soviets" must not be overlooked.

The principal restriction on the power of the local soviets was budgetary. All local expenditures and taxes had to be approved by higher authorities. Again uncompromising power at the center thwarted the forces of decentralization.

THE BILL OF RIGHTS

The 1918 Constitution also provided a bill of rights which emphasized the revolutionary nature of the regime. Freedom of speech, press, association, assembly, and access to education were reserved for the working class.

The church, formerly subsidized by the government, was separated from the state, and freedom of religious and antireligious propaganda was granted.

Work became a duty in accord with the declaration "He who does not work shall not eat."

Application of these rights was difficult for those who did not accept the party's definitions. Thus the right of assembly was denied to so-called counterrevolutionary elements. These elements, in the eyes of the party, turned out to be anyone who opposed Bolshevik policy.

Freedom of religious propaganda was limited by party pressure on printing plants to refuse to publish religious tracts.

At first, antireligious propaganda took the most violent forms. Churches were looted and burned. Priests were attacked. The Militant League of the Godless was formed to fight all religions.

After the mid-1930's this activity was moderate. Today a small number of churches are open for worship. There are several seminaries for the training of Orthodox priests. But the party continues to discourage worship. It prevents anyone who believes in God from gaining a responsible position in the state or other institutions of society. The youth of Russia are prime targets for the party's atheistic, antireligious indoctrination.

The right to vote was denied by the Constitution to the so-called exploiter-class businessmen, former police officials, monks, and priests. The voting system was set up to secure higher representation for workers in order to balance the mass of peasants who, it was feared, would be hostile to Communist domination.

The Constitution made no mention of the most important political fact of all: that the Bolsheviks were the real source of authority in the new Russia. In fact the Constitution did not mention the Bolshevik party. Clearly the party sought to veil, even though thinly, its complete control over the state.

Gradually, after the Bolshevik victory in the Civil War, the once-rebellious areas inhabited by national minorities in the Ukraine, the Caucasus, and in central Asia were brought back under Russian control. With their return, formal changes were made in the constitutional structure.

THE USSR APPEARS

In 1924 the name of the state was changed to reflect the increasingly multinational character of the country. The R.S.F.S.R., the Russian Soviet Federated Socialist Republic, became the U.S.S.R., the Union of Soviet Socialist Republics. There have been various numbers of these republics over the years. Today there are fifteen, including the R.S.F.S.R. Smaller national groups were organized into autonomous republics and regions, but the assortment of designations meant little. Supreme power remained in the hands of the Congress of Soviets; little local initiative was allowed.

The Congress of Soviets elected the two-chamber Central Executive Committee. One house, the Council of Nationalities, was based on territorial representation, somewhat like the United States Senate, with a certain number of delegates from each republic, regardless of population. The second house was to be the Council of the Union, somewhat along the lines of the U.S. House of Representatives, where representation is proportional to population.

Unlike the U.S. system, however, the real power never passed from the hands of the one, all-powerful Communist party, the Bolsheviks-Communists. Various committees and chambers, therefore, were little more than a democratic façade behind which the dictatorial party functioned.

SOVIET GOVERNMENT AND THE COMMUNIST PARTY

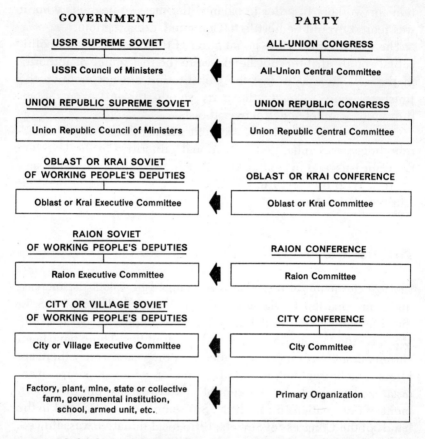

At each level of government there is a comparable party organization.

Oblast = territory or province
Krai = special region
Raion = district or township

One of the main reasons for this elaborate shell of government was to soothe the many nationalities which made up the Soviet state and to attract support from other national groups along the fringes of the vast Russian plain.

Attempts by certain union republics, especially the Ukraine, to develop genuinely autonomous institutions and rights, in line with their native traditions, were rigorously suppressed by the party.

STALIN'S CONSTITUTION

By 1936 Stalin considered it necessary to introduce a new constitution. He believed that the changes in Soviet society, as a result of the economic and cultural transformation of the country toward the Communist image, necessitated such a step.

Stalin reasoned that since there were no longer any antagonistic classes in Russia—only two friendly classes of peasants and workers—unrestricted universal suffrage could be introduced and the unequal representation of workers over peasants abolished. Elections henceforth, he decreed, would be secret. But the underlying significance of these concessions was revealed when Stalin added: "I must admit that . . . in the U.S.S.R. only one party can exist, the Communist. . . ." Again, what appeared to the citizen to be an important extension of his rights did nothing whatever to disturb the changeless authoritarian power of the party and its leaders.

Why bother to draft a new constitution and to submit it to the people for discussions since no amount of public debate would change as much as a comma? Part of the reason lies in the character of the Soviet system as a Communist totalitarian regime. Both Lenin and Stalin understood the value of keeping the masses and the party hierarchy in touch with each other without allowing the masses any real power. No party, no matter how conspiratorial or disciplined, could rule a population which was either entirely hostile or passively resistant. The system of soviets provided a ready device for giving the people a sense of participation in the government. Changing a constitution was part of this technique which the party used to provide for the peoples' political exercise.

Anyone who has witnessed a Soviet election will testify to the holiday atmosphere that prevails and the vigorous campaigning of the nominees—all representing the same party. The voter may register disapproval, of course, by scratching out the name of this or that nominee, but this, too, is hardly more than a safety valve for letting off voter steam.

Elections to soviets give the party a chance to reward citizens who have faithfully carried out its orders. A two-week trip to Moscow with all expenses paid by the state, the prestige of being a deputy to the Supreme Soviet, and the opportunity to hear and see the leaders of the state and party are modest compensation for a population which is denied the right of real choice.

Another main reason for this constitutional structure was to try to persuade people in the West, in this crucial period of the 1930's, that the Soviet Union was moving toward genuine democracy.

CONSTITUTIONAL RIGHTS VERSUS SOVIET REALITY

As one reads the Soviet Constitution of 1936, its similarity to many of the rights listed in the Constitution of the United States becomes apparent. There are some rights proclaimed in the Soviet document which do not appear in the American law, such as the right of any republic in the U.S.S.R. "to secede freely," the right to work, and the right to rest and leisure. Equal rights are proclaimed for women, as well as the prohibition of racial or national discrimination. Can all these rights be hollow, too?

The answer lies in viewing these rights against the background of Soviet reality. The answer also lies in the determination of the Communist party to monopolize the definition of these rights.

The right to work is not the right to choose one's work, but to work in disciplined subordination to state purposes; to work for a state-established wage in a state-controlled enterprise which forbids strikes or demonstrations of any sort.

The right of racial equality must be weighed against the Soviet anti-Semitic campaigns of 1939 and those from 1947-1953, against the large-scale deportation of whole segments of the population during World War II for security reasons, and against the monopoly by so-called Great Russians in leading positions in many of the union republics.

The 1936 Constitution, plus the Law on the Judiciary, 1938, created a new judicial system with a supreme court and several levels of local courts. The Supreme Court has no power to declare acts of the Supreme Soviet unconstitutional, as does the United States Supreme Court over the laws passed by Congress.

Furthermore, in the eyes of leading Soviet jurists, there can be no contradiction between the law and the policy of the party.

Other judicial rights, familiar and cherished by non-Communist nations, such as the right to defense by counsel, have been completely flouted in the political trials of the Soviet Union.

The office of public prosecutor (roughly comparable to that of the U.S. state's attorney or prosecutor) is designed to prevent anyone from being arrested except with its sanction or the sanction of a judge. Soviet citizens who have been arrested by the secret police maintain, however, that this provision does not provide immunity from such dangers as false arrest.

No constitutional declaration or device in the Soviet Union, whatever it may claim to guarantee – universal suffrage, civil rights, fair trial – has ever altered the fundamental character of Communist party power supremacy. The revised constitution (ordered by Khrushchev at the April 1962 meeting of the Supreme Soviet in Moscow), designed, said Khrushchev, to reflect the present stage of "the full-fledged construction of communism," is unlikely to alter the dictatorship of the party.

III. PEOPLE UNDER COMMUNISM

It is difficult for anyone of a non-Communist nation to imagine just how the Soviet system works in the everyday life of many of the Russian people because of the gap between what communism claims and what actually prevails in the U.S.S.R. What is the actual effect of the party organization and the state institutions which it controls upon Soviet people? Here is how the party has touched the lives of several Russians.

IVAN, THE RELIABLE PARTY MEMBER

Ivan is a draftsman, age 63. He works in a state-owned industrial plant. A veteran Bolshevik, he joined the party before the revolutionary seizure of power in 1917. Because of his long service to the party, a distinguished war record, and personal honesty, he is greatly respected by his neighbors and fellow party members.

Ivan's factory is a large one; therefore, the primary party organization in Ivan's community is also large – more than three hundred members – and requires the services of a full-time party secretary and a party bureau.

In the fifteen years that Ivan has worked at the factory, there have been seven different party secretaries. The first man was arrested in 1947 for embezzling party funds. During his five-year term of office he had built up what is called a "family nest." This is a private clique organized secretly and informally for mutual protection against inspections and various other party checks. In the "nest" at Ivan's plant were the director of the plant, the plant secret police official, several leading party workers, and the party secretary. They all shared the stolen party money.

The next party secretary was a veteran party committee member of Jewish background. He was purged by Stalin during an anti-Semitic outburst which preceded Stalin's general party purge in 1953.

He was succeeded by a protégé of Malenkov, but in 1957, when Khrushchev defeated Malenkov in the struggle for control of the party, a Khrushchev man took over party affairs in Ivan's district.

The next party secretary was another Jewish man, a veteran who had been liberated in 1955 from a forced-labor camp. He was replaced by a young secretary who was ousted when the plant failed to meet its production quota in 1960.

His successor, the present secretary, has succeeded in spurring the plant to overfulfill the planned production quotas set for it by the government. For this achievement he probably will soon be promoted to a higher, regional party office.

Despite his long tenure in the party, Ivan gives advice only when it is asked for. He helps conduct local party propaganda activities among nonparty members at the factory. He also works on the local workers' newspaper and on production of posters urging harder work; he helps form evening reading circles and organizes holiday outings.

The primary organization of Ivan's local party is also responsible for making certain that there is no mismanagement in the factory. Ivan recently helped uncover a ring of petty thieves who had taken lumber from the factory yard after work at night to build a summer cottage for themselves. (The building materials were not available on the open market.) For stealing state property they were given long prison terms.

MASHA, THE DEDICATED PARTY WORKER

Masha is a dedicated Communist. When she became eighteen, she was eligible for party membership. Her father urged her to apply. She had to file a declaration.

Her training for eventual party membership had begun when her father enrolled her at the age of nine in the Young Pioneers (Communist youth organization for children from age nine to fifteen).

Almost every Russian child is a member of the Young Pioneers. Masha was part of a "link" of twelve who elected their own leader. Their "link" was united into a brigade of forty members which in turn chose five children to represent it. Masha was soon one of the five. Devotedly, she read and memorized the stories of Lenin's life and the stories of the Soviet heroes of World War II. She soon became the outstanding member of her brigade in reciting political themes.

Masha's dedication to the Young Pioneers even led her to rebuke her father for permitting her grandmother to continue to attend the local church. Masha brought her "link" home one day to expose her grandmother to atheistic propaganda. Thereafter, Masha rarely spoke to her grandmother.

When she was fourteen, Masha applied for membership and was accepted in the Komsomol (Komsomol: short for Russian words meaning Communist Union of Youth, an organization created in 1918 to train young people from age fourteen to twenty-three for Communist party membership) after having been recommended by one of her father's fellow party members. The Komsomol selection process was more demanding than the Pioneers' had been, and membership responsibilities were also greater. Masha was required to engage in systematic study of Marxism-Leninism, active participation in the political life of the city, and social vigilance against drunkenness and rowdyism. She took her duties seriously but found herself in a small minority. Masha took every legitimate opportunity to denounce those whom she considered slackers and careerists.

During this period she became an expert marksman in the Komsomol-sponsored paramilitary shooting matches. She also lectured on Marxism-Leninism for her primary organization and served as a brigade leader for the Pioneers. She avidly read the official organization newspaper, *Komsomolskaya Pravda* ("The Truth of the Komsomols"), and accompanied her father to political meetings. When she was seventeen she volunteered for summer farm work in the new projects of central Asia and enrolled in a parachute training course.

Her tough-minded, almost fanatically loyal approach to the Komsomol was unusual. She complained of the general indifference and even occasional hostility of some of its members to Communist goals. Most of her girl friends thought of the Komsomol as a social club which offered dances, excursions, and musicales.

They cared little about political lectures. There were others, however, classified as opportunists who were mainly interested in furthering their careers.

Masha will continue her education and eventually she will become an engineer. Her dedication to the party is her first interest in life, above education, family, and friends.

IGOR, THE DISILLUSIONED STUDENT

Igor, another young student, has a consuming interest in biological science. Though he, too, had been a member of the Young Pioneers and hoped to join the Komsomols, his reasons for membership were not political. He liked the nature excursions and laboratory work which the Pioneers encouraged. When he could, he skipped the political talks.

He complained to his parents that the lecturers in Marxism sounded foolish when they discussed science, for they seemed to know very little about the subject.

Igor joined the Komsomol, because there was little chance otherwise of his getting into Moscow University to study biology. Igor's parents explained that it was important for Igor's future rise in the field of biology to avoid political criticism. Therefore, he should attend political lectures though he thought them dull.

Igor's disillusionment with Communist controls deepened when he discovered that some of the books on plant genetics he wanted to read could be obtained only by special permission from his

The training of party members begins at an early age. Very small children may become Little Octobrists. Older boys and girls may become Young Pioneers. Trained youth leaders organize games, plays, picnics, take the children on field trips and to summer camp, instill patriotic doctrine and party ideals. Recognition and awards for outstanding merit are given.

teacher because they were kept in a locked section of the library. When he read them, he discovered that they contained experimental evidence which contradicted what he was taught in class and in Marxism-Leninism courses.

Igor began to realize the great power which the party exercised in controlling science and the individual. When he reported to his class on his outside reading, he was severely reprimanded by the teacher and was investigated by a special delegation of the Komsomol. He was forced to apologize formally and to rewrite his report. He resolved that, in the future he would carefully draw conclusions which would satisfy the instructor. Igor had made the adjustment reluctantly, but it was the only way in which he could continue his studies.

BORIS, POLITICAL PRISONER

Boris was a major in the Red Army during World War II. He was one of the few holding such high rank who were not party members. Late in the war Boris served as an officer in the Soviet occupation army in Czechoslovakia. Later he was stationed in Vienna, Prague, and, finally, Berlin. He saw at first hand the way of life of people in central Europe.

Even during the depressing days following the war, he was astonished at the material comforts, food supplies, and general well-being of the Czechs, Austrians, Hungarians, and to a lesser extent the Germans, compared with what he knew to be conditions in Russia.

On occasion he cautiously discussed this contrast with fellow officers. They warned him to be silent lest he be arrested. A fellow officer, who was also a Communist party member, reported Boris' conversations to the political leader of the regiment. It was the latter's responsibility to supervise Communist party propaganda and indoctrination among the men of the regiment.

Before the party organization could take action, however, Boris was arrested by the secret police, who had received a report from their informer in the regiment. The police checked Boris' personal history files and discovered that his mother had participated in a demonstration to secure religious rights in 1928 and had been arrested but released. Although Boris himself was not a religious man, his mother's experience was used as incriminating evidence that his family background was corrupt. Boris was permitted no defense counsel. He was tried by a special police court, found guilty, stripped of his rank, and sent to a forced-labor camp at Vorkuta in northern Russia.

He worked there for seven years. His family knew nothing of his whereabouts and believed that he had been killed in Germany. After Stalin's death most of the political prisoners in Vorkuta were released, and Boris made his long way home, a prematurely old man. His decorations and rank were restored.

ELENA, THE JUDGE

Elena is a judge in a local people's court, as well as being a wife and mother.

Elena's court is crowded with cases. Sometimes twenty or thirty cases must be rushed through in a day to keep pace with the overload. Like all judges and public prosecutors in the Soviet Union, Elena is a party member.

Generally the party does not interfere with minor cases, unless a party member is involved. In one divorce case involving a party member, however, the regional party secretary issued a directive as to the verdict the court was to render, and Elena was obliged to carry it out.

Most citizens represent themselves in court, because to hire a defender from the local "collective board of lawyers" would cost an average worker as much as a week's pay. Apparently there is no Russian equivalent of a public defender in the United States, who is as freely available to give legal counsel to people unable to afford a lawyer's services.

Among the most successful lawyers, Elena has observed, is one famed for his "political power counseling." He is a man who knows not only the law but the politics that may bear on a case. Thus he knows whom to write, whom to bribe, and even which words of defense most nearly fit the political mood of the time. Each of these insights is calculated to minimize his client's penalties.

Elena has little or no contact with Soviet secret police courts, where legal safeguards are virtually nonexistent for the accused. Soviet legal reforms in 1958 restrained the interference of secret police in judicial procedures. Political prisoners have been freed, and trials for political crimes have sharply declined. On the other

Visitors to the U.S.S.R. always remark at the number of women doing work ordinarily done by men elsewhere. It is commonplace to see women sweeping streets, working at construction jobs, acting in all sorts of official capacities. The young woman is a People's judge.

SOVFOTO

hand a party decision in 1962 introduced the death penalty for embezzlement of state funds, an offense which had become increasingly frequent.

Perhaps the most striking difference between Elena and her counterparts in other, non-Communist nations—the United States, for example—is her belief that the law relates to political loyalty to the Communist party rather than to the rights of the individual.

SOVIET CITIZENS AND THE PARTY TODAY

Russian families, even when they are composed of loyal party members, rarely discuss their innermost feelings about the workings of the strict political system within which they live.

It is particularly interesting for an outsider to note that the realities of Soviet society are frequently quite different from the theories of Marx and Lenin and from the rights proclaimed by Stalin and his successors.

Visitors to the Soviet Union discover a widespread lack of political knowledge among the people, not only about the systems of other nations but about their own system.

Bernadine Bailey

"The press is the only weapon with whose aid the party every day speaks to the working class in the language of the party. You cannot find in the world another such flexible apparatus as the press, and there is no means through which the party can so well connect its ideological threads with the working class," said Joseph Stalin in the early days of the revolution. The press has always been a powerful instrument in the hands of the party. Workers who do not buy daily papers have an opportunity to read the news from papers posted on bulletin boards.

When asked what they would change in their system if they had the chance, the replies often are as contradictory as they are varied.

Some would replace the dictatorship of the party with a dictatorship of the intelligentsia, that group of learned and also socially and politically conscious citizens whose early members fought the oppressions of tsarism. Other Russians would like to have a multiparty political system. Others would wish only for more cultural freedom.

AUTHORITY OF THE POLITICAL SYSTEM

Americans who have lived in the Soviet Union for any period of time generally agree that the basic Soviet political system is quite stable, that Communist party authority and control is both vigorous and durable. Under present conditions and probably through all circumstances short of a major military disaster to the U.S.S.R., there seems almost no chance of open revolt or even mass disaffection.

This does not mean, however, that all or even most of the people are satisfied with the system. But the degrees of dissatisfaction are hard to measure because people have little opportunity to express themselves.

The hard core of Communist party members and other important people have more to gain than to lose by keeping the regime as it is. This group is constantly growing as the Soviet economy strengthens and more and better-paying jobs become available.

Although one small group (widely scattered and uninfluential) may be totally alienated and hostile, the great majority of U.S.S.R. citizens can best be described as generally indifferent to politics, but not uncomplaining when the system chafes their personal lives. The peasants are the most disgruntled group. In the cities the foreigner often will hear Russians say "You have it better, don't you?" Then they hasten to add, "Give us a few years and we will catch up with you."

SUMMARY

When Lenin's revolutionaries seized power in the political and social turmoil of 1917, they knew little of the practical necessities of ruling the enormous Russian state. Thus, for a half century, they and their successors have mixed ideology and power, opportunism, terror and concessions, in constructing the Soviet Communist state. Politics and government have been a drastic departure from Western democratic traditions, and the gulf between East and West has spread as the dictatorial nature of the state has become clearer.

The structure of the Soviet government runs parallel to the structure of the Communist party. The powerful presence of the party is felt at every point in Soviet society. So supreme is the party that elections, legislatures, courts, the law, and many civil liberties are allowed and practiced only in terms of party, not individual, interests. Thus neither the individual nor his collective image, the nation, has identity in the Soviet Union outside the context of the Communist party. But because of political indifference among many Soviet citizens there is little active opposition to the regime and no clear idea of what changes in the system would be welcome.

Still, so long as there is no agreed-upon method of transferring authority after the death of the leader, be he Lenin, Stalin, or Khrushchev, the Communist party is faced with the recurring threat that the struggle for power will become violent and costly.

TERMS TO KNOW

Presidium	Secretariat	soviet
Congress of Soviets	Central Committee	Komsomol
Council of Nationalities	Council of the Union	Young Pioneers

QUESTIONS ON THE CHAPTER

1. About how many Communist party members are there in the Soviet Union? These constitute what percentage of the total population?
2. What is the function of the purge under communism?

3. Who was responsible for the purges carried out in 1937 and 1938? State some of the possible reasons behind these purges.

4. Who were the leaders eliminated as rivals of Khrushchev following the death of Joseph Stalin?

5. Explain why Lenin was at first suspicious of the soviets (councils of workers' deputies). How did Trotsky view these soviets?

6. According to Stalin's Constitution of 1936, all elections were to be free and secret. Explain how the Communist party maintained its control and power in spite of "free" elections.

7. Describe the Communist interpretation of the citizens' rights set forth in the Soviet Constitution of 1936.

8. What is the general attitude toward politics held by people in the U.S.S.R.?

QUESTIONS FOR DISCUSSION

1. Compare the methods by which Stalin seized power after Lenin's death, and the methods by which Khrushchev seized power following Stalin's death.

2. Both the United States and the Soviet Union have constitutions guaranteeing the rights of citizens. Discuss the interpretation and application of these rights in both countries.

3. In the Soviet Union there is only one political party, and its membership is restricted by establishing rigid qualifications for admittance. Contrast this situation with political activity in Western democracies in terms of elections, party competition, party responsibility, and membership in political parties.

4. The Soviets use the word "democratic" to describe the functions of the Soviet government and the Communist party. The Western World views the same word in a completely different light. Suggest other words or terms which have different meanings to the Communist and Western worlds and explain the varying connotations. What implications does this disagreement on meanings of words and terms have for negotiations between the Soviets and the Western democracies?

BIBLIOGRAPHY

For Reference: □ Brzezinski, Zbigniew, *The Permanent Purge: Politics in Soviet Totalitarianism.* Harvard University Press, 1956. □ Carson, George B., Jr., *Russia Since 1917.* American Historical Association, Service Center for Teachers of History, 1962. □ Fainsod, Merle, *How Russia is Ruled.* Harvard University Press, 1961. □ Kulski, W. W., *The Soviet Regime: Communism in Practice.* Syracuse University Press, 1956. □ Meissner, Boris, *The Communist Party of the Soviet Union.* Frederick A. Praeger, Inc., 1956. □ Mosely, Philip, and others, *Russia Since Stalin: Old Trends and New Problems.* Annals of the American Academy of Political and Social Science, volume 303: January 1956. □ Wolfe, Bertram, *Communist Totalitarianism: Keys to the Soviet System.* Beacon Press, 1961. For Further Reading: □ Kasenkina, Oksana, *Leap to Freedom.* J. B. Lippincott Company, 1949. □ Koestler, Arthur, *Darkness at Noon.* The Macmillan Company, 1941. □ Kravchenko, Victor, *I Chose Freedom.* Garden City Publishing Company, 1947.

CHAPTER **5**

ECONOMICS IN THE USSR

*By maintaining harsh controls
over all aspects of economic life,
Soviet planners
have changed a backward economy
into one which challenges
the free economy of the Western World.*

Today the Soviet Union ranks second only to the United States in industrial productivity. Soviet leaders are predicting that by 1980 their Soviet economic utopia will lead the world.

What lies in the background of the surprising economic change in a nation which less than a half century ago was an underdeveloped area?

To begin with fundamentals: The Soviet economy is highly centralized, just as Soviet government and politics are centralized. The elements of the economy—factories, tractors, tools, huge farms, resources, capital—are owned and operated by the government. Workers are strictly regimented.

This controlled economy is highly unlike the basic economic structure in most non-Communist countries where the economy is decentralized, largely privately owned and operated, consumer

Day-shift workers leaving the big iron and steel works at Magnitogorsk in the Ural Mountain area. Heavy industry—the production of steel, the construction of hydroelectric plants, canals, and the like—has been given priority in the U.S.S.R.

directed, and based on the interplay of supply and demand.

In the Soviet Union many of the crucial decisions which have shaped the Soviet economy have been politically, rather than economically, inspired. In 1928, for example, the Soviet government decided to launch a crash program to industrialize the country and collectivize the peasantry. But this program was as much a scheme to strengthen and consolidate political power as to improve the economic life of the nation.

Aside from its spectacular growth, the Soviet economy demands attention because it undergirds virtually every dimension of the Soviet challenge to the non-Communist world.

The military threat of the Soviet Union to the Free World, is based upon the productive capacity of its factories, the technological skills of its scientists and engineers, and the ability of its economic structure in general to withstand the strains and tensions of an immensely costly arms race.

The political thrust of the Soviet Union depends for success, in large part, on the appeal of the Soviet economic system to the underdeveloped, emerging nations who seek to increase their industrial production in the most rapid way possible.

Does the Soviet system offer the quick formula for world power status? If so, how can these countries accept the economic system without emulating the totalitarian political controls which enable the Soviet economy to function as it does? These are serious questions.

The purely economic threat of the Soviet system is less acute. At the present time the United States is fully capable of producing consumer goods and agricultural products for foreign trade in greater quantity and of superior quality. On the other hand Soviet efforts to export high-grade, heavy industrial products and the Soviet state monopoly of foreign trade are factors in the economic rivalry which cannot be minimized.

ECONOMIC PROBLEMS THE BOLSHEVIKS FACED

The fundamental decisions which have shaped the structure of the Soviet economy were taken in the late 1920's, after a period of uncertainty which divided Soviet leaders contending for supremacy into several groups.

When the Bolsheviks seized power in November 1917, the Russian economy was in a state of complete chaos. War and the revolution had completely shattered the old autocratic society. The Bolsheviks were anxious to hasten this deterioration in order to destroy the economic power of the nobility and the small middle class. Yet the Bolsheviks needed food from the countryside and manufactured goods from the factories to check widespread dissatisfaction. The policy devised to answer these contradictory needs was called War Communism.

WAR COMMUNISM

War Communism lasted from 1917 to 1921 and was a mixture of primitive Communist theory and practical necessity, contrived in a desperate attempt to mobilize men and materials for Russia's survival. Although the peasants were allowed to use the land as they wished, they had to surrender property title to the government. Grain was urgently needed to stave off famine. In many cases it had to be requisitioned from hostile peasants.

The basic industries were nationalized. A highly centralized economic administration began to take shape. Labor discipline was restored in the face of workers' resistance. Food, fuel, and housing shortages were turned into economic weapons with which to destroy the upper classes.

War Communism helped the Bolsheviks produce and distribute just enough to bolster their victory in the Civil War. By 1920 it was clear that this period of stopgap economics had reached the end of its usefulness. The practice of requisitioning grain had become so oppressive that the peasants were in open revolt. The population of towns and cities had diminished in a startling fashion. Industrial production had fallen to less than 10 per cent of the 1914 level. Hunger was everywhere.

THE NEW ECONOMIC POLICY

Waiting for the workers' revolution in western Europe that never came, the revolutionaries were forced to seek a compromise with the peasants. The series of concessions which Lenin and his followers made to the peasants and workers in 1921 became known as the New Economic Policy, or NEP.

The NEP was designed to give the Bolsheviks a breathing space in the unabating political, economic, and social turmoil of post-revolutionary Russia. Strength and stability regained, they would then push toward their final goal — establishment of the Communist state. The NEP lasted until 1928.

During NEP a large measure of capitalism was restored, particularly in agriculture and trade. Peasants were given land tenure under law, were permitted to rent land and hire labor. Grain requisitioning was replaced by a *tax in kind* (payment in crops or livestock), and the peasants — in the fashion of capitalist farmers — were permitted to sell their surplus privately wherever they chose. Within a year or two food was once again flowing into the cities.

Although the most important heavy industries, the banks, and foreign trade were still controlled by the state, private capitalist stores and small factories were permitted to operate. Some large companies were even rented to private individuals to be run for profit. Heavy industry, however, "the commanding heights," as Lenin called it, remained securely in state hands.

THE NEED FOR INDUSTRIALIZATION

Despite a strong economic recovery, the Bolsheviks still faced a serious conflict. The popular base for their rule continued to be the workers, the proletariat. Opposition continued to come from the peasantry. The question now became how to increase the number of workers and reduce the influence of peasants in order to stabilize power.

As long as revolution did not break out elsewhere in the world, the Bolsheviks needed to develop their military and economic strength to resist what they considered to be a united and hostile capitalist world. The theoretical basis for the Bolshevik seizure of power had been the Marxist ideal of meeting all the material needs of the people.

Thus industrialization became necessary for three reasons: (1) to increase the number of workers and thereby broaden the base of Bolshevik strength, (2) to thwart the designs of what the Bolsheviks called an encircling hostile capitalist world, and (3) to fulfill the Marxist promise that the revolution would satisfy everybody's material needs.

The why of industrializing was clear, but the how remained the central issue of the 1920's. The solution that was finally adopted laid the foundation for the Soviet economy we know today. In the struggle over industrial policy, Bukharin, Trotsky, Zinoviev, Kamenev, and Stalin were principal figures.

BUKHARIN'S APPROACH

One group in the Bolshevik party, the rightists, claimed that industrialization would have to be very gradual and that the urban classes for the most part would have to bear the costs. The spokesman for this group, Nikolai Bukharin (Stalin supported him at first), wanted to avoid antagonizing the peasants by using repressive measures. At the same time he did not think that the peasants constituted an overriding danger to the regime so long as their material needs were met. Therefore, he suggested that the state encourage peasants to increase their production by offering them various price concessions and a wider selection of consumer goods and by promising higher farm incomes for those peasants who coöperated.

The state, then, Bukharin planned, could sell some of the surplus grain abroad and use the profit to invest in industrial machinery. As industry grew, its own profits could be plowed back into capital investment—improved and enlarged plants and equipment. Furthermore, peasant savings could be tapped by the government through taxes and borrowing. In short, Bukharin proposed a gradual process of industrialization based on a prosperous peasantry. He further believed that the high degree of mechanization of agriculture resulting from the development of socialist industry would eventually persuade the peasants to organize into huge collective farms. Thus Bukharin foresaw a peaceful transition from capitalism to socialism in the countryside to match the transition in the factories.

THE LEFTISTS—THEIR APPROACH

Trotsky, Zinoviev, and Kamenev—the leftists—opposed Bukharin's point of view. (Stalin eventually took their opinions for his own, but only after having purged them in his drive for control of the party and the state.)

This group pointed out that the state needed much more capital for industrialization than Bukharin realized. Certainly it needed far more than could be provided by the peasants in a market economy or a capitalist agricultural system. Investments would also be needed for the development of transportation and social services, as well as industry, in order to raise the general level of the economy to the point where industrial production could be most effectively utilized.

Modern industry requires that large initial investments be followed over a long period of time with continuing capital input. Under Bukharin's piecemeal investment scheme, the leftists argued, both production of consumer goods and production of such heavy-industry items as mining equipment, machine tools, cement, bricks, electrical equipment, paint, glass, and metals

USSR—USA: AREA, ARABLE LAND, POPULATION

Area *(excludes water areas)*		8,609,876 *square miles* 3,548,974 *square miles*	
Arable Land	*each unit=500,000 square miles*	861,000 *square miles* 850,000 *square miles*	
Population *(1960)*	*each unit=10,000,000 persons*	214,400,000 179,323,000	

USSR ■   USA ■

USSR—USA: AGRICULTURE 1960

	UNIT *(In Millions)*	USSR	USA
Grain	*bushels*	4110.0	6852.0
Rice (1959)	*tons*	00.2	2.7
Sugar Beets	*tons*	56.0	16.4
Cotton	*bales*	6.8	14.3
Potatoes	*hundredweight*	1851.9	257.4
Livestock (1959)		70.8	93.9

would take too long and peasant dissatisfaction would persist.

In addition, the leftists pointed out, it was politically dangerous to allow a prosperous capitalist peasantry to exist for long. The regime would be placing its trust in the good will of a group which was the enemy of the proletariat.

Therefore, the leftists advised wholesale reconstruction of agriculture in order to force peasants to produce surplus food without incentives and thus provide the capital needed for industrialization, the heaviest burden falling upon the peasantry.

Stalin sided first with Bukharin's group in order to discredit Trotsky and his followers. Then in 1928 he reversed himself and adopted many of the proposals of the, by then, discredited leftists in order to defeat Bukharin.

STALIN'S PLAN: COLLECTIVIZE AND INDUSTRIALIZE

Stalin's campaign in 1928 was twofold: to force all Russian peasants to give up their privately held land and form collective or state farms, and to launch a five-year plan to accomplish the rapid growth of heavy industry. This decision unleashed a tide of suffering and misery across Russia, but it also signaled an economic surge, the effects of which the world is still trying to gauge.

THE COLLECTIVE FARMS (KOLKHOZY)

Stalin sought to turn the poor against the well-to-do peasants, kulaks (*kulak:* "the fist"), in order to split the group and weaken it. At the same time he expropriated the grain and livestock of the prosperous peasants. Then he ordered all peasants to join collective or state farms.

In these collectives, or kolkhozy, most of the land was owned by the collective itself. Each peasant was permitted to keep a small garden plot, a limited number of chickens, and a cow for his personal needs. All other livestock was placed under the collective ownership of the kolkhoz. As for what to plant and how much, these decisions were made by planners in Moscow, rather than by local authorities.

The kolkhoz was required to pay a tax in kind. It was in the form of a quota or norm for different crops and livestock. If the kolkhoz produced more than its quota, it might decide for itself whether to sell the surplus to the government at a fixed price, sell it on the private but now restricted market, or consume it. There were great pressures, of course, to sell surplus to the state.

In theory the collective farm was to elect its own chairman, but in fact this important official was usually selected by the party from its ranks. He served as the ear of the party in the countryside and as disciplinary agent as well.

In order to assure control of the countryside, the party established machine tractor stations (MTS) in strategic locations to manage all mechanized farm equipment. Loyal workers and party bureaucrats were put in charge of the farm equipment in order to provide an iron framework of proletarian strength in the countryside. The kolkhoz had to rent the machines in order to cultivate and harvest its fields. Since payments to the state were in kind, the MTS served also as collection agencies. Through its work in helping the kolkhoz meet its quotas, the MTS became deeply involved in the workaday operations of the collective and provided the state an additional check on the efficiency and honesty of the peasant collectives.

THE STATE FARMS (SOVKHOZY)

Collective farms, however, did not represent Stalin's long-range goal in reorganizing the countryside. The kolkhozy was merely an intermediary step to the state farms, or sovkhozy, which remain to this day the Communists' ideal for the organization of the rural areas. The state farm is owned and operated by the state. The peasants work on the farm for daily wages in the manner of factory workers. There are no private garden plots nor is there any freedom to dispose of surpluses. Each sovkhoz specializes in some form of farming—dairying, grain, or stock raising. The hub of the farm is a group of administrative offices, dormitories, kitchens and communal dining rooms, repair shops, and usually an agricultural school.

The object of the state farms is to simplify agricultural planning and commodity distribution and to destroy the peasant mentality by converting the peasant into an hourly wage earner. The insistence by Soviet leaders that they intend to wipe out the differences between rural and urban labor simply means that the state farms will ultimately replace the collectives and the mass of the Russian peasantry will be "proletarianized." Soviet leaders count on this transition to eliminate the last vestiges of hostility to the party that have lingered in the Russian countryside.

PEASANT RESISTANCE

All elements of the peasantry, the poor as well as the well-to-do, stoutly resisted the Stalin order to collectivize. In many cases state and party organizers who were sent into the countryside were attacked. Reliable reports from the Volga area told of organizers who were seized and burned in bales of hay.

The party countered peasant resistance with its own brand of toughness: arrests, deportations, and the use of heavily armed troops to induce collectivization with bayonets and bullets. The peasants were not easily suppressed, however. They reacted even more violently, slaughtering their cattle and burning their crops to prevent them from being seized for the collectives.

Through the 1930's the regime alternated tactics of brute force and economic incentives, a typically Communist carrot-and-stick formula. The incentives were in the form of tax advantages, shares in state credits, seed and fertilizer distribution, and, of course, use of the MTS machinery.

By 1939 collectivization was almost universal in the Soviet Union. The price paid was immense. Millions of peasants literally had been uprooted and exiled. Stunted livestock production still showed the wounds of collectivization. Between one and three million peasants died from starvation during the worst years of Stalin's collectivization drive.

But the increasingly powerful Communist dictator achieved his main economic purpose—to guarantee a fixed supply of food and raw materials for the cities and factories. This flow of goods opened the way for the rapid industrialization of the Soviet economy.

THE FIRST FIVE-YEAR PLAN

With an equal disregard for the wishes of the mass of workers, Stalin launched the First Five-Year Plan in industry (1928-1932). After the nationalization of all industrial enterprise, the organization of industry was placed under the control of the Council of People's Commissars (Council of Ministers after 1946) which, with the assistance of the State Planning Commission (Gosplan), made policy and laid out the general plans for all industry.

At the next level of authority was the individual commissariat (ministry) which administered certain sectors of the economy, such as heavy industry, light industry, and ferrous metals. These commissariats, with jurisdiction over thousands of mines and industrial enterprises scattered from one end of the country to another, controlled every facet of their particular segment of the economy. Under the ministries, several chief administrations were organized to take charge of certain special problems within each industry — research and procurement, for example.

Usually a third level of authority was organized around a trust that included several plants or mines with either similar problems or a common location. At the bottom was the individual enterprise or factory. The structure was partially reorganized in 1957. However, the chain of command remained intact. The most important person in determining the actual production of goods in this hierarchy is the factory manager or director at the local level.

PRODUCTION GOALS

At Stalin's insistence, the industrial planners who had been assembled to draw up an economic plan for the entire country, set very high production goals. Gosplan then drew up a complex plan which provided the maximum and minimum production goals in every aspect of economic life, from steel to shoelaces. It took into account every factor from weather to population growth. It allocated raw materials, set priorities for use of transportation facilities, and planned resettlement of hundreds of thousands of Russians.

Never before had the world seen anything like this — an attempt to control and direct the entire resources of a nation toward a particular set of goals established in detail beforehand by an army of engineers, statisticians, and other technicians working in offices far removed from the people or machines they manipulated.

Every power of the state and party was mobilized to assist this grandiose five-year design. Steel production was to rise from 4.2 million to 10 million tons, coal from 35 million to 150 million tons, electric power from 5 million to 22 million kilowatt-hours.

ARCTIC
OCEAN

Bering
Sea

Barents
Sea

Baltic Sea

Black Sea

Caspian Sea

Sea of
Okhotsk

PACIFIC OCEAN

Sea of
Japan

200 400 600 800
MILES

POPULATION
Each dot represents 20,000 people

WORKER DISSENSION; TRADE UNIONS SHACKLED

If the anarchic traditions of the peasantry had to be curbed and
crushed, so also did the desire of the workers for wage equality and
independent unions have to be overcome. During the 1920's, the
trade unions had enjoyed greater independence than ever before
or since. They had been able to obtain wage increases and had even
exerted some influence on matters of high policy. But during the
First Five-Year Plan, Stalin purged the union leadership and
brought the organizations under strict control. The unions were
committed only to encouraging production. They had lost all right
to represent the workers in bargaining with the state. They became,
in Stalin's own words, a transmission belt to carry orders from the
state to the workers.

PUNISHMENT AND PROPAGANDA

The workers now found themselves helpless to resist the party's
imposition of rigid labor discipline. In order to keep workers from
changing jobs in search of better conditions, the party introduced a

system of internal passports; penalties against absenteeism, including loss of ration cards and living quarters; and finally, in 1938, labor books. These labor books contained a full record of a worker's previous employment and remained in the possession of the factory in which he was employed. He could not get a job without presenting the book. Because labor was in such short supply, factory managers rarely would surrender a labor book.

Severe punishment was imposed for lateness, petty thievery, and hooliganism. By 1940 a state decree bound all workers to their jobs and threatened heavy penalties for any job changes. Thus the worker and the peasant were bound to state service in a manner which grimly resembled conditions in 17th-century Russia.

STAKHANOVISM

But force alone could not spur a complex economic plan in so vast a nation. The enormous propaganda and agitation department of the Communist party Secretariat now was thrown into the battle for production. In the press, over the radio, the word went out to factories, farms, schools, clubs, and the local soviets — produce, produce, produce! The arts, literature, the cinema, were all harnessed to the state's economic purpose in exhorting greater efforts

Collective farms are operated like factories. This collective farm is in Kazakhstan in central Asia. In the foreground are piles of grain; beyond the farm buildings are workers' dwellings. Stretching into the distance is the steppe.

and sacrifices. The party even tried to kindle a spirit of adventure and romanticism to overcome the obstacles which were blocking the economic progress of the country.

Rewards and incentives were offered to those who fulfilled or over-fulfilled their production quotas. In 1935 in the Donets basin, a miner named Stakhanov dug 102 tons of coal in a six-hour shift (the average had been 6 or 7 tons); overnight his name heralded an entire movement—Stakhanovism, the smashing of individual production records. Stakhanovites received high pay and many other privileges. They were given paid vacations at state resorts, free transportation, better living quarters.

The system of relating material benefits to production—denounced as exploitation by leading Bolsheviks before the revolution—was being given added impetus. Once again the workers' ideal of equal wages was sacrificed to the overriding needs of the state, as interpreted by Stalin and the party.

MORE FIVE-YEAR PLANS

Second and Third Five-Year Plans followed in rapid succession. Large numbers of foreign technicians were brought in to help build some of the most complex enterprises. American engineers

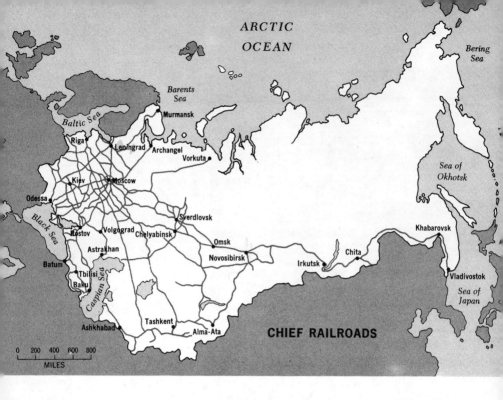

built the great Dneprostroi Dam, the great tractor works at Stalin-grad (changed to Volgograd in 1961 during the de-Stalinization campaign triggered by Premier Khrushchev), and a huge steel factory at Magnitogorsk.

Despite great effort, many of the goals of these plans were not realized. By 1939 the Soviet Union was not a highly indus-trialized country at all, in terms of per capita production. It had slipped to third place in steel production, behind the United States and a resurgent Germany. On the other hand, its petroleum pro-duction had moved up to second place, behind the United States; its electric power output had made startling gains; and its coal production had doubled. More important than these figures, how-ever, was the fact that a heavy industrial base for the future was being constructed.

THE GERMANS ATTACK

The German attack on the Soviet Union in June 1941 interrupted the Third Five-Year Plan and diverted all of the country's resources into war production. The heavy industrial base which Stalin was

Homer Smith

Railroad lines are well maintained and managed. These men are being given additional training as engineers.

building played a decisive role in turning out the tanks, planes, and guns which helped repel and finally defeat the Nazis on the eastern (Russian) front. In a heroic effort the state organized and carried out a transfer of heavy industrial plants from areas threatened by German occupation to the safety of the Ural Mountain area. This wholesale transplanting of industry at great cost and often over great distances was a key factor in preserving the war potential of Soviet industry.

Although the United States sent masses of war materiel to Soviet Russia through lend-lease, this equipment did not arrive in bulk until the Red Army had scored a dramatic victory at Stalingrad, which destroyed the German strategic reserve and proved to be one of the turning points in the war. American equipment did help greatly, however, to speed the advance of the Red Army after Stalingrad.

WAR'S AFTERMATH

By the end of the war the western areas of Russia, much of the Ukraine, and the Caucasus were devastated. The United States offered economic aid to the U.S.S.R. within the framework of the Marshall Plan, which was helping Europe recover, but Stalin rejected this as interference by the United States in Soviet domestic affairs.

Stalin believed that the Marshall Plan would weaken the independence of the Soviet economy and undermine its socialist base. Therefore, he denounced the plan as an imperialist plot, telling the Russian people that they had to shoulder the burden of reconstruction alone in the face of a hostile capitalist world. Again Stalin used the bugbear of a foreign threat to frighten the Russian people and discourage economic coöperation with the West.

FOURTH FIVE-YEAR PLAN

In 1946 Stalin announced plans for a new Five-Year Plan, aimed at reconstruction of war-damaged areas and acceleration of industrial expansion. The progress of the postwar reconstruction was interrupted, however, by the Korean war. Unexpected American resistance to Communist aggression threw Soviet leadership into confusion and forced a step-up in defense spending. By the time Stalin died in 1953, the Soviet economy was moving toward another serious predicament. Overcentralization, lack of local initiative, and excessive fear bred by Stalinist terror had sharply reduced the efficiency of the industrial sector and was causing serious shortages and recurrent crises throughout the farmlands.

ECONOMIC REORGANIZATION AFTER STALIN

Stalin's successors have made no effort to change the basic goals of the Soviet economy — industrialization and collectivization — but they have been more flexible in employing a wide range of economic means to achieve their ends.

Investments in military strength, for example, have increased since Stalin's death. Heavy industry has maintained its high rate of growth. The new leadership, especially under Premier Nikita S. Khrushchev, boasts that the Soviet Union will soon overtake and surpass the production of the United States. In order to carry out his plans, Khrushchev launched in 1959 an ambitious Seven-Year Plan, including a reorganization of Soviet industry and agriculture.

KHRUSHCHEV'S REFORMS

In 1957 Khrushchev's reforms focused on replacing the centralized industrial ministries with regional grouping under the authority of the State Planning Commission (Gosplan) in order to overcome serious waste and confusion and to make better use of local resources. This reform in no way affected the central planning and overall coördination of the economy. It did, however, affect the administration of economic plans and constituted a decentralization of industrial management.

The reorganization of the economy has overcome several major problems, such as duplication of function by two ministries. The Soviet press has cited the case of two steamship companies operating under different ministries on the same river. The steamer of one company sailed empty in one direction, and the steamer of the other sailed empty in the opposite direction. In one important mining area, lead and tin were extracted while other important minerals which were uncovered in the process were thrown away because they fell under the control of another ministry.

Furthermore, the rivalry between economics ministries to overfulfill their plans in order to receive rewards and consolidate their power led to ruthless competition for available resources and often a breakdown in coöperation between complementary ministries.

While the new reorganization has solved some of these problems, it has merely shifted others and created some new ones. There are now more than 100 regional groups in the country, and each one of these has a large staff; but the problem of localism has now replaced that of centralism. In any situation facing the regional grouping which offers a choice, the local authorities will usually decide to do what will benefit their region, regardless of how it may affect the country as a whole.

In other instances crucial deliveries of scrap and manganese ore to the iron and steel industries were jeopardized by the decentralization of functions. The Soviet system, however, cannot tolerate this sort of disjointed operation. It is based on a planned, nationwide economy which requires the coöperation of economic regions and the closely coördinated shipment of materials and semifinished goods from one region to another.

A tractor factory in Minsk, for example, relies for its materials upon more than 100 other enterprises outside the jurisdiction of its home area in the Byelorussian regional grouping. Whenever there is excessive concern over local needs, the designs of the Gosplan are disrupted.

The chairman of the Tambov Regional Economic Soviet in early 1962, complained in the *Journal of Soviet Economic Affairs* that "The excessive complexity of Gosplan's apparatus accounts for the fact that branch administrations of the central planning agency have restored the departmental barriers which were removed in 1957." Each branch administration, he charged, "defends only its own interests."

REFORMING THE REFORM

Attempts to overcome this regionalism by relying on the discretionary powers of the party secretaries, who are supposed to defend the national plan, have failed. In many cases the reputation of the party secretaries rests upon their helping fulfill the plan in their locality. Therefore, they tend to encourage regionalism to protect themselves (and, in consequence, undermine the state plan). Thus this regional parochialism of Khrushchev's day seems merely to have replaced ministerial parochialism of Stalinist times.

The system has placed enormous responsibility on Gosplan to draw up the national and republic budgets, to make decisions on new investments, and to manage supply and distribution.

Gosplan tried to exercise direct supervision of the national plan by receiving reports and sending teams of inspectors. In many cases Gosplan absorbed many of the key functions of the former national economic ministries. Of course, Gosplan continued to operate under the supervision of the Council of Ministers (the Soviet cabinet) and the Presidium (the highest policy-making body in the Communist party). Because of the great powers of Gosplan and the problems arising from localism, the trend toward even greater centralization of power appeared certain. However, the regional groupings fulfilled the useful function of making possible a more efficient allocation of local resources.

REORGANIZATION IN AGRICULTURE

Khrushchev ordered a similar reorganization in agriculture. Many of the machine tractor stations were abolished and their equipment

ECONOMIC COMPARISONS II

USSR — USA: TRADE [1959]

EXPORTS	USSR	USA
Machinery and Industrial Equipment	$ 5,185,920,000	$6,156,000,000
Steel	1,435,562,000	161,000,000
Iron Ore	957,930,000	34,000,000
Petroleum	1,535,130,000	480,000,000
Timber	1,153,290,000	24,000,000
Grain	2,162,280,000	1,414,000,000
TOTAL	$12,430,112,000	$8,269,000,000
IMPORTS		
Machinery and Industrial Equipment	$6,001,770,000	$2,429,000,000
Metal Ores	1,469,640,000	1,431,000,000
Textile Raw Materials	1,462,980,000	249,000,000
TOTAL	$8,934,390,000	$4,109,000,000

USSR — USA: GROSS NATIONAL PRODUCT

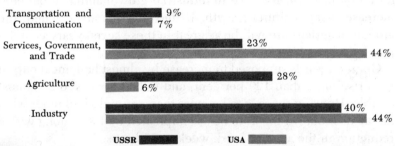

Transportation and Communication — 9% / 7%

Services, Government, and Trade — 23% / 44%

Agriculture — 28% / 6%

Industry — 40% / 44%

USSR   USA

USSR — USA: CONSUMER GOODS PRODUCED [1961]

	UNITS	USSR	USA
Passenger cars	*thousands*	149.0	5542.8
Trucks and buses	*thousands*	406.0	1134.0
Television sets	*millions*	2.0	6.2
Radios	*millions*	4.2	17.4
Meat	*million metric tons*	4.3	12.4
Butter	*thousand metric tons*	894.0	677.7

sold to other, more successful collective farms. Premier Khrushchev hoped in this way to eliminate what had become an inefficient and burdensome institution and to permit the collective farms to use the equipment in the way they most needed it. Furthermore, this move tended to strengthen the large and highly productive collective farms, which were in a position to absorb their weaker neighbors and thereby create even larger farms. The goal remained the same — transformation of collectives into state farms.

At the same time Khrushchev had gambled heavily on increasing the agricultural output by plowing up 45 million acres of grassland in northern Kazakhstan in a move to create a new grain region. This semiarid region did not prove very suitable for grain production, however. During dry years successive huge dust bowls developed there.

THE SEVEN-YEAR PLAN

Side by side with reorganization of industry and agriculture, the Communist party launched a Seven-Year Plan (1959-1965), calling for an 80 per cent increase in industrial growth and a 70 per cent increase in agricultural growth. If these targets are reached, the growth in agriculture will be as great in these seven years as in the previous forty years of Soviet history.

Grain output is supposed to increase by almost half, meat output is to rise more than 100 per cent, and milk output is to be almost double. Housing space is to be more than one and a half times what it was in 1958. All this is to be accomplished by 1965, along with a reduction in the average work week to 35 hours.

Can the Soviet economy achieve these goals? Has the reorganization of agriculture and industry solved long-standing problems? Will the Soviet Union overtake and surpass the economic pace of the United States? How will continued Soviet economic growth affect the underdeveloped nations of the world?

GROWTH IN THE SOVIET ECONOMY

The answers to these questions lie in understanding the many facets of Soviet economic growth. One way to measure the performance of the Soviet economy is by the yardstick economists call the Gross National Product (GNP). Measurements are in terms of an index or percentage of annual growth. GNP is the total value of all goods and services produced in an economy: everything from highway construction to toys, medical services, and motion picture entertainment.

Economists separate GNP into consumption, or that part which is used up, and investment, or that part which is used to create new capital and productive potential. They also seek to find out how much of the GNP comes from various sectors of the economy — agriculture, industry, and various services.

Estimates about the growth of an economy can be made by determining how much the GNP increases from year to year. This is done by figuring out the percentage rate of growth. Thus, if the GNP were 100 billion dollars in 1960 and 150 billion dollars in 1961, the percentage increase would be 50.

INDUSTRIAL PRODUCTION
AS AN INDEX TO ECONOMIC GROWTH

Industrial production is one of the most important areas of the Soviet GNP. Production figures would offer a valuable set of year-to-year comparisons if we had access to them. Soviet statistics, however, are notoriously unreliable. Furthermore, Soviet economists have often presented misleading growth figures by basing their calculations upon unusual years. For example, they may base the industrial index (yearly percentage increase in industrial production) upon the prices of 1926-1927, which were much lower than in later years when most of the industrial goods were produced.

Even after allowing for these economic quirks, economists in the United States still disagree on the rate of Soviet economic growth. In general, economists concede that the percentage of industrial growth was greater in the early phases of industrialization than at present. This is understandable because production expansion obviously appears more extensive when there is so much to be done. Perhaps a fair figure for the first two five-year plans and the years of postwar reconstruction would be from 15 to 18 per cent growth in the GNP, a very high rate. After 1950 the growth probably slipped to between 10 and 12 per cent, but the percentage is still high compared with that of the United States.

USSR—USA: EMPLOYMENT [1959]

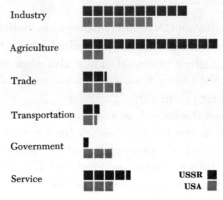

Industry

Agriculture

Trade

Transportation

Government

Service

USSR ■
USA ■

each unit=3 million workers

USSR—USA: MEDICAL SERVICES [1969]

	USSR	USA
Hospitals	26,348	6,845
Hospital Beds	1,618,000	1,613,000
No. of Hospital Beds per 1000 pop.	7.7	9.9
Physicians	380,000	236,818
No. of Physicians per 1000 pop.	1.8	1.3

USSR—USA: TRANSPORTATION [1960]

	USSR	USA
Railroads	78,180 *miles*	230,000 *miles*
Roads	935,783 *miles*	3,478,787 *miles*
Shipping	2,380,573 *tons*	32,601,000 *tons*
	1,113 *ships*	2,934 *ships*
Aviation	257,780 *route miles*	223,287 *route miles*

It is difficult, also, to figure out the average annual rate of industrial growth in the United States, because during the depression from 1929 to 1939 there was no increase, while during World War II, it was more than 16 per cent. Neither period was representative. After World War II, the increase in the United States approximated 4.3 per cent a year. This percentage is high compared with other countries of the West, but substantially below the Soviet rate.

THE AGRICULTURAL FACTOR IN THE GNP

This discussion has been about the rate of industrial growth, only one facet of the GNP. If Soviet agricultural production is averaged with the industrial production, then the high figure for industrial production is reduced. Soviet agriculture has not recovered from the debilitating effects of encounters with collectivization.

SERVICES AS PART OF THE GROSS NATIONAL PRODUCT

In addition the higher standard of living in the United States leads to a greater rise in spending for services than for industrial products, the demand for which has been more fully satisfied. For these reasons, it is necessary to add the element of services to industrial and agricultural production to find out the total comparable GNP of the two countries. The result is a further decline in the Soviet annual average, but it still shows a fairly constant growth in the GNP of 6 to 7 per cent a year, as compared with 3.7 per cent in the United States.

Therefore, whether we base our comparison strictly on industrial growth or on the growth of the entire economy, the Soviet Union is moving ahead more rapidly than is the United States. In part this is the basis for Premier Khrushchev's claim that the Soviet economy will lead the world in the not too distant future.

THE ROLE OF CENTRALIZED CONTROLS

How have the Russians been able to establish and maintain this pace of economic growth? There are two important factors for inquirers to consider.

First, centralized control of raw materials and man power has enabled the Russians to reduce consumption by the population and concentrate the economic forces of the country on productive investment, buildings, machine tools, and equipment of various kinds. By forcing the Russian people to wait for consumer goods, which could easily have been produced, Soviet leaders have been able to build up the productive capacity of heavy industry.

Second, the huge man power resources of the Soviet Union have been an important consideration. The steady growth of the population and the large reservoir of labor in the countryside before 1928, have enabled the government to throw large numbers of workers into critical undertakings at key moments. Furthermore, technological progress has kept pace with the demands of industry.

CAN THE GROWTH RATE OF THE U.S.S.R. BE MAINTAINED?

Can the economy of the Soviet Union maintain its rapid rate of growth? There are a number of factors which point to a slowing down of the present growth rate.

To begin with, the question "Where will the labor supply come from?" suggests one argument against continued growth at the present pace. The surplus of man power from the countryside is being used up and cannot be replaced. Greater labor productivity may take up part of the slack. Greater productivity, however, calls for an increased educational level of workers and improvements

in technology and organization. Automation, for example, has considerably increased production in the United States and, to a more limited extent, in the Soviet Union.

Another antigrowth argument is that the Soviet economy still is less efficient than that of the United States. The consequent wastefulness makes it too weak to compete with the capitalist economies of the West, in single countries or in powerful blocs such as the Common Market (European Economic Community).

It is true that the Soviet economy is not so efficient as the U.S. economy in terms of output relative to input. For example, Russia uses more coal (input) to generate electric power (output) than the United States. It is also true that an American worker produces more per hour than a Soviet worker. Consequently, American labor productivity is superior.

However, Soviet economists foresee great improvements in these situations, especially in the amount of electrical energy available to industry. The Soviet planners realize the importance of providing workers with mechanical power to increase labor productivity. This becomes apparent in the startling fact that since World War II the consumption of electrical power per worker has increased at a greater *rate* in the Soviet Union than in the United States. Yet a comparison shows that in 1957 the Soviet consumption of electrical power per worker was only 45 per cent of that in the United States.

Inefficiency is magnified in the agricultural sector of the Soviet Union. Planners have paid less attention to agricultural labor than to industrial labor.

Housing, an acute problem in the U.S.S.R., is being solved in cities and towns by the construction of such bulky, barrack-like apartment buildings as these, which extend for miles in a new section of Moscow. Walls of the buildings are prefabricated. Construction is markedly inferior to American standards. Rents are low, but space allotments per family are limited. Tens of thousands of families are on waiting lists for apartments in new buildings like these. The large tower of Moscow University appears in the background.

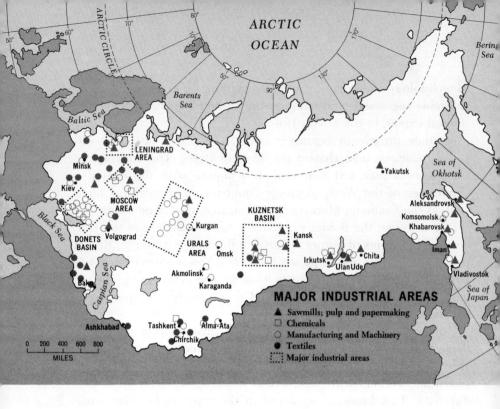

MAJOR INDUSTRIAL AREAS

▲ Sawmills; pulp and papermaking
☐ Chemicals
○ Manufacturing and Machinery
● Textiles
┆┄┆ Major industrial areas

DOES PLANNING GUARANTEE GROWTH?

It is difficult to estimate the effect of planning on the growth of the Soviet economy. Many economists contend that central economic planning can lead only to confusion and stagnation. Yet a number of recent developments in the realm of economic theories of long-range planning have produced some remarkable results. Ironically enough most of these developments have taken place in the free enterprise, open market economy of the United States and not in the rigidly supervised economy of the Soviet Union. In fact Soviet planners have been reluctant till recently to accept the findings of some of their own leading theoreticians regarding the usefulness of computers in planning. Businessmen and government officials in the United States have been using elaborate methods of planning for several decades. Through mathematical analysis and projection, they are able to select from many choices a solution to a problem which most efficiently utilizes productive resources. Aided by these electronic calculations, they are able to coördinate vast enterprises and plan many weeks or months in advance, or analyze quantities of statistics relating to past performances. These methods have nothing to do with socialism, of course, but it is not difficult to imagine the impact of such streamlined methods on an economy planned and directed from one central agency. Just in solving the Soviet Union's enormous problems in allocating and coördinating resources, the effect could be startling.

Although Soviet economists and planners seem to be groping their way toward an acceptance of the value of these methods, it has taken them a long time to reach this conclusion. One reason for their hesitation has been the belief that mathematical tools of analysis are bourgeois in origin and therefore unacceptable.

Ideological assumptions have blinded them not only to the advances made by the leading theoreticians of the non-Communist world but also to the findings of their own countrymen. Under the leaders who succeeded Stalin, interest has been renewed, and progress in large-scale planning may advance dramatically if Soviet economists are allowed to employ these mathematical tools.

PRICES IN THE SOVIET ECONOMY

The Soviet economy still suffers from many cases of disrupted coördination between different branches of industry and a lopsided price system; prices in the Soviet Union are not set by supply and demand, as in most Western nations, but by administrative order from the government. Soviet economists have often underestimated the real cost of worn-out and outmoded factories and equipment in figuring prices. They completely ignore such factors as rent and capital in their calculations. If prices do not correspond to real costs in terms of rent, capital, labor, and depreciation, then the planners find it difficult to know which is really the cheapest way of doing something.

THE ROLE OF INCENTIVES AND PENALTIES

Another criticism of the Soviet economy relates to incentives. Outsiders familiar only with the profit motive and the pride of individual enterprise occasionally charge that the Soviet system coldly drains away the essential motivations needed to spur workers toward economic goals. Yet if we examine the Soviet economic system carefully, we find it well stocked with its own brand of incentives. The Soviet factory manager, for example, is promised such rewards as higher pay, bonuses, the use of an automobile, travel on expense account, a country home, vacations at exclusive state-run summer resorts, in return for increased production.

Penalties for failure in the Soviet Union are much harsher than in a non-Communist nation. In fact, there is much less personal security among the Soviet managerial elite than among their American counterparts. At one end of the penalty scale a manager may merely lose his job for failing to carry out the state plan. At the other extreme he may be accused of criminal negligence and even of economic crimes against the state, thereby facing a long prison term or, in severe cases, execution.

The Soviet press reports numerous examples of plant managers who have resorted to illegal means to obtain raw materials when expected shipments did not arrive. Fear of punishment for failing may drive the manager to violate the law. In most cases the threat of punishment tends to lurk in the background as a reminder to managers that failure, indolence, and laxity are not permitted. These are what we might call negative incentives, but they also play a role in keeping the manager obedient and his plant productive.

Workers are exposed to a variety of incentives and pressures, from bonuses to coercion. Today, as with the wage incentives in the very first year of the Soviet state and in Stalin's time, a skilled worker may make from three to four and a half times the salary of an unskilled worker in the same factory. This differential is much greater than that in almost any American industry. Workers in industries which the government considers important are paid premium wages. Most Soviet workers and many American workers are paid according to the number of items they produce. This is piece-rate payment rather than hourly pay. For exceeding production quotas, workers receive wage increases. Dangerous and unattractive work, such as that in remote locations, also earns especially high pay.

Medals also are a form of reward for the worker who produces well. Heroes of socialist labor are honored throughout the country, mentioned prominently in factory newspapers, and perhaps even named to important trade-union committees or local government positions. These rewards are much less prominent on the collective farms, where peasants, traditionally suspicious of government supervisors, have shown little enthusiasm for increasing productivity.

Henri Cartier Bresson: MAGNUM

Women workers in a Soviet dress factory. Posted on the red honor bulletin board in the background are pictures of the most productive workers in department 2.

Since World War II and especially since Stalin's death, coercive measures to increase labor productivity have been sharply curtailed. The restrictive labor laws which remain are interpreted more leniently than before. Punishments for tardiness, which ranged up to four months in prison, have been abolished. The emphasis has definitely turned toward positive incentives.

Some Westerners expect Soviet workers or peasants to be discouraged from working because of the realization that their system is not providing the high standard of living which exists widely outside Russia. This view fails to take into account the fact that most Soviet workers know very little about the West. Whatever comparisons they make are more likely to involve their fellow Soviet citizens and the conditions in times past.

The Soviet regime welcomes economic comparisons with the tsarist period. However, today's wage levels of Soviet workers are still low, even though they have almost doubled since the end of World War II. It is doubtful that the real wages of Soviet workers have increased beyond the level of 1928, before the First Five-Year Plan was introduced by Stalin.

On the other hand, the younger Soviet workers compare their standards of living today favorably with those of the years following 1928 when wages became minimal. People from the United States who visit the Soviet Union may often hear it said: "We do not have it as good as you Americans yet, but it is much better here today than it was ten or fifteen years ago."

Hope for the continued growth of the economy, for an ever rising standard of living, and for a better life for one's family serves as an important incentive to Soviet workers and peasants.

GROWTH IN QUANTITY, NOT QUALITY

We must not forget, however, that the growth we speak of here is growth in quantity and not quality. Growth in quality is much more difficult to measure. Managers, workers, and peasants who are concerned primarily with fulfilling their quotas are liable not to pay much attention to the quality of the goods they produce so long as they fulfill their part of the state plan.

A first-hand look at Soviet life convinces the foreigner that building materials and consumer goods are of poor quality. In 1959 one of the new large apartment buildings in northern Moscow settled badly and had to be evacuated, condemned, and torn down. The shoddy quality of both the outside and inside of many new buildings is obvious even to the casual observer.

FAMILIES AND THE SOVIET ECONOMY

Often families consisting of mother, father, grandmother, and child live together in a single large room in Moscow apartment houses. The room may be partitioned into three sections for a measure of privacy, but this leaves little room for furniture. The rents are low, in the range of $5 a month, but both parents must work to meet their obligations. If grandmother is not present to act as nursemaid, the child attends a day nursery.

Families who have lived in Moscow for several years are able to place their names on a preferential list to move into one of the new apartments in the southwestern section of the city. Tens of thousands of others are on waiting lists.

These families often share a bathroom and kitchen with as many as three other families. In a typical week, one family may be assigned dinnertime use of the kitchen only after 10 P.M. Telephones in Moscow apartments are as communal as the bathtubs and stoves. There is very little privacy for any of the families.

If they work late, husbands and wives may find the city's open markets closed, and they then must shop at large state-run stores such as GUM ("State Department Store") in downtown Moscow. Long lines of customers wind toward the meat and fruit counters. In winter there is unlikely to be much choice of fresh vegetables, perhaps only beets and cabbage if potatoes are sold out. It may take as long as two hours to shop. The wait for a bus may be a long one also. The fare is approximately two and a half cents.

To buy a car, the Soviet citizen may have to save for years and order it almost as far in advance.

The Soviet citizen must sometimes wait in line for an hour to buy movie tickets a week in advance.

Books are inexpensive; a good hard-cover novel might cost 80 cents. Clothing is expensive and the average worker may have only one good suit, which is likely to be old. Women often make their own dresses. The material for one simple dress may cost up to $50, or two weeks' salary for a female schoolteacher.

Soviet citizens complain about the quality of many consumer goods. In 1960 large numbers of Soviet-made shoes could not be sold because the Russian consumer did not like either the style or the quality. Instead they bought Czech or Hungarian imports. But rejection of consumer goods in this manner is not frequent. When shortages are great people buy whatever happens to be available.

As the quantity of consumer goods increases, state enterprises may well find that the people will no longer accept poor quality products. Then revaluation of the demand for consumer goods will have to be made.

PRIVATE ENTERPRISE

An even more marked disregard for quality shows up in collective farm production. Government stores sell meat and vegetables which do not nearly measure up to American standards. More significant is the great difference in quality between goods sold in the state stores from collective farm quotas and those sold in the open market by peasants who have brought produce from their private garden plots. The cut and quality of meat and the size and taste of fruits and vegetables grown in the private fields are far superior to that of those produced for the state. The prices are higher, of course, but many are willing to pay for extra quality.

ПРИВЕТ ВСЕМ БОРЦ[АМ]
ПРОТИВ ПОДЖИГАТЕ[ЛЕЙ]

Periodically the government has tried to reduce the size of the garden plots in order to reduce the amount of time and effort the peasant lavishes on his cherished land. Often peasants are punished for having encroached on the collective property by surreptitiously advancing their fences a few feet each year.

In other words the desire for private enterprise is not dead. The cash return for privately produced food is so attractive that the peasant spends as much time as he can in his garden plot.

THE RATE OF INVESTMENT

Continued growth of the Soviet economy depends also upon high rate of investment, particularly in capital goods, the heavy productive equipment of major industry. But in the face of rising demands for more consumer goods, how can the Soviet Union maintain its present high rate of capital investment?

Soviet planners know that they need only divert a small percentage of total investment into consumer goods production in order to increase the living standards enough to keep worker morale up. The Seven-Year Plan we have mentioned makes this clear. It calls for no change in the basic pattern of investment in Soviet heavy industry through 1965.

HOW TECHNOLOGICAL PROGRESS
AFFECTS THE SOVIET ECONOMY

Technological progress has long been a factor in Soviet economic development. Scientific inventions which can be applied to industry to save both labor and capital may well be critical in maintaining Soviet economic growth. When Stalin launched the First

A truck assembly line in a Moscow factory. Machinery and methods do not seem to be impressively modern to the visitor. Plant safety standards do not appear to be high. State-operated companies like this one provide housing at prescribed rentals for as many workers as possible. Plants also provide health services, library and recreational facilities, nursery facilities for children of working parents, paid vacations, and workers' clubs in the country for vacations. Characteristic of every work area are large red signs like the one above the workers' heads here, carrying propaganda slogans and admonitions to work harder, to produce more, to be patriotic. The sign above greets all who "work against warmongers."

Five-Year Plan, Soviet planners were able to borrow the latest technological advances from the West and apply them to their own problems. In many ways being a backward nation was an advantage. There was no need to convert old industrial plants or spend time and money to find through trial and error the best methods of industrializing. In many cases the pioneering work had already been done in the most advanced western economies.

Today the technologically matured Soviet economy faces the problem of developing its own inventions and techniques in order to move ahead. Modern technological progress requires large investments in both basic and practical research. However, the Soviet system has shown a reluctance to support pure science because of the uncertainty of its producing something of immediate, practical value. Basic research is not concerned with practical applications but with broadening the horizons of knowledge.

SCIENCE AND THE ECONOMY

Pure science is threatened not only by narrowly practical planners but by the ideological rigidities in the commitments of Soviet leaders to Marxism-Leninism. In the past there have been attempts by the leadership to force crude Marxist formulas upon scientists in order to maintain the validity of their philosophical system. These conflicts between Communist theory and the experimental findings of Soviet scientists have sometimes been resolved in favor of the scientists and sometimes in favor of the single-purpose Marxists.

Since Stalin's death, many of the more rigid controls on scientific inquiry have been relaxed, and the scientists who have become party members may now be in a better position to protect the integrity of their work. It remains to be seen, however, whether the leaders of the party can afford to endorse scientific work which might undermine the very ideological foundations upon which their power rests.

Meanwhile great emphasis has been placed upon applied research. Large organizations have been created by the state simply to find useful applications for new scientific discoveries. These organizations suffer from bureaucratic conservatism (fear of expensive but possibly revolutionary innovations), overcentralization (too much standardization), and lack of imagination, due, perhaps, to the cautions that envelop such a controlled system.

The most striking and frank admission of this problem in the Soviet Union can be found in the controversial novel *Not by Bread Alone,* by Vladimir Dudintsev (1918–   ), in which a talented inventor finds it difficult and dangerous to persuade state bureaucrats to adopt a new pipe-casting machine.

IN THE FUTURE

In the near future of the Soviet economy, it appears likely that the Soviet Union will attain many of the industrial goals set by the Seven-Year Plan. It appears less likely that the targets in consumer goods, housing, and agriculture will be reached. In 1961 and 1962, serious shortcomings in the agricultural sector forced Premier Khrushchev to carry out widespread purges of key personnel at the regional and republic levels. As usual administrators, not the system or the planners, were blamed.

TAXATION

The remaining key factor in this foreshortened study of the Soviet economic system is taxation, the means of paying for the operation

Many Russians visit exhibits of Soviet-made automobiles, but few have the means to buy a car of their own. The chart in the background dramatizes increased production.

Paul's Photos

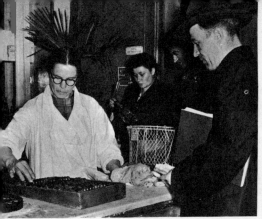

Cornell Capa: MAGNUM

Food is still not abundant. Stores are small and old-fashioned. Some self-service "supermarkets" like these above exist in Moscow. Note particularly the cashier at the checkout desk using an abacus to total the sale. A skilled user of an abacus can calculate with great speed. Many shoppers inspect merchandise in GUM department store, Moscow's largest (right), but purchases are small.

of this complex economy. The Soviet economy still runs on a money basis, and currency flows between private citizens and the state as well as between economic agencies of the state. To pay for such necessities as education, defense, and administrative expenses, the state collects taxes.

The Soviet citizen has no voice in deciding the amount or form of tax to be levied; he may not always be sure precisely how much tax he is paying, since the bulk of Soviet taxes are hidden and indirect. This is noteworthy if only because Lenin denounced indirect taxes as reactionary and supported the idea of direct and progressive taxes.

The Soviet income tax is very small as is the inheritance tax. Most of the tax revenue comes from the turnover tax, which provides almost half of the income of the state. This is a tax on all consumer goods sold in the Soviet Union and often amounts to double the economic value or price of the item bought. The price of a movie ticket in Moscow, for example, is 3.3 rubles which in terms of earning power represents almost one hour's wages for an average worker. This figures to about $1.75 in American money. Of this amount, 1.6 rubles is the economic value of the ticket and is used to pay salaries of the cinema workers, to pay for electric consumption, for film rental, and even to provide a profit for the government as the owner of the movie house. The remaining 1.7 rubles is the turnover tax which goes to the state treasury to be used in any fashion the planners see fit.

Cornell Capa: MAGNUM

The turnover tax is easy and inexpensive to collect. However, it affects all people equally without regard to income. In this sense, it discriminates against those who earn least. How can this be in a state which claims to be socialist? Soviet theorists have had little success in explaining this to the population. Aware of the character of the tax, Soviet planners have done their best to hide the true amount of the turnover tax from the people. There is nothing on a sales slip to indicate how much of the price goes for the turnover tax. Not even the retailer knows this secret. As with the organization of labor and the rate of investment, so with taxes, the needs of the state again overshadow the desire of the individual.

SUMMARY

The spectacular growth of Soviet industry (which has grown sixfold since 1928) has not improved the standard of living of a majority of the population since that time. Furthermore, it is clear that this growth has not been the result of the application of a socialist system to Russia, because it would be impossible to call either the Soviet way or tax system socialist.

Rather, the industrial advance can be explained as the imposition of certain industrial goals by a totalitarian dictatorship upon a technologically and economically backward country. It is this model which appeals to many countries in the world today. Much like prerevolutionary Russia, these countries have never enjoyed political freedoms. Their leadership frequently tends to be authoritarian. The great emphasis throughout the world upon economic power as a measure of a progressive society serves as a strong inducement for the people of these countries to accept the system which seems to give them the greatest chance of achieving their aims quickly. However, under the Soviet system, the sacrifices have not only been material, in terms of lives lost and resources wasted, but cultural and intellectual as well.

The implications of a totalitarian system upon the cultural life of the individual and his consciousness are all too frequently ignored in any scale of values which measures success in material terms. The next chapter examines those implications in detail.

Elliott Erwitt: MAGNUM

TERMS TO KNOW

War Communism	New Economic Policy (NEP)	sovkhoz
kulaks	Gross National Product (GNP)	Stakhanovism
turnover tax	Gosplan	kolkhoz

QUESTIONS ON THE CHAPTER

1. For what reasons did the Bolshevik leaders institute the policy of War Communism?

2. Give three reasons for the Bolsheviks' desire to industrialize Russia.

3. Explain the chief differences between the collective farms and the state farms.

4. By what means did the state combat peasant resistance to the collectivization of agriculture?

5. How did the Communist party discourage lateness to work, absenteeism, and job-changing among the industrial workers?
6. Why did Stalin reject Marshall Plan aid from the United States after World War II?
7. Explain why it is difficult to figure accurately the rates of Soviet economic growth and American average annual industrial growth.
8. What two factors point to a future reduction in the rate of Soviet economic growth?
9. How does the pricing system of the Soviet Union differ from that of a free-enterprise economy?
10. What are some of the incentives used in Soviet industry to increase production? Give an example of a negative incentive.
11. Describe some of the differences in quality of farm produce sold in state stores and that which is sold on the open market in the Soviet Union.
12. Name some of the taxes which are collected in the Soviet Union. In what way does the present Soviet tax system contradict Lenin's ideas on taxation?

QUESTIONS FOR DISCUSSION

1. Every economic system has problems involving prices, costs, investments, allocation of resources, and labor. Compare some of the approaches to these problems in the planned economy of the U.S.S.R. and the market economy of the United States (for example, prices in the U.S.S.R. are set by government order and prices in the United States are governed by supply and demand).
2. The basic goals of the Soviet economy have always been industrialization and collectivization. What implications does this have for the improvement of the quality and quantity of consumer goods in the Soviet Union? What implications does this have for competition in the world's industrial markets?
3. It has been said that the rapid industrial growth of the Soviet economy can be attributed to the imposing of certain goals, by a totalitarian government, on a technologically backward country. Discuss some of the problems that have arisen in Soviet industry as a result of the imposing of these goals (for example, duplication of services).

BIBLIOGRAPHY

For Reference: □ Campbell, Robert W., *Soviet Economic Power.* Houghton Mifflin Company, 1960.   □ Katkoff, Vladimir, *Soviet Economy, 1940-1965.* Dangery Publishing Company, 1961.   □ Schwartz, Harry, *Russia's Soviet Economy.* Prentice-Hall, Inc., 1954. **For Further Reading:**   □ Lee, Baldwin, *Capitalism and Other Economic Systems.* C-A-S-E Economic Literacy Series, Number 2. Council for Advancement of Secondary Education, 1959.   □ Lawrence, John, *A History of Russia.* Chapters 20-23. New American Library, 1962. *Saturday Review,* January 21, 1961, "Inside the Soviet Economy."

CHAPTER **6**

CULTURAL AND INTELLECTUAL
LIFE IN THE USSR

The control of culture
poses a basic question to the Soviets:
What degree of freedom
can be granted artists and intellectuals
without endangering the totalitarian system?

There have actually been three revolutions in Russia. The first revolution was political, when the Communists seized power in 1917. The second revolution was economic, when, under Stalin's dictatorship, the party began to collectivize and industrialize Russia. The third and final revolution was cultural, when the party launched its drive to create a new social order. In this chapter the third revolution is discussed.

Never before has Western civilization seen such an extreme degree of control over culture and intellect. These controls constitute a unique attempt in the history of the world to isolate a nation from any ideas or images which their rulers deem harmful while at the same time imposing an entirely new set of values.

The Soviet record stands in definite contrast to the Western World's traditionally strong commitment to an open society with

Elliott Erwitt: MAGNUM

Young Russians are as interested in the exploration of space as young Americans. Popular science lectures at the Moscow Planetarium are a great attraction.

broad cultural and intellectual freedom. The controls and the ideals which the Soviet regime seeks to superimpose on the minds of the people under it are, however, an indispensable part of the totalitarian way of life in the Soviet Union.

MARXISM-LENINISM, THE CONSTANT GUIDELINE

Since Marxism claims to be an all-encompassing body of knowledge, its supporters maintain that Marxism is valid in every sphere of human activity. Whatever is to be judged, whether it is a painting or a scientific discovery, the guide for the Communist party is invariable: Does it measure up to the values set down in Communist ideology?

According to the Marxist-Leninist viewpoint, creative art and science spring from the social and economic environment in which they appear. This is an immense oversimplification of a very complex process and leaves much to be explained. For example, if all art and science produced before the Soviet period in Russia (or anywhere else in the world) arose from the class system which prevailed at that time, how then can this art or science have any validity for the proletarian Soviet Union?

On the other hand, if this art or science has universal and time-less qualities which continue to make it valid, how then can it be a product of a class culture? Soviet theoreticians raise even deeper questions when they try to dodge these problems by explaining that some art and some scientific ideas were ahead of their time and, in fact, foreshadowed a Communist system. If ideas could foreshadow communism, then what happens to the Marxist theory that ideas are secondary to material conditions and dependent upon them for their existence? Thus, as will become increasingly apparent through the study of this chapter, the philosophical foundations of Soviet controls over creativity are very shaky indeed.

Despite the present-day inconsistencies and contradictions in their preachings on cultural and intellectual problems, Soviet leaders still try to find social meaning in all art. In the sciences, Soviet theoreticians still try to fit new and complex scientific find-ings into outworn theories. The attempt to judge art, science, and all intellectual life in terms of politics has ended up in stripping these artistic and scientific disciplines of their independent func-tions and harnessing them to the power of the Communist party.

POLITICS, NOT CULTURE, IS PARAMOUNT

Stalin's revolution to fit creative thinking into a Communist strait jacket was a personal as well as a political measure to increase his control over Russia. Marx and Lenin had said very little about the implications of their philosophical systems for the creative arts and sciences. Marx and Lenin had rather conventional taste in art and literature. They knew little about science. When the Bolshe-viks took power in 1917, they paid much less attention to the prob-lem of what to do about intellectual life than to the burning politi-cal and economic questions of the day. Their immediate concern was to prevent any opposition to the state which could root itself in the intellectual community.

The Bolsheviks would not permit the printing of any propaganda which criticized the state, whether or not it appeared in the guise of art. At the same time they launched a two-pronged campaign to weaken the power of the church as a cultural force and to recruit the intellectual elite of the old Russian society to work for them in important positions until they could train the needed Bolshevik personnel to replace them.

THE ATTACK ON THE CHURCH

From 1917 to 1928 the party moved cautiously in many fields to instill a new set of Bolshevik values in the minds of the Russian people. Since Marx and Lenin considered religion to be an opiate of the masses, the church was an early and prime target. Lenin hoped that a combination of persecution and changing socioeconomic conditions would weaken the church's influence in society. Although the antichurch drive was not massive—lest the masses become uncontrollably alarmed—it was methodical. Church properties were confiscated, church marriages were not recognized by the state, and children under eighteen were barred from religious instruction. The Militant League of the Godless was formed to preach atheism.

Priests were persecuted, churches occasionally were looted by hot-headed young Communists. In 1922 a large number of Russian Orthodox and Roman Catholic priests were tried and condemned for antistate activity. But the struggle against the church was not effective and by the mid-1920's a compromise had been established based on the church's promise not to interfere in political matters

Respected Soviet authority: Two volumes of the *Great Soviet Encyclopedia* which when completed will comprise about 45 volumes. Soviet propaganda pervades its pages. A reader learns, for example, that the White House is a nest of warmaking intrigue, that Harvard is a hotbed of reaction, that the Dearborn, Michigan, police force is owned by the Ford Motor Company. The rather uncomplimentary pictures in the open volume above are of Washington, D.C.

and Bolshevik assurance that persecution would be stopped. Antireligious propaganda continued, of course, as sanctioned by the 1922 Soviet Constitution.

THE PARTY ATTACK ON EDUCATION

The Bolshevik campaign against traditional education was not much more decisive than was its drive against the church.

At first the party tried to adapt the most extreme experimental educational ideas of the West, abolishing discipline and allowing Russian school children complete freedom in the classroom. Many of the old classic subjects disappeared; curricula were completely reorganized. And, of course, strong doses of Communist ideology were injected into all class schedules.

Under the leadership of Marxist historian Mikhail N. Pokrovsky, universities were reorganized. Communist teachers were scattered throughout the country to check on nonparty teachers, who were then in a majority. Special Communist universities were established to train new teachers in the strictest party manner. Students were encouraged to denounce teachers whose views did not correspond with those of the party.

Bolshevik-controlled research institutes sought to strengthen the party's influence among intellectuals, especially in the fields of history and economics.

This vigorous attention to higher education reflected the Bolshevik party's recognition of its own educational weaknesses. As late as 1927, fewer than 1 per cent of its members had received a university degree. Despite Bolshevik efforts to reform the schools of Russia, they continued to be centers of antiparty attitudes.

THE PARTY ATTACK ON THE FAMILY

At the same time the party encouraged the independence of children from parents and home life, and the emancipation of women from domestic responsibilities. Divorce became little more than a matter of announcing one's intention to leave home.

By attacking the traditional authority of school and family in Russian life, the party was seeking to shatter old values before substituting its own new one.

LIMITED FREEDOM IN THE ARTS AND SCIENCES

The Bolsheviks' first commissar of education proclaimed that a revolutionary government ought to preserve the right of individual creation. Accordingly artists and writers greeted the revolution as a liberating force which would help them shake off stodgy conventions of the prerevolutionary past and what they considered to be the crude tastes of the middle class.

In some cases this reaction against the past was so strong that the government had to step in with reminders that the classics of Russian literature and art had much to offer the Soviet people and were not to be dismissed quite so thoughtlessly.

Artists, composers, and writers soon realized, however, that the revolution had brought them anything but liberation, and dark disillusionment set in. Some fled, including musicians Igor Stravinsky, Sergei Rachmaninov, and, for a time, Sergei Prokofiev, the author Ivan Bunin, and artists Alexander Benois and Ilya Repin. Others remained, setting up independent organizations for the encouragement and spread of their art and ideas. This time of mixed feelings and uncertainty produced a variety of artistic styles that were at once exciting and bewildering.

Some of the finest works of the Soviet period were produced during the period of the 1920's. Alexander Blok's mystic-symbolist poem *The Twelve* tried to identify the revolution with the second coming of Christ, twelve Red Army men symbolizing the disciples. Boris Pasternak's lyric poem *My Sister Life* was free of political overtones, rich with imagery. Mikhail Sholokhov's epic novel *The Silent Don* described with objective and human sympathy the terrible Civil War period in the Cossack country of Russia. Leonid Leonov's novel *The Thief* portrayed the struggle between the old society and the new in a manner reminiscent of Dostoevsky.

Many of these early Soviet period writings dealt with the heroism of the Civil War. Others were lyrical, having little or no political content. Very few satisfied the hope of the party for a literature which would reflect Bolshevik values. The party looked with frank distaste upon much of the writing, art, and music of this period, charging that it was unintelligible to the barely literate masses.

In architecture the 1920's produced the so-called constructivist style. Vladimir Tatlin, the leading architect of the group, insisted that metal, concrete, and glass replace stone and wood as building materials. He idealized a "machine" style matched to the dynamic, streamlined, and efficient characteristics he saw in industrial society.

Although many of Tatlin's plans never left the drawing board, they did reflect the revulsion of the young architects of the 1920's toward 19th-century architectural frills. The new functional form of the American skyscraper captivated many of these men. Again the mass of Russian workers simply could not understand these ultramodern styles or the terminology of the constructivists.

Motor rhythms, factory whistles, and the sounds of machinery resounded in symphonic music, as in Dimitri Shostakovich's *Second Symphony*. But the public had little appreciation for these experiments, either.

The easel painters also had their eyes on machinery and industrial designs. One of them wrote: "We shall seize upon the storm of the revolution, put into it the pulse of American life, and produce a work that will be as accurate as a chronometer. . . ." They banded together and called themselves futurists and suprematists and dedicated themselves to producing works of art, in the manner of a cobbler hammering out shoes, as a "socially useful" product. On one state holiday, the futurist painters doused the lawns, flower beds, and trees in front of the Bolshoi Theater in Moscow with paint. "Streets are our brushes, the squares our palettes," sang the enraptured poet Vladimir Mayakovsky.

There were Russian branches of Western artistic cults. One Soviet cubist produced a geometric sculpture of Mikhail Bakunin, the 19th-century Russian revolutionary, which so infuriated the workmen assigned to erect it that they smashed it. For the artists, the 1920's were heydays of free expression, but for the public they were little more than years of revolting artistic confusion. Stalin later took advantage of this lack of understanding on the part of the people to bring artists into the grip of the Soviet state, where style and content could be rigidly controlled.

EXPERIMENTATION COMES TO AN END

The great age of experimentation in the arts began to draw to a close in the late 1920's, as Stalin prepared to mobilize the total energies of the party and state for an enormous crash program to industrialize Russia. Intellectual life was to serve the state in Stalin's plan.

Paul's Photos

Contrasts: At the right, a present-day student art exhibit of safely representational works. At the left, Vladimir Tatlin's model of a tower commemorating the Third International. The proposed monument, created in the 1920's and never erected, was to have been 100 meters higher than the Eiffel Tower, with components that revolve at different speeds. Tatlin was an innovator. He was one of the inventors of suspended sculpture and one of the first to make mobile sculptures.

Stalin well knew the power of a small group of dedicated intellectuals. The Revolution of 1917 had been led by just such a group. He realized that sensitive intellectuals, protesting the inhumanity and cultural stagnation of autocratic tsars and subservient churchmen, had dramatically influenced Russian cultural history in the 19th century. No independent intellectual class could be allowed freedom enough to rally an opposition. In Stalin's words, writers and artists were to become "the engineers of the human soul."

The cultural revolution was even more vast in its conception than the earlier political and economic revolutions. It aimed at creating an entirely new Soviet man. This process continues unabated in the Soviet Union today, but has fallen far shorter of success than the other revolutions. In its wake lie countless ruined careers, vast areas of intellectual blight, and in many fields a residue of mediocrity.

CULTURAL LIFE MOBILIZED

In 1929 Stalin decided to mobilize literature, the theater, and the motion-picture industry for a full-scale campaign to communize the cultural outlook of the nation. Publishing houses were informed of the type of books they were to publish, and the themes to be suggested to writers. Such subjects as industrial construction, the fight against external aggression and internal subversion, and life on collective farms were preferred. The party officially endorsed the most Marxist of the many writers' organizations, the Russian Association of Proletarian Writers, and directed it to promote the mobilization plan.

Similar "proletarian" goals were simultaneously proclaimed for art, music, and literature. Experiments in styles were to be replaced by more traditional concepts designed to explain to workers and peasants the tasks before them. Scientists were ordered "to stop daydreaming" and settle down to solving the practical construction problems facing the state.

In 1931 the party ordered the reorganization of the entire Russian school system. Traditional patterns of study were again imposed: mathematics, Russian language, chemistry, geography, physics, and history returned to the classroom, as did examinations. Teachers were reinvested with their former authority.

THE PATTERN OF CULTURAL REVOLUTION

In this Stalin-directed process of creating a new culture in Soviet Russia, three distinct trends emerged: (1) the attempt to set down a theory of artistic truth called socialist realism, (2) the attempt to reintroduce patriotism in the outlook of the Russian people, and (3) the attempt to organize all intellectuals into separate groups which could be controlled and directed by party members.

In 1932 the Culture and Propaganda Department of the Central Committee of the Communist party was instructed to provide systematic guidance in all areas of Soviet intellectual theory, practice, and personnel. Its twelve sections governed a vast range of activities: party and political literature, party schools, technical propaganda, mass propaganda, newspapers, schools, scientific establishments, journals, scientific literature, creative literature, culture among collective farmers and workers, motion pictures.

Within a few years, all independent organizations of writers and artists were liquidated. The Russian Association of Proletarian Writers had presumptuously tried to develop its own theory of literature, and, proletarian though it was, the party could not tolerate *any* competition in its drive for cultural uniformity. In its place, unions for writers and artists were set up by the party to regiment all practicing members of the arts. Key party personnel were placed at the head of these organizations with orders to ensure loyalty and unity on the part of the members.

Since the state controlled all printing presses, movie houses, theaters, museums, exhibition halls, studios, as well as the film industry and concert orchestras, it was almost impossible for the creative artist to reach the public without first bowing to the state.

All leading scientific personnel were brought into the newly reorganized Academy of Sciences of the U.S.S.R.

All of the new Stalinist theories for the arts, humanities, and sciences reflected the party dictator's overriding concern for the political and economic problems of the Soviet Union and for the reawakening in the Russian people of a national pride.

SOCIALIST REALISM

The most significant of these theories and the one which became the standard by which every creative work was henceforth to be judged was socialist realism. According to Stalin, socialist realism meant the portrayal of reality in its revolutionary development in order to remake and reëducate the workers in the spirit of socialism. All creative arts were to depict Soviet reality as it would be, or ought to be, rather than as the U.S.S.R. actually was.

There was to be no attempt to discourage or confuse the workers and peasants by painting a despairing picture of life. No melancholy or morbid themes were to appear. Life was to be shown as optimistic and happy. Artists, writers, and musicians were to abandon inner personal experiences which others could not be expected to understand. Music was to be melodic, not harsh and dissonant. Art was to avoid the abstract. Architecture was to avoid streamlined styles. Ballet was to keep strictly to classic choreography. Modern dance and jazz were outlawed. Art for art's sake was denounced as decadent or formalistic.

All creativity had to reflect "the social command," that is, the needs of the Soviet society. Above all, the creative artist was not to separate himself from the masses, but rather to idealize them. Art must exude *partiinost,* the spirit of the party, its plans and hopes, its discipline and dogmas.

The interpretation of this doctrine was left to the highest party officials, including Stalin himself. Lenin's few comments on literature were now cited as sacred. They were quoted endlessly by those who sought to dictate the new Communist values.

FIVE-YEAR PLAN FOR THE ARTS

Socialist realism was even put on a five-year plan for art and literature in order to focus creative work on the problems of industrialization and collectivization.

Much of the creative output of this period was far inferior to earlier Soviet work. An exception, however, was Valentin Katayev's novel *Time Forward*, which dealt with the attempt of a brigade of workers at a great industrial plant in the Ural Mountains to break a production record during a single shift. The problem constantly confronting the writers during the early 1930's was the need to portray party members always as pure and good and their enemies as scheming and evil. Only the boldest artist risked abandoning these stereotypes. Mikhail Sholokhov's novel *Seeds of Tomorrow* manages to achieve an unusually realistic picture of life during these hard times.

Artists and musicians were slower to react to these Soviet-disciplined years, perhaps because by the very nature of their work and its limited audience their art did not serve the needs of the state so well as did literature. Except for those artists who chose to withdraw from the public and paint for themselves and their friends, which was legal but discouraged, the majority of artists suffered more than writers.

The predominant subjects included portraits of Lenin and Stalin (it was unwise to paint other political leaders because of the threat of purge which hung over Russia in the 1930's), landscapes of collective farms, dams, railroad constructions, and heroes of labor.

PURGE IN THE ARTS

By 1936 the party concluded that artists, writers, and musicians had reacted much too slowly to the social command. It unleashed a purge which made grimly clear that artistic deviation was as much a crime against the state as stealing or treason. Dimitri

Shostakovich, one of the leading composers of the Soviet Union, was the first object of attack. He was accused of destroying harmony and melody in music and substituting dissonances and ugliness.

Special conferences of musicians, organized by the party, denounced leading Western composers as false models leading into blind alleys of creativity. The works of Arnold Schönberg, Arthur Honegger, and Alban Berg, and of the U.S. composers Charles Ives and Aaron Copland, ceased to be heard in Soviet concert halls. Shostakovich's *Fourth Symphony* and his opera *Lady Macbeth of the Mtsensk District* lay unperformed for more than twenty years. Several influential composers were denounced; almost all Jewish composers were arrested, and shortly they vanished. Some composers apologized publicly. Shostakovich and Prokofiev turned to music based on folk tunes, abandoning experimentation.

Artists who distorted human figures, drew formless lines, or portrayed misery and poverty were similarly denounced. These works, charged the official Soviet critics, reflected naturalism, not socialist realism. The Russian countryside appeared the way it was, instead of the way socialism was going to make it. Many paintings were taken down from the walls of the leading museums of Moscow and Leningrad and stored in special closed funds where only carefully screened persons were allowed to view them. These included many by Vincent Van Gogh, Paul Gauguin, Georges Seurat, Henri Matisse, Georges Rouault, and Pablo Picasso, as well as the Russians Marc Chagall and Vasili Kandinsky. Many of these paintings remain locked in storage today.

Attacks on literary figures were occasionally followed by arrests and even execution. In 1937 alone, the works of sixty authors were attacked and proscribed. The authors were accused of being fascist spies, terrorists, and enemies of the people, terms which ordinarily signaled the most severe punishments.

It must be remembered that these people were not engaged in political activity or espionage. Their crime simply was that they wrote books and poems which did not conform to what the Communist party wanted the Russian people to read.

THE FIVE-YEAR PLANS AND THE SCIENCES

During the period of the Five-Year Plans, Bolshevik theorists also tried to impose Marxist theories upon the various sciences. The result was to break down the independent position of Soviet scientists and bring them under tighter state control. But the Bolsheviks were too unlettered in the sciences to restructure physics, chemistry, and biology with their dialectical materialism. The party attacked certain leading theories, such as relativity and quantum mechanics in physics, but the Russian scientists went right ahead teaching and developing their work on these problems. Only in the field of biology was there an important exception to this indifference.

In 1937 Trofim Lysenko, an unknown naturalist, attacked the entire school of Soviet genetics as hostile to the ideas of Marxism, substituting his own concepts. These concepts won favor from Stalin himself. Marxism, declared Lysenko, teaches that all phenomena in life can be explained only in environmental terms. In genetics, therefore, characteristics acquired through environmental influences are inherited. This was contrary to theories then widely accepted in the West and advocated at the time by leading Soviet geneticists as well. They taught that inheritance is a very complex process, largely accidental, unpredictable, and uncontrollable.

This was not Marxian, however, Lysenko announced, nor was it practical (or politic, he might have added). Soviet leaders, after all, were working to change the political and economic structure of Russian society and thereby alter the human nature of the Soviet people and create an entirely new Soviet man.

Lysenko also offered a quick and easy way to improve livestock and agriculture. He claimed that with chemicals not only could plants be made to germinate earlier and therefore overcome some of Russia's serious soil and climate problems, but that this favorable characteristic of early germination could be passed on to the next generation of seeds and plants.

Stalin saw great possibilities for opening up vast hitherto unusable lands to cultivation, and he encouraged Lysenko. As a result Nikolai A. Vavilov, the leading Russian geneticist, was removed from his important positions, arrested, and sent to a concentration camp, where he died in 1942.

Lysenko was given control of Soviet genetics. He purged it of its leading scientists and introduced his own theories. This reign of terror set Soviet genetics back a generation or more. The height of Lysenko's power came after World War II, in 1948, when he was publicly endorsed by Stalin. He proceeded to complete his purge of geneticists and even rewrote Russia's biology textbooks.

REVIVAL OF RUSSIAN NATIONALISM

Stalin sought to strengthen the state and his own position by appealing to a basic love of the Russian people for their homeland. With great political cunning, Stalin sought to make everything Communist, Russian and everything Russian, Communist.

Stalin's propagandists advanced arguments to show that Russia was best suited for the development of socialism, that its history, its cultural, and its intellectual life had prepared it better than any other country for the coming of communism. In cultural and intellectual fields Stalin then tried to do what he had done for the ideological and political life of Russia in the 1920's, when he claimed that because of the country's peculiar circumstances, it could build socialism in one country without waiting for a revolution to occur elsewhere.

REWRITING HISTORY

One of the amazing attempts by Stalin to expedite his cultural-intellectual revolution was the rewriting of Russian history. Until 1932, Russian historians had been under the thumb of Mikhail N. Pokrovsky, the Marxist historian. He believed that history had to be written in terms of social and economic changes, that political events and, above all, great historical personalities were insignificant.

Pokrovsky tried to fit developments in Russian history into universal categories. He extolled international class solidarity and condemned Russia's historical heritage as wretched, reactionary, and barbaric. He leveled some of his sharpest charges at the role of Christianity in Russia. Supported first by Lenin and then by Stalin, Pokrovsky ruthlessly eliminated his scholarly critics from their posts and ran Soviet education with an iron hand.

When Pokrovsky died, however, Stalin decided that his views could no longer serve the needs of the state. He demanded a complete overhaul of the teaching of history and eventually of the whole Soviet educational system. So complete was Stalin's unexpected about-face that Pokrovsky was denounced as a vulgarizer of Marx, a teacher of sociological abstractions instead of history.

All school textbooks had to be rewritten and Pokrovsky's works had to be withdrawn from libraries and bookstores. Two themes

A marriage ceremony in Russia today consists of signing a marriage document. The government, having once discouraged family life, now encourages stable marriages.

were to keynote the new teaching of history: (1) the glorious role of the Russian people, and (2) the importance of Russian leaders of the past.

Russian military figures such as Generals Mikhail Kutuzov, who helped defeat Napoleon in 1812, and Alexander Suvorov, who fought against French revolutionary armies in Switzerland and in Italy, now became national heroes. These were the men whom Pokrovsky had once denounced as reactionary tsarist generals, hangmen of peasants. Peter the Great was singled out as a progressive statesman. His exploitation of the peasants was glossed over. The adaptation of Christianity by Russia in the 10th century was praised as "an act of progress in the history of the Russian people."

The colonization by the Russians of such national areas as the Ukraine and Georgia had been denounced by Pokrovsky as predatory imperialism. It was now explained as a lesser evil for the inhabitants of those areas than absorption by Turkey or Persia, because Russia was a more advanced country. Whatever seemed inconvenient or contradictory was suppressed.

Even the history of the Russian Revolution was rewritten. Stalin was made to appear as Lenin's right-hand man. The names of those men whom Stalin had liquidated in the purges were eliminated.

178

The very existence of some people who lived and fought during the revolutionary years was bluntly denied. Revolutionary figures such as Trotsky disappeared or were buried under mountains of abuse. Western historians who wrote differently were attacked in the most sensational and abusive terms as "vile, slandering members of Trotskyite bandit gangs."

Books which Stalin considered harmful to the new history were removed from library shelves and put in special closed funds. Today many remain available only to students having written permission from high-ranking academic authorities.

History had become the pawn of politics, just like art and science and literature. Standards of reliability, accuracy, intellectual honesty, caution, and thoroughness were replaced by the "social command." Worship of historical heroes opened the way to deification of Stalin. Stalin, of course, basked in the reflected light of the hero worship which was all but prescribed by the new histories. The rising tide of nationalism which followed the rewriting of history flowed into all Soviet intellectual life.

CHURCH AND STATE

Indirectly the Russian Orthodox Church benefited from this campaign of nationalism. Subjected to severe persecution in 1929-1930, it sought to make peace with the Soviet authorities by praying for Soviet leaders (much as the church had prayed for the conquering pagan Mongol leaders in the 13th century) and rejecting foreign charges that the Russian church was persecuted. Some priests even supported industrialization and collectivization. Stalin began to see the value of relaxing pressure on the church, and from the mid-1930's persecution was tempered again.

Stalin's gamble with the church appeared to pay off during World War II when the church took an active role in supporting the struggle against Nazi Germany. The metropolitan, the head of the Russian Orthodox Church, even declared Stalin to be "the divinely anointed leader of the nation." Church leaders, in return, were decorated and appointed to important committees. More churches were opened, and even a few seminaries and monasteries were allowed to operate. None of this signaled any basic departure from the party's atheistic position, merely a tactical adjustment of its antichurch campaign.

FAMILY AND STATE

In the mid-1930's a drive was launched to reëstablish standards of personal morality, standards familiar in the West but subject to the whims of the revolution in Russia. Divorce was made more difficult. The family was now praised as the center of the socialist society. Motherhood medals and state subsidies were bestowed on large families. But Stalinist virtue had its peculiarities: "a Soviet person cannot simply love someone without criticism, without political and moral watchfulness." Stalin attempted to turn even love into politics.

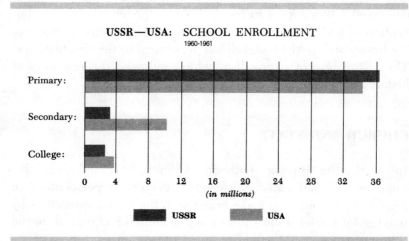

USSR—USA: SCHOOL ENROLLMENT
1960-1961

CULTURAL ACTIVITY DURING WORLD WAR II

During World War II, the party's control of the creative arts and, to a certain degree, science was relaxed. Freed from writing solely on economic themes, writers poured out their hatred against the invaders in countless war stories. Some of these stories, emphasizing ordinary human, but hardly Marxist, hopes and fears, were outstanding: Konstantin Simonov's *Days and Nights*, for example, which dealt with the siege of Stalingrad.

The party needed to divert all its energies to winning the war. Stalin hoped further that an easing of cultural restrictions would placate his Western allies, on whom he was relying for military aid and lend-lease equipment. Increased contacts between Westerners and Soviet citizens led to hopes that after the war the cultural line of the party would soften and Western influences would mix with Russian as in the prerevolutionary days and the 1920's.

But these hopes were dashed when Stalin decided, after the war, that his power would be seriously threatened by continued good relations with the West in politics, economics, or culture. From 1946 to his death in 1953, he tried to isolate Soviet culture behind an "iron curtain" as never before. Intellectual life in the Soviet Union, with the exception of advances in physics, fell to a low point in these years.

THE NEW GUIDELINES OF ZHDANOV

The party aimed first to bring culture back under its guidance and control, second to eliminate foreign influences, and third to break up cliques of intellectuals who had entrenched themselves so strongly in their chosen fields that they threatened to escape party controls.

The party spokesman who laid down the newly rigid guidelines was Andrei A. Zhdanov. His name became synonymous with the period of repression which followed. In 1946 he denounced two popular writers, the humorist Mikhail Zoshchenko, who wrote a story about a monkey which escaped from a zoo in Leningrad but which soon hurried back when it found out what life outside was like, and the poetess Anna Akhmatova, for her love poems with religious overtones.

There was too much pessimism for Zhdanov, and a tendency to turn away from the high road of socialist life to the narrow road of personal experience. "How is it possible," Zhdanov asked, "to turn over to them [the literary figures of the day] the upbringing of our youth?"

He described much Soviet music as vulgar imitations of foreign music. Shostakovich, Prokofiev, Aram Khatchaturian, and Dimitri Kabalevsky were singled out as the main culprits.

The party press and propaganda organs unleashed a storm of criticism against the limited freedoms of the wartime period. They stirred up a "hate America" campaign which extended to all aspects of culture and demanded a return to the tenets of socialist realism. Among the leading propaganda organs were *Pravda*, the party newspaper, *Izvestia*, the government newspaper, *Kommunist*, the party journal, *Sovietskaya Kultura*, the literary journal, and *Krokodil*, the satirical magazine.

Scientists who had freshly reëstablished fruitful relations with their Western colleagues came under attack for criticizing Lysenko, the bumbling but Stalin-backed geneticist, and for trying to build a "general world-wide biology."

"There is not and cannot be a single world science," declared the party. "Only Soviet science can be free of distortion; only Soviet science can lead mankind." Scientific coöperation with the West was denounced, Western science was condemned as rotten, and Soviet scientists were forbidden even to quote from Western scientific literature.

Russian physicists and chemists, on the other hand, received little more than a stern rebuke for accepting Western scientific theories. Only the biologists had suffered from the Lysenko purges. The physicists and chemists had to promise to take into consideration the materialist basis of Marxian dialectics and had to absorb a measure of ideological heckling on such matters as quantum mechanics, but few lost their posts. They were too highly valued by the regime. In their experiments they were allowed free rein.

But Western scientists did not suspect the behind-the-scenes progress of their Soviet counterparts and were more than a little surprised when the Russians achieved thermonuclear explosions simultaneously with the West, and when they moved ahead of the United States in great particle accelerators and rocketry.

In theoretical work in pure science, however, the Soviet scientists showed less spectacular gains, largely because Communist theoreticians object to potential threats in the areas of the materialist dogmas of Marx.

Philosophy and history were also under siege during the years of the Zhdanov terror. Soviet philosophers were taken to task for failing to give sufficient emphasis to Russian philosophical predecessors of Karl Marx.

A series of purges swept through the ranks of Soviet historians. Many were denounced for having failed to glorify Russian national traditions. The distinguished Professor Evgeny Tarle was ordered to rewrite his history of the Russian campaign of 1812 against Napoleon, because the party felt he had overemphasized the effect of geography and climate in the defeat of the French. Stalin apparently thought that this same interpretation might be transferred to the Russian campaign of 1941-1945 against the Nazis and weaken the theory that he and the party, not the breadth of the Russian plain or the cruel depths of its winter, had brought about the Soviet victory.

ANTI-SEMITISM

The most sinister aspect of the reassertion of party controls over cultural life was the mounting wave of anti-Semitism which reached its peak just before Stalin's death.

Jews in the Soviet Union had always formed an important minority of scientific specialists, writers, and musicians. In the purges of the 1930's, veteran Jewish Bolsheviks were executed. Zinoviev, Kamenev, and Trotsky (exiled and assassinated in 1940 by a Stalinist agent) were among them. After that time virtually no Jewish names appeared in the highest ranks of the party. Lazar Kaganovich was the sole exception.

The Soviet government for a while encouraged Jewish nationalism. But after the founding of the state of Israel in 1948 and the attack on Western culture, the party stepped up its drive to weaken Jewish culture in the U.S.S.R. Apparently it feared cultural and intellectual links between Russian and Israeli Jews. All publications in Yiddish were forbidden. The Yiddish theater was closed in 1949. Unofficial discrimination was practiced against Jews in universities and certain professions. By 1952 almost all the leaders of Jewish culture had been shot, and widespread fear had developed among the Jewish population.

STALIN AND THE LANGUAGE CONTROVERSY

In the midst of these tense times, Stalin began a controversy over language. One explanation for his personal intervention in this cultural area was that he apparently began to fear that some of Zhdanov's followers were building private empires by discrediting their opponents. As in 1930, when he denounced the Pokrovsky school of history, Stalin condemned the extremists, intending thereby to discipline all who thought they could place themselves above the party. He rebuked the followers of Nikolai Marr, a leading Marxist language specialist, for maintaining that the structure of language reflected the class struggle. This, he said, was a vulgar distortion of Marx.

On the other hand, Stalin pointed out that the Russian language had absorbed all other languages with which it had come in contact throughout history and could, therefore, be called a victorious language. He even foresaw the use of Russian as a "zonal language" after the world revolution and, finally, as playing an important part in developing the world language of communism.

It was the 1930's all over again in an attempt to show the intellectual community its mission: to fuse Marxism and Russian national traditions under Communist party guidance.

But all Stalin's efforts in this direction led only to stagnation and fear throughout the world of Russian culture and intellectual life. When he died in 1953, creative work was being carried on only in the most furtive manner by scientists who did not name their theories, by artists who painted behind closed doors, by writers who wrote rough drafts but did not publish. As in the political and economic spheres, so also in culture, Stalin's successors would need to lift the pall of fear which was stifling creativity. The challenge, the party realized, was to remove the fear without implying any softening of party control over the minds of men.

THE THAW

A period called "the thaw" began slowly in 1953 and built toward a high point in 1956 before declining to a point of uneasy stability in 1960. This partial relaxation of Stalinist controls over Soviet cultural and intellectual affairs took its name from the title of a novel by Ilya Ehrenburg. Published in the fall of 1953, *The Thaw* broke with almost all of the traditions of socialist realism in its theme and development, though the style remained basically reportorial. Ehrenburg exposed the cynicism, injustice, frustrations, and sadness of life in the Soviet Union. He described human weaknesses in a frank and sympathetic manner. Since Ehrenburg was thought to have the ear of high party officials, the appearance of the book was widely interpreted in the U.S.S.R. as the signal for a more honest appraisal of Soviet reality in the arts. No one knew how far one might go in honest expression.

During the next half-dozen years artists and writers, scientists and musicians cautiously probed for the limits to which they might go before incurring the wrath of the party. These proved to be the most exciting and intellectually stimulating years in Soviet cultural history since the late 1920's.

With Premier Nikita Khrushchev's startling speech to the Twentieth Congress of the Communist party in 1956, in which he strongly denounced Stalin for having created a "cult of personality" which crushed creativity and expression, the slackening of party controls on the arts and sciences received the highest sanction.

There followed a series of proclamations and demands from the party that the dull art of the past give way to something new and fresh, that the bonds on intellectual life which Stalin had tied be loosened, that imagination be freed. The appeal for honest criticism and sincerity aroused the intellectuals from their long-forced hibernation, and open discussions echoed through the Soviet press, scholarly journals, and meetings of artists.

Writers who had been executed (Isak Babel was one) were honored posthumously; works of others, like Anna Akhmatova, who had fallen into disfavor, were republished. Many of the discussions focused on Vladimir Dudintsev's novel *Not by Bread Alone*, which exposed abuses in the party, in the state bureaucracy, and even in the secret police. A strong element of individualism emerged from its story of a talented inventor's futile struggle to overcome the oppressions of the Soviet bureaucracy.

By this time the intellectual ferment had spread to all fields: history, philosophy, biology, music, and painting. Everywhere it was asked: "How far may we go?" "What is permissible?" "Are the bars really down on creativity?" "Is the party really renouncing control, or is it just maneuvering to assert control more subtly?"

In the post-Stalin 1950's, therefore, we encounter an almost bewildering variety of opinion and criticism. At no time did the party lose control of the situation. When necessary, it was easily able to tighten its grip on cultural life.

REBELS, NEO-LENINISTS, CONSERVATIVES, AND NEO-STALINISTS

Generally, there are four tendencies to notice in this current period of ferment in the creative arts, putting aside, for a moment,

Elliott Erwitt: MAGNUM

Two traditions: Religion, once openly discouraged, is now at least tolerated. A few ecclesiastical academies train priests today. The Russian theater continues the tradition of fine ballet and meticulous training of dancers.

other disciplines such as science, history, and philosophy. Reflecting these tendencies were groups we shall call: (1) rebels, (2) neo-Leninists, (3) conservatives, (4) neo-Stalinists.

THE REBELS

The rebels comprise the smallest and most radical body of unleashed intellectuals, opposed to socialist realism and party controls over the arts. They want complete freedom of expression, either with or without state subsidies, and the end of party-dictated regimentation. The rebels favor atonal music and Western jazz in all its forms. They like abstract and expressionist art, including all the avant-garde movements of the West. In ballet, in theater, and to a limited degree in literature, they hope for experimentation in form and design. They are a young group, highly critical of many aspects of Soviet life. They gain much of their inspiration from books, reproductions of paintings, and phonograph records brought back to Russia by Soviet citizens traveling in the West, and from

cultural exchange with the United States, which also brings news of Western culture to Russia.

THE NEO-LENINISTS

The neo-Leninists favor broadening the definition of socialist realism, short of accepting the more extreme innovations proposed by the rebels. They urge less stringent bureaucratic party control and more freedom to the creative artists themselves to share in guiding the evolution of the arts in the Soviet Union. Their slogan could well be "Back to Lenin." Thus it is not inappropriate to call them neo-Leninists.

This group takes the party's demand for greater honesty literally, without attempting to go beyond what is considered to be a sincere and helpful portrayal of Soviet reality. The members are patriotic. They look to the great Russian traditions of the past as their guide and inspiration. As writers they are interested not so much in new forms as in greater variety of subject matter and emotional range. As artists and musicians they wish to enlarge the artistic range of socialist realism to include certain styles heretofore excluded, such as the impressionism of Claude Monet in art, Claude Debussy and Maurice Ravel in music, or moderate expressionism such as early Picasso in art and Richard Strauss and Gustav Mahler in music.

In this group are many well-known figures. Therefore, the group bore the brunt of the campaign to liberalize Soviet cultural life in this contemporary period. Some of these artists, writers, and musicians are Mikhail Alpatov, art critic; Igor Grabar, painter; Dimitri Shostakovich, composer; Evgeny Evtushenko, poet; Konstantin Paustovsky and Vladimir Dudintsev, writers.

THE CONSERVATIVES

The conservatives, a still more cautious group of artists, call vaguely for an end to conformity. This group includes such well-known authors as Konstantin Simonov and Mikhail Sholokhov. This too is a large group. The conservatives have been unwilling to define precisely what they mean by ending conformity. Their brand of criticism appears almost formal and artificial, aiming primarily at removing the worst Stalinist abuses including the exaltation of Stalin himself. In general, their view is supported by Premier Khrushchev.

THE NEO-STALINISTS

Finally there are the neo-Stalinists, the unshakable defenders of the old system. They maintain that any attempt to correct abuses will result in creating more dangerous ones. This group is composed of people who have little apparent talent or who have mortgaged their talents to the demands of the state in order to be personally successful.

The conservatives and a few of the more cautious neo-Leninists appear to have won powerful support from the party. For them, 1958 was the decisive year, for it was then that Nikita S. Khrushchev succeeded in consolidating his political position against all opposition. It also was the year of the most startling result of the de-Stalinization campaign in the arts: the publication, in Italy, of Boris Pasternak's first novel, *Doctor Zhivago*. This bold literary incident brought home to the party the great dangers inherent in "the thaw."

Soviet publishers rejected the manuscript of *Doctor Zhivago*. Pasternak was informed in writing that his novel renounced the socialist revolution, adopted a renegade position with respect to Soviet life, and made a hero of a treacherous individual. While remarking on some passages of rare beauty, the publishers denounced the book as a political sermon aimed against the interests of the Soviet people. American readers can judge for themselves the value of the book by reading it in English. It has been published in several other languages, including Russian, but it has never been published in the Soviet Union.

In private meetings with Soviet intellectuals, high-ranking Communist party officials later admitted that it was a mistake not to have published a small edition of the book in the U.S.S.R., if only to blunt the edge of sharp Western criticism over the treatment of the book and its author. Partly on the basis of having written *Doctor Zhivago*, together with his main body of creative work in poetry, Pasternak was awarded the Nobel prize for literature in 1958, but under pressure from the Soviet government, he was obliged to decline the prize.

To the Communist party, Pasternak was a holdover from the 19th-century intellectual who maintained that his talent owed no allegiance other than to itself. The party must have feared that "the thaw" as epitomized in the Zhivago experience would unleash the pent-up forces of individualism. And slowly, since. then, ideological debates have been brought under control. The old terrorist methods of Stalinism are gone, but equally firm (if less drastic) limitations persist.

The hopes of the neo-Leninists have been dimmed, although not extinguished entirely. It remains to be seen what long-run effect the acceptance by the party of the moderate position will have upon Soviet creativity. The big question is still unanswered: Can the Communists hold the forces of individual expression in check with this intermediate position between terror and freedom?

CULTURAL EXCHANGE

One of the main obstacles to holding the intellectual community in check is the Soviet decision to engage in peaceful cultural competition with the West. This has brought a cultural exchange between the United States and the Soviet Union, for example, in a hitherto unprecedented degree. Beginning officially in 1958, a series of agreements between the U.S. and the U.S.S.R. provided for the exchange of university students and professors, concert artists, scientists, exhibitions, ballet and dance troupes, jazz bands, movies, and groups of writers, artists, and composers. These were followed by agreements with Western European countries.

Even before these agreements, the Soviet decision to permit increasing numbers of Western tourists to visit the Soviet Union and a small, select number of carefully chosen Soviet tourists to visit the West opened a broad avenue for the exchange of opinions and cultural impressions.

Experts in various fields have found their counterparts in Soviet or American delegations eager to exchange views. Many of these discussions have been much franker than could have been antici- pated, given the long years of Soviet isolation and exposure to anti-American propaganda. The warm, spontaneous receptions which have greeted representatives of the American intellectual and cultural community—such as that afforded pianist Van Cliburn —have demonstrated the failure of Soviet propaganda to paint American culture, as Zhdanov put it, as a world of "gangsters and chorus girls."

On the other hand, Americans have had a chance to judge some of the outstanding examples of Soviet culture, such as the classic ballet, the Moiseyev ballet, and pianists like Sviatoslav Richter and Emil Gilels. The general impression in the West has been that some of the Soviet arts have maintained a high degree of professional and artistic excellence through turbulent years. However, it has also been noticed that there has been scant innovation or originality in the creative arts of the Soviet Union, and very little in the performing arts, since the late 1920's.

In the 1960's Soviet leaders find themselves in a predicament over continuing of the cultural exchange. They want to show their cultural advances, yet they cannot easily control the culture which foreigners bring in.

SOVIET SCIENCE SINCE STALIN

Especially impressive to Westerners have been the achievements in some branches of the Soviet sciences since Stalin's death. Soviet scientists have been given greater freedom from party interference than creative artists have. Now, as in Stalin's time, their work is considered important to the security of the state and the progress of the Communist world revolution. Scientific life in the Soviet Union is concentrated in the Academy of Sciences, which maintains 118 research institutes in the natural sciences.

The academy's most impressive achievements in attempting to centralize the planning and carrying out of scientific work have been in areas of military importance and in areas where until recently Soviet developments have lagged behind those of the West.

In the development of some of the world's most powerful rocket engines, nuclear weapons, and electronic computers, and in the fields of automation and biology, Soviet scientists and engineers have made remarkable progress. These major areas, however, emphasize applied science.

As in art, so in science, originality is a personal, not a centralized, matter. No amount of state support or planning can create genius or schedule the birth of an idea. No government can plan breakthroughs into unexplored areas of physics or chemistry or astronomy until a freely creative mind shows the way. A state can only mobilize resources to exploit ideas.

There is little of major creative significance to be measured in Soviet science. From 1901 to 1962, only five Russians have won Nobel prizes (one in medicine and physiology in 1904, three in physics in 1958, one in chemistry in 1956). During the same period, 19 U.S. scientists have been honored in physics, 12 in chemistry, 27 in medicine and physiology. One U.S. university alone (the University of California) has produced more Nobel prize winners than the U.S.S.R.

The Nobel prizes are by no means an entirely accurate measure of scientific creativity, but they do give some idea of the really fundamental and original work being carried on throughout the world. Nobel prize-caliber scientists have bloomed in an atmosphere of free inquiry. It remains to be seen whether the Soviet Union can achieve excellence in an atmosphere which is closed and controlled or whether it will have to give way, inch by inch, to a more open society in order to encourage the scientific progress upon which its future hinges.

SOVIET EDUCATION TODAY

To achieve long-range goals of world domination, Communist leadership relies more and more heavily upon the training of specialists and technicians in all fields.

Since the first Russian earth satellite, Sputnik I (1957), many efforts have been made to compare the Soviet and American educational systems, with mixed and inconclusive results.

Those who have studied under both systems in recent years are probably in the best position to offer some judgment. They warn, however, that because each system aims to achieve entirely different goals, the comparison is almost impossible to make in any meaningful way.

The Soviet system aims to produce technicians and specialists for industrial and administrative posts, and to indoctrinate the mass of the people with Communist ideology.

The American system aims to develop the critical and analytical mind, to encourage the creative, imaginative thinker. Those who wish to specialize are permitted to sharpen the focus of their education in graduate studies.

The most satisfactory way to evaluate the Soviet educational system is to compare its achievements with its goals.

Elliott Erwitt: MAGNUM

Architecture and interior decoration of buildings in the U.S.S.R. show unimagina-
tive uniformity of design. This is the waiting room in the airport at Kiev.

In the matter of Communist indoctrination, the Soviet leaders
have recently been critical of the job being done by Soviet schools.
Exchange students to the Soviet Union have noticed that the
indoctrination course required of all Russian students, entitled
History of the Party, is considered to be a waste of time by large
numbers of students.

Indifference, cheating on examinations, and outright scorn in
the classroom are by-products of this student antagonism.

Many highly trained Soviet specialists in ideology defend
their ideological position by citing Marx and Lenin, but often
are unable to adapt these ideas to changing times and new problems. Top students in the sciences and arts deeply resent party
interference in their work. Soviet scholars in all fields privately
scoff at the need to mention Lenin and Marx in the prefaces to
works on every topic from paleontology to Pushkin.

It must be noted that by this time many scholars in the Soviet
Union have accepted the assumptions of Marxism-Leninism and
unconsciously reveal a pattern of thinking which arises from
these assumptions. One young Soviet startled an American his-

torian by remarking, "Both American and Russian intellectuals are trapped by the political and economic systems in which they live. The only difference is that we Russians know this, but you do not."

The Soviet attempt to train specialists has been more effective in chemistry, physics, geography, geology, some branches of medicine, and astronomy. The benefits from such training have been channeled almost entirely into state activities. Medical care and public health for the average Russian do not compare with that in Western Europe or the United States. But Soviet achievements in certain surgical pursuits have been noteworthy.

In the humanities and social sciences, Soviet achievements, measured even by Soviet standards, have been woefully inadequate. Physiology has vegetated under the dogmatic insistence on outdated theories of Ivan Pavlov (the first Russian Nobel prize winner, incidentally). Economics has suffered from sterile rehashing of Marx and, more recently, an unwillingness to accept new statistical and mathematical methods for solving problems of planning.

History has consisted of little more than trying to apply Marxism-Leninism to every country in every period of time. Much of the rich historical source material gathering dust in Russian archives goes untouched from one year to the next. Literary criticism and philosophy are in a deplorable state.

One of the aims of Premier Khrushchev's de-Stalinization campaign was to shake scholars loose from their intellectual ruts. But memories of Stalinist terror and fear of making mistakes in interpreting Communist ideology and socialist realism which will cost them their jobs have made these people cautious.

EDUCATIONAL REFORMS

The party also has charged the Soviet educational system with producing loafers with a sense of superiority over other members of society. Premier Khrushchev declared that education has become separated from life. To arrest this tendency, he launched a school-reform program in 1958 to combine physical and mental labor. By combining mental and physical disciplines, Khrushchev hopes to prevent the emergence of a new class of educated Russians who might adopt a dangerous separateness from the regime.

At the same time, the regime faces a labor-shortage problem

which if not solved by automation must be solved by pressing more youth into the productive labor force.

The educational reform seeks to siphon off into technical and trade schools, or directly into industry, those students who show little promise of doing outstanding academic work in the universities. The promise of free higher education for all has been withdrawn. University students are expected to work in factories or farms during the summer and spend some part of the school year volunteering for construction work in the cities on free Saturdays and Sundays. After graduation all but the very top university graduates must work three years before applying for graduate work. This plan is to discourage too many from going into higher education simply to escape the drudgery of physical labor. There has been a noticeable lack of enthusiasm for the new program among Russian students.

While trying to prevent any elitism (a sense of intellectual superiority) among those receiving higher education, the regime may well be encouraging it, for only the best students are encouraged to complete their education without interruption. They are singled out as special cases to a greater extent than ever before.

However, there is little evidence that a new Soviet intelligentsia is arising to criticize the regime and champion the rights of the downtrodden masses. There is no question that the Soviet intellectuals live better than most of the rest of the Soviet population. They enjoy special privileges and prestige but they are closely controlled by the party, nevertheless. Thus the intellectuals, whether factory managers, artists, army officers, or teachers, form no pressure groups, have no political power outside their membership in the Communist party.

Party loyalties override all others. The situation may change, however, if the opportunities are restricted, say, for the sons and daughters of the present intellectuals to move up the ladder of social prestige because of the status of parents. What will happen to those who are unable to achieve the status of their parents? Will they become discontented? Will they react like the young intelligentsia of the 19th century when they found that the outlets for their creative energy and talent were blocked by the state?

Top Soviet leaders are challenged also by signs of ferment among university students stirred by the Hungarian and Polish revolutions and the attacks on Stalin. As in the 19th century, the universities of the Soviet Union are the seedbeds of discontent.

Until 1956 this opposition was covert and splintered. But the brutal Soviet suppression of the Hungarian freedom fighters, many of whom were students, aroused the Soviet students. Their outbursts made clear they they had not been molded into Stalinist puppets. Their viewpoints differ widely, but many are strongly at variance with Communist party goals. Such discontent often mellows, however, as the students move into responsible jobs.

Organization of the opposition is extremely difficult under conditions of Soviet totalitarianism. So long as the party maintains its grip on the control system of the state and the assignment of jobs, the student opposition is virtually helpless.

SUMMARY

After Stalin's death, the Soviet Communist regime tried to awaken the intellectual life of the U.S.S.R. from its long Stalinist seclusion without, however, relaxing its ultimate control over creativity.

This risky mission may have been accomplished as of 1960, when Premier Khrushchev said that he was satisfied with the general attitude of Soviet intellectuals.

After a brief period of limited freedom during the 1920's, the Communist party tried to assert its control over all aspects of the

Culture is officially popularized throughout Russia. Houses of culture, where games, amateur programs, lectures, and rallies are held, are as familiar in the U.S.S.R. as are YMCA's in the U.S. Assemblies, large demonstrations are a part of citizens' public life. The May Day demonstration (right) honored Yuri Gagarin, cosmonaut.

Elliott Erwitt: MAGNUM

intellectual and cultural life of the U.S.S.R. Stalin aimed at organizing all intellectuals and guiding their thoughts and work along the lines best suited to serve the needs of the state.

The doctrine of socialist realism imposed on the creative artists the obligation to paint a rosy picture of life in the Soviet Union. Biologists were forced to accept unproven speculations as Marxist truth. Historians were told to rewrite history in order to glorify Stalin and the Russian people. The church was persecuted, and then used by the state as an organ of propaganda. In this way any potential opposition to Stalin's rule was nipped in the bud.

When the party devoted all its energies to winning World War II, the control system was relaxed. Soon after the war, the Zhdanov decrees in arts and sciences reasserted the role of the party in guiding the intellectual life of the country. Many nonconformist artists were purged. Jewish intellectuals suffered most, because Stalin suspected them of sympathy with the West.

During "the thaw" some of the rigid Stalinist controls were dropped or softened. For the first time in many years, voices of protest against party dictation could be heard. But Khrushchev upheld the power of the party to control the arts.

In order to strengthen the development of scientific research and provide for much needed man power, Khrushchev introduced an education reform. The best students are allowed to complete their studies without interruption. Others are forced to work part time.

The Soviet leaders are now trying to compete with the West culturally as well as industrially. How can they open the doors

Marc Riboud: MAGNUM

Marc Riboud: MAGNUM

to the people and ideas of the free world and still maintain their ideological control over the Russians?

Should the party sense an excess of intellectual boldness, it may turn again to heavy-handed restrictions. On the other hand these intellectual thrusts may succeed in chipping away party control little by little. There are no indications at present that the Soviet regime will either resort to Stalinist terror or entirely unleash the creative capacities of the Soviet Union.

Jim Blair

TERMS TO KNOW

socialist realism	*Kommunist*	*partiinost*
neo-Leninists	*Krokodil*	*Izvestia*
neo-Stalinists	*Pravda*	*Sovietskaya Kultura*

QUESTIONS ON THE CHAPTER

1. What was the ultimate purpose of the Communists' cultural revolution?

2. In what ways did the Communist party carry out its attack on religion during the 1920's?

3. Tell about some of the measures taken by the Communists to inject Communist ideology into the Russian educational system.

4. As the period of artistic experimentation drew to a close in the late 1920's, what were some of the actions taken by Stalin to communize Russia's cultural outlook?

5. What were the three chief trends that emerged from Stalin's process of creating a new Soviet culture?

6. Explain Stalin's concept of socialist realism.

7. In the 1930's many authors, composers, and painters were persecuted by the Soviet government. State some of the accusations made against creative artists such as Dimitri Shostakovich.

8. Many Soviet textbooks have been rewritten to promote Communist ideology. Give one example of this, and explain why Stalin thought it necessary to order the rewriting of the book.

9. For what reasons did Soviet publishers reject Boris Pasternak's prize-winning book *Doctor Zhivago?*

10. Compare the chief aims of Soviet education with the aims of education in the United States.

11. Soviet scientific achievements have been most noteworthy in certain fields. Name some of these achievements.

12. In the Soviet Union, which branches of study in the humanities and social sciences have been most inadequate in their achievements?

QUESTIONS FOR DISCUSSION

1. Western civilization has never seen such an extreme degree of control over culture and intellect as that which has been, and still is, practiced in the Soviet Union. Discuss some of the possible reasons for this strict control of art and ideas in the Soviet Union.

2. Textbooks in the Soviet Union have been rewritten or replaced over a period of many years. Textbooks in the Western World also are rewritten or reinterpreted. Discuss some of the differences between rewriting history, for example, in the Soviet sense, and reinterpreting history through scholarly research.

3. According to the Marxist-Leninist viewpoint, art and science are shaped by the prevailing class system and economic system in any given country. What reasons can you give to refute this viewpoint?

4. In the Soviet Union, there are four chief groups reflecting tendencies in the field of creative art: a) the rebels, b) the neo-Leninists, c) the conservatives, and d) the neo-Stalinists. Discuss briefly the major differences among these groups. For example, compare their distinguishing characteristics and aims.

BIBLIOGRAPHY

For Reference: □ Bauer, Raymond A.; Inkeles, Alex; and Kluckhohn, Clyde, *How the Soviet System Works.* Random House, 1960. □ Gunther, John, *Inside Russia Today.* Harper and Brothers, 1958. □ Levine, Irving R., *Main Street, USSR.* Anchor Books, 1959. □ State Historical Society of Wisconsin, *A Soviet View of the American Past.* The Society, 1960. **For Further Reading:** □ Dudintsev, Vladimir, *Not by Bread Alone.* E. P. Dutton & Company, 1957. □ Leonov, Leonid, *Thief.* Vintage Press, 1960. □ Orwell, George, *Animal Farm.* Harcourt, Brace & Company, 1946. □ Pasternak, Boris, *Doctor Zhivago.* Pantheon Books, Inc., 1958.

CHAPTER 7

THE USSR
AND INTERNATIONAL RELATIONS

*The confusing zigzags
of Soviet foreign policy
and the tactical shifts of Red groups
the world over tend to obscure
but fail to disguise
the Communist goal of world domination.*

To understand the evolution of Soviet foreign policy, we must turn again to the early days of the Communist party. From the beginning, Lenin put great emphasis on the close connection between a revolution in Russia and the world revolution. He theorized that Russia was ripe for revolution because it was a backward country, exploited by the industrial countries of the West. When World War I broke out in 1914, Lenin worked actively to bring about Russia's defeat, hoping that defeat would trigger internal revolution.

Once having taken power, he desperately wanted a general peace, because the might of the German Army menaced his new and hard-won power. The Russian Army was a shambles. The Bolsheviks had no position of strength from which to bargain for an end of hostilities. Anything less than a general peace—a limited Russo-German peace alone, for example—would tend to strengthen Germany, Lenin believed, and further delay the world revolution.

Delegates assembled at the Twenty-second Congress of the Communist party held in the Kremlin's new Palace of Congresses in October 1961.

Thus, as the first act of Soviet foreign policy, the Bolsheviks, naïvely and dutifully Marxist, called upon the peoples of the world for an end to the war. There should be no territorial exchanges, they declared, nor any payments of war indemnities.

The plea for peace failed. The Bolsheviks then had to decide whether to continue fighting the Germans or whether to do as Lenin urged, seek peace on any terms in order to protect the Bolshevik grip on the government of Russia.

Lenin finally won by arguing that a revolutionary war might not touch off the European revolution in time to save the Russian Revolution. In such circumstances all Bolshevik efforts toward revolt in Russia would have been fruitless. By signing a peace, however, the Bolsheviks could continue to work for the spread of the revolution to Europe by other means.

I. PEACE-AT-ANY-PRICE DIPLOMACY

Lenin's peace-at-any-price policy took the form of the Treaty of Brest Litovsk, signed with Germany and Austria-Hungary in March 1918. The treaty took Russia out of the war and became the first plank in the platform of Bolshevik foreign policy. Always a practical politician, Lenin refused to pursue elusive world revolution at the expense of losing power at home.

The terms of the treaty were extremely demanding: Russia gave up 40 per cent of its industry and industrial population through territorial losses, and 70 per cent of its iron and steel industry. As a result of the Treaty of Brest Litovsk, many of the nationalities of the old empire split away from the Bolsheviks. Russia lost the Ukraine, Finland, the Baltic States, most of the Polish provinces, the Transcaucasus, and central Asia.

Some of these areas became independent states. Others, like the Ukraine, fell under the control of the occupying German forces. But to the Bolsheviks the cost did not seem too much to pay to retain their power.

ALLIED INTERVENTION

To the Western Allies fighting Germany, the Treaty of Brest Litovsk was the worst imaginable disaster. It freed the Germans from a war on two fronts, allowing them to swing their forces to the western front. Thus the Allies began to look for some way to reconstitute an eastern front against the Germans.

Intervention in Russia by British, United States, French, and Japanese troops was the way chosen. Other motives also contributed to the decision to intervene. The Japanese were primarily interested in carving out territories in Pacific Russia. The Americans were interested mostly in preventing military supplies which had been sent to Russia from falling into German hands. The British and French wanted to prevent the Germans from transferring troops to the west.

However, when World War I finally ended in 1918, the British, United States, French, and Japanese occupation troops remained in Russia, much to the surprise of the Bolsheviks. Some of the Allied leaders considered using their troops in Russia either to force the Bolsheviks to pay off debts incurred by the prerevolutionary tsarist regime or to overthrow the Bolshevik regime by supporting the growing factions of anti-Bolsheviks in Russia, the White Russians. Furthermore, the European powers feared that postwar chaos in the area would make eastern Europe easy prey for the revolution-exporting Bolsheviks.

The end of the war and the mounting resistance inside Russia, now supported by foreign powers, posed serious problems for the Soviet leadership. The breathing space gained by signing the Treaty of Brest Litovsk was over.

RISING TIDE OF REVOLUTION

The Bolsheviks tried to negotiate settlements with the Allies, but negotiation failed. Therefore, they turned their attention to another aspect of their foreign policy: social revolution.

They had fertile ground for experimenting with revolution. Between the end of the war in the fall of 1918 and the signing of the Versailles Peace Treaty in the late spring of 1919, eastern Europe's three great empires were overwhelmed by domestic troubles. In the German, Austro-Hungarian, and Ottoman empires, authority largely had broken down and economic life was badly disrupted. Defeat and disillusion bred despair and violence. The chaos foreseen by the western European powers was on the rise. In the winter of 1918-1919, revolts and revolutions broke out in major German cities; a left-wing Socialist regime was set up in Hungary and in the German province of Bavaria. Although these revolts were soon suppressed, they were closely watched by the Bolsheviks. A revolution led by Mustafa Kemal Pasha (Kemal Atatürk) spread throughout the Ottoman Empire and resulted in the establishment of the Turkish Republic (1923).

THE COMINTERN IS FOUNDED

In the constant hope of spreading revolution throughout the West, Lenin called for the formation of the Third International in March 1919, to unite all Communist party members. He estimated that this step would menace the Western powers then sitting at the Versailles Peace Congress (which had excluded the Russians).

The First International—called the International Workingmen's Association (1864-1876), which Karl Marx himself had helped found—had, in Lenin's estimation, "laid the foundation of the proletarian, international struggle."

The Second International (1889-1914) had virtually collapsed as a result of the war. Nevertheless, Lenin said, the Second Inter-

USSR: WESTERN BOUNDARIES
1914 TO THE PRESENT

- - - - - RUSSIA 1914 ——— USSR 1929 ▒ USSR Today

national had "marked the epoch in which the soil was prepared for a broad, mass, widespread movement in a number of countries."

Now the Third, or Communist, International (or, abbreviated, Comintern) would begin "to effect the world wide dictatorship of the proletariat" that the Soviet Union was already "enacting."

Lenin wanted the Comintern to serve as the command post of world revolution. He wanted it to be well disciplined and centrally controlled so that it could stand solidly as a Bolshevik organization and not shatter during an international crisis.

The Russian Communists, with their prestige, experience, money, and the power to persuade or force compliance with their wishes, soon controlled the Comintern. Made in the image of the Bolshevik organization, the Comintern became a reliable instrument of Soviet foreign policy. Decisions made in Moscow were binding on all members of the Comintern everywhere.

Exacting instructions on methods of infiltrating mass organizations – trade unions, the army, farmers' associations, social affairs pressure groups, and other industrial, cultural, and civic organizations – were issued to all members by the Comintern. All Communist parties were ordered to carry on illegal and underground, as well as legal, work. As a result of strict rules, such as the provision for periodic purges, only the most revolutionary elements in the world socialist movement joined the Comintern.

To find out why men throughout the world became Communists it would really be necessary to study the history of each national party individually. However, there were reasons common to many or all parties. Disillusioned intellectuals found a sophisticated and tough-minded philosophy in Marxism-Leninism. Disgruntled workers and peasants saw a quick solution to the problems of unemployment, poverty, class discrimination. Communism offered the politically ambitious and unscrupulous a key to power. Finally, communism appealed to many who thought that it alone could save man from the worst abuses and yet preserve for him the many blessings of industrialization.

Many of the Communist parties that began to appear throughout the world were very small, but this did not trouble Lenin. More than numbers, he sought loyalty to his ideas.

Meanwhile in Russia it was becoming clear to the Bolshevik leaders that the extreme revolutionary policies of the Comintern were becoming a political liability. The West had not been able to destroy Bolshevism (although it really had not tried very hard to support the anti-Bolshevik, White Russian forces during the Civil War), and the Bolsheviks had failed to export their revolutionary ways beyond Russia's frontiers. As 1921 arrived, an uneasy stalemate prevailed.

COMMUNIST-CAPITALIST COEXISTENCE

At the Third Congress of the Communist party of the Soviet Union in 1921, Lenin warned that the full tide of European revolution was receding. Political and economic stability in the West was blocking further Communist advances. A temporary equilibrium between capitalism and socialism existed, he explained. Foreshadowing the later Khrushchev doctrine of "peaceful coexistence," Lenin asserted that it was possible for two systems to exist side by side, "for a short time, of course."

During that "short time," the Comintern dutifully agreed, "unreserved support of Soviet Russia is the very first duty of Communists of all countries." Because there was little chance of spreading world revolution, the Communists everywhere were told to support revolution where it had succeeded—in Russia. It was in this way that Communists in other countries, as well as the Comintern, became agents of Soviet foreign policy.

With no sign that revolutions were due in the advanced capitalist countries—they had not occurred during the war or during the chaotic postwar period—Lenin turned his attention to the backward countries of Asia. The movement of the colonial peoples against their Western "overlords," Lenin stated, "perhaps will play a far greater revolutionary role than we expect."

More and more, Lenin turned away from Marx's idea of a revolution in the industrialized countries and focused on revolution in backward countries.

RETURN TO DIPLOMACY

With their hopes for world revolution stymied for the time being, the Bolsheviks were forced to adopt a new tactic in foreign policy: greater emphasis on traditional, rather than revolutionary, means of conduct in international affairs.

Between 1921 and 1924 their diplomatic tactics aimed at three goals: (1) reëstablishment of normal diplomatic relations with capitalist countries in order to reduce the mounting economic and political isolation of the Soviet Union; (2) signing of friendship agreements with the governments of neighboring countries to prevent them from becoming stepping stones for new Allied interventions; (3) encouraging the so-called backward countries to throw off western European economic and political controls and establish independent regimes. Points one and two reflected Russian fears of new attacks from the west; point three was plainly tinged with the ingrained Bolshevik dedication to the Marxian idea of revolution as modified by Lenin.

Bearing these goals in mind, it is clear why the Soviet Union signed peace treaties with the Baltic States and Poland in 1920-1921, and then a series of commercial agreements with Great Britain, Italy, and Austria. These were followed by political agreements with Germany (at Rapallo, in 1922); then with the new Turkish regime of Kemal Atatürk; with the new Iranian regime of Reza Shah; with the Afghan government; and with the new revolutionary movement in China called the *Kuomintang,* under the leadership of Sun Yat-sen. Ironically, in light of current history, Chiang Kai-shek, the present-day leader of Nationalist China (Formosa), went to the Soviet Union to study military tactics under this agreement.

Despite these diplomatic gains, the Communists still did not completely abandon the idea of fostering revolutions in the industrial nations of the West. Therefore, when the opportunity arose in 1923-1924, the Comintern called upon Communists in Germany and Bulgaria to take up arms. But these last gasps of violent revolutionary activity before World War II were badly timed and quickly crushed.

When Lenin died in 1924, Soviet foreign policy was in a state of flux. Lenin had identified the interests of the world revolution with the national interests of the Soviet Union. What was good for one had to be good for the other. But, to the time of his death, he was not certain what policy would best advance the power of Russia and the world revolution. He had clearly become skeptical about the need for a revolution in the West to save the Soviet Union. It was left to Stalin to draw the logical conclusion from this belief, that is, the chief aim of Soviet foreign policy ought to be the strengthening of the Soviet state. When the state was powerful enough, it could serve as a base for world revolution.

II. "SOCIALISM IN ONE COUNTRY" IN ACTION

The most important practical result of Stalin's policy was a much more cautious Soviet attitude toward the development of Communist-led revolutions in countries friendly to the Soviet Union. Stalin was even more skeptical than Lenin about the value of these foreign revolutions.

In 1927, for example, Stalin ordered the Chinese Communists to continue to coöperate with the new Chinese Nationalist leader, Chiang Kai-shek, despite Chiang's persecution of the Communists.

Battered by Chiang on the one hand and frustrated by the Russians on the other, the Chinese Communists went underground. The Chinese Communist leaders, including Mao Tse-tung, never forgot the lesson of not relying on Moscow's orders.

Stalin's policy of maintaining traditional diplomatic relations with the West also had its ups and downs in the 1920's. By 1927 the Soviet Union had been recognized by most of the European powers. The Soviet Union had signed, in 1928, the Kellogg-Briand Pact outlawing war as well as a number of other nonaggression pacts with its immediate neighbors and Germany. On the other hand Germany appeared to be drawing closer to France and Great Britain, a sure sign of danger in the eyes of the Bolshevik leaders. Britain, having recognized Russia in 1924, had broken off diplomatic relations with the Soviet Union in 1927.

Thus, in 1928, Stalin felt pressed to redouble his efforts to make his nation secure from external attack. As depressions swept many of the world's economies, he feared that the capitalist powers might try to launch a war to recover from their economic plight. Furthermore he had just begun the great effort to industrialize and collectivize the U.S.S.R. In order to concentrate on implementing the First Five-Year Plan, Stalin began to pull Soviet Russia back into semi-isolation and left external affairs—especially combatting any Western coalition against him—to the Comintern.

The Comintern, reverting to its earlier policy, veered sharply to the left, proclaiming the need for all-out revolutionary action. Stalin supported the shift in order to discredit the Comintern supporters of Bukharin (who opposed Stalin's drive for collectivization) and to harass the democratic Socialists of the West, especially the German Socialists, whom he suspected of seeking closer relations with other Western powers.

Stalin's attack on the German Socialists through the German Communists turned out to be a serious miscalculation. The Socialists formed the bulwark of the republican government in Germany. By weakening them, Stalin only aided the rise of the Nazi party under Adolf Hitler. Caught between the twin fires, Hitler and Stalin, the Socialists literally begged the Soviet embassy in Berlin to reverse the German Communist assault so that its strength might be joined with that of the Socialists in battling the Hitlerite threat. But the request was refused. Germany's democratic government, overwhelmed by many problems in addition to Communist agitation and subversion, fell easy prey to Hitler in 1932. To the Communists, Hitler's triumph seemed to be the last gasp of capitalism in Germany.

The Communists completely misunderstood the character of Hitler's movement and the appeal of his program. In Stalin's eyes, Hitler had the merit of being a violent enemy of Western democracy. Stalin could be certain, therefore, that Germany would not become an ally of any of the Western countries who had intervened in Russian affairs during the Civil War. He was willing to sacrifice the German Communist party, as he had the Chinese Communist party, to win more time for Russian domestic progress in collectivization and industrialization.

Let the Western powers squabble among themselves; let Russia go about its domestic business. How wrong Stalin's reasoning proved to be! Hitler carried out a bloody and much more thorough massacre of the Communists than had Chiang Kai-shek. The German Communist party was all but destroyed. It had been the most powerful Communist organization outside Russia.

COLLECTIVE SECURITY

Hitler launched in Germany a program of rearmament and war-like diplomacy. Finally the Soviet leaders awakened to the error of their German policy. Once again the direction of Soviet foreign policy shifted. Diplomats were urgently instructed to work harder to strengthen a policy of collective security against a Nazi drive toward Russia. In the Far East there was the smoldering threat of Japanese aggression on Russia's distant, defenseless Pacific flank.

Events had moved swiftly. Hitler became chancellor of Germany (January 1933); Germany quit the League of Nations (October

During the German invasion of the U.S.S.R., cities like Stalingrad (called Volgograd today) were almost leveled. American equipment like the jeeps shown here helped Russians turn the invaders back.

1933); the United States, under President Franklin D. Roosevelt, recognized the Soviet Union as the government of Russia (November 1933); the Soviet Union joined the League of Nations, which it had long denounced as a "capitalist club" (September 1934); the Soviet Union signed mutual defense treaties with France and Czechoslovakia (May 1935) to throw up a defense on three sides of Germany. Finally the disastrous Comintern policy was sharply reversed. Communist parties everywhere were urged to drop their revolutionary slogans and support any anti-Hitler groups, including the much-maligned western democratic Socialists.

THE POPULAR FRONT

This new direction to Comintern policy, the attempt to coöperate with anti-Hitler groups, was called the Popular Front.

The Popular-Front tactic aimed at two political targets. The first was to rally support in all countries against Naziism, the main threat to Soviet security at the time. The second was to take advantage of the world disturbance to create new types of governments, so-called popular democracies. These popular democracies would be an intermediate stage between capitalism and the full-blown Communist dictatorship of the proletariat.

As one of the leaders of the Comintern, Georgi Dimitrov, put it: "When carrying out the policy of the [Popular Front] against fascism and war . . . the Communists do not lose sight of the historic need for the revolutionary overthrow of capitalism which has outlived its day and for the achievement of socialism, which brings emancipation to the working class and the whole of mankind."

DECLINE OF COLLECTIVE SECURITY

The results of collective security efforts against Germany and Japan were discouraging to both the Russians and their Western allies. The Soviet Union feared that the Western powers were always ready to make a deal with the aggressor at Russia's expense. The Western leaders thought that the Soviet Union appeared eager to embroil them in a war with Hitler during which the Soviet Union would stand aloof until it could intervene on the side which promised most.

Furthermore, there was a nagging fear among the leaders of the West that the Soviet Union regarded war between Western powers as the best means of undermining their democratic social structure. This would set the stage for the social revolution which would demolish democracy completely.

Thus Western diplomats found themselves wrestling with two fears: (1) Hitler's mania for conquest, and (2) Soviet Russia's commitment to social upheaval and the spread of communism.

The Spanish Civil War (1936-1939), in which both communism (the Russians) and fascism (Italians and Germans) battled for a foothold deep in western Europe, added to Western alarm. After the war broke out in the summer of 1936, Germany and Italy sent supplies to General Francisco Franco, in violation of previous agreements of nonintervention. What started as a civil crisis in a backward and disorganized country began to mushroom into a world controversy of ideologies.

The Soviet Union countered with aid to the Spanish Popular Front government, in which Spanish Communists were a small but influential segment. Stalin's purpose apparently was to force France and Great Britain to follow suit and to involve them in war with Hitler (Germany) and Mussolini (Italy).

Although France contributed minor aid to the Spanish Popular Front government, Britain did not intervene. The Soviet Union could not supply the Spanish Republicans indefinitely. Thus Moscow's problem became one of extricating itself as quickly as possible from intervention in Spain while keeping German and Italian forces occupied there. At the same time, Stalin carried out a ruthless purge of the advisers he had sent to Spain, apparently because they seemed sincerely committed to the fight for communism in Spain regardless of the danger of enlarged war with Germany and Italy. There was danger also that the spontaneous enthusiasm of the Russian Communists in Spain might lead to the formation of a splinter group within the Comintern advocating all-out revolutionary activity. Stalin felt nothing but fury for disaffection in the international Communist movement. Once again a foreign Communist party, the Spanish this time, was sacrificed for the protection of the Soviet Union.

The final hammer blows against the fragile edifice of collective security were struck in 1938 when Hitler invaded and annexed Austria (March), and when Britain, France, and Italy agreed at Munich (September) to allow Hitler to partition Czechoslovakia.

The Soviet Union was excluded from the Munich conference between Adolf Hitler, Benito Mussolini of Italy, Neville Chamberlain of Great Britain, and Édouard Daladier of France, which decided the fate of Czechoslovakia. So far as Moscow was concerned, the Munich conference removed all doubt that the policy of collective security was bankrupt. In Stalin's view, his fears might be justified: the Western powers would make a deal with the aggressor (Germany) at Russia's expense just as they had in the case of Czechoslovakia. Therefore, preparations were begun in the Soviet capital to reach some kind of understanding with Hitler to deter him from eastward expansion.

In August 1939, a 10-year Nazi-Soviet nonaggression pact was signed. It divided eastern Europe into two spheres of influence and provided that Germany and the U.S.S.R. would remain neutral toward each other in the event of war. The surprised Communist parties of Europe were once again ordered to attack the western democratic Socialists.

WORLD WAR II AND SOVIET NEUTRALITY

Stalin realized that by signing the treaty he freed Hitler of a fear of war on two fronts. He thus opened the way for the Nazi invasion of Poland Sept. 1, 1939, and the beginning of World War II.

Stalin counted on remaining neutral in this war, hoping, however, to bring under direct Soviet control the areas in eastern Europe assigned to him by the pact: eastern Poland, the Baltic States (Latvia, Lithuania, Estonia), Finland, and the Romanian province of Bessarabia. Then, behind this broad defensive buffer zone along the Russian western frontier, he might wait patiently until a stalemate had been reached in the west and then intervene and decide the outcome. Unfortunately for the U.S.S.R., Stalin again miscalculated both Hitler's intentions and his strength. This error soon cost the Soviet Union untold losses and suffering.

As soon as the war broke out, Stalin moved to carry out his design. The Red Army occupied eastern Poland in 1939 and the Baltic States in 1940. Both areas were incorporated into the Soviet Union. The Soviet attempt to dominate Finland ended in a war which exposed the military weakness of the Red Army. Though tiny Finland was beaten eventually and lost some territory, it did not lose its independence. Because of its aggression against Finland, the Soviet Union was expelled from the League of Nations in December 1940.

Despite acquiring this zone of protecton on the west, Stalin was alarmed by the swift Nazi victories over Poland and France in 1939-1940. In order to further strengthen defenses on the west, Stalin demanded control over eastern Bulgaria and German help against Finland and Turkey. But Hitler's plans swerved at this point. Unable to invade Britain, he decided to crush Russia in order to deprive Britain of its only remaining potential ally on the Continent. It was a fateful decision.

Stalin was warned by several governments and intelligence sources that Hitler planned to attack in June 1941. But the Soviet dictator refused to believe that his policy was about to fail again. Soviet leaders tried desperately to keep out of the war. Up to the last moment they persisted in sending Germany the raw materials and supplies promised in their treaty of 1939. When the Nazi attack came (June 22, 1941), the Red Army was grossly unprepared and suffered terribly from Stalin's miscalculation.

WORLD WAR II AND THE GRAND ALLIANCE

Throughout Soviet participation (1941-1945) in World War II the single-minded Soviet goal was to destroy the enemy. A Nazi victory on the vast Eurasian plain, they realized, would mean the end of the Communist system in Russia. The Soviet foreign policy designed to protect that system, evolved during three periods of World War II: the defensive battles from 1941 to 1943, the Soviet offensives from 1943 to early 1945, and the post-Yalta disagreements, from early 1945 until mid-1945.

THE YEARS OF DEFENSIVE BATTLES (1941-1943)

During the period from June 1941 to the battle of Stalingrad in 1943, Soviet foreign policy reverted to two familiar approaches to world affairs. First, a series of agreements was negotiated with the Western powers and exiled representatives of governments overrun by the Nazis. From these countries, the Soviet Union wanted military supplies and fighting assistance against the Germans. This was the grand alliance. Second, the Communist parties of

Europe were urged to coöperate with all anti-Nazi forces and to wage all-out guerrilla war against the Nazis in order to ease the Nazi pressures on the Soviet Union.

The Germans were stopped at Moscow and Leningrad in 1941 as the Russian winter clenched all movement in its frigid grip, but another Nazi phalanx drove deep into southern Russia in 1942. By then the German supply lines were long and vulnerable; the Red Army was beginning to stiffen its resistance. The mass uprising of Russians against their Soviet masters, which the Germans were counting on to further weaken Russian resistance, never materialized. The Russian people found the Nazi invaders cruel and merciless overlords who even maintained the collective farm system in order to make the forced delivery of grain supplies easier.

Against this grim backdrop, Stalin's appeal to the people to defend their homes (not communism this time) met a ready response. When the Nazi war machine stalled and was battered at the gates of Stalingrad, the "invincible" German Army initiative was turned. The Red Army counterattacked in force.

THE SOVIET OFFENSIVES (1943–EARLY 1945)

Emboldened by victory over the Nazi armies, Stalin now pressed the Allied nations for political concessions in eastern Europe. At conferences with the United States and Great Britain, he insisted that the 1941 Soviet frontier with Poland be accepted as the future frontier and that the Polish government display a friendly – which in this case meant subservient – attitude toward Moscow. (The Poles refused, and diplomatic relations with Moscow were broken.) Stalin also won from Churchill (but not from Roosevelt) the recognition of a Soviet sphere of influence in most eastern European countries except Greece.

To placate the Allies, in the light of these strong territorial demands, Stalin announced the dissolution of the Comintern in 1943. By then, however, the Comintern had already lost most of its power to the Secretariat of the Communist party of the Soviet Union, the new control center of world communism.

As the Red Army had driven the Germans back across the old Soviet frontiers and entered Bulgaria, Hungary, Romania, and Poland, it had carried in its van thousands of local Communists who had fled to Moscow before and during the war. Now they returned to prepare the way for new Communist seizures of power.

Communist parties in eastern Europe, either on Stalin's orders (as in Poland) or against his wishes (as in Yugoslavia), began to eliminate opposition elements in preparation for the liberation by the sweeping Red Army.

Stalin sought to restrain the more vigorous among these Communist groups because he did not want to antagonize the Allies and because he wanted the local Communists to await the arrival of the Red Army before seizing local power. Stalin showed the same strong suspicion of the independent Communist leaders in eastern Europe that he displayed earlier toward their counterparts in Germany, China, and Spain. His break with Marshal Tito of Yugoslavia was rooted in these wartime quarrels.

In western Europe, the Communist parties of France and Italy obeyed Stalin's instructions to devote their main energies to fighting against the Germans. Stalin's long-range hope was that this tactic would enhance the reputation of the Communists in their homelands and win for them a strong voice in the formation of postwar governments. To the extent to which these parties could influence the policies of France and Italy, they were urged to join in coalition governments which Stalin hoped could be transformed into the popular democracies described by the 1935 meeting of the Comintern Congress.

As Stalin felt the growth of Soviet power, he sought to use that power, as he had promised in 1925, as a base from which to spread world revolution.

POST-YALTA DISAGREEMENTS (EARLY 1945–MID-1945)

At the Yalta Conference in early 1945, the Big Three (the United States, Britain, and the Soviet Union) agreed to settle the political problems of eastern Europe by permitting free elections by all democratic parties, a coalition Polish government of Communists and non-Communists, and recognition of the 1941 Soviet-Polish frontier. The Soviet Union flagrantly violated these agreements later.

In retrospect, the Allies realized their mistake in not clarifying what the Soviet Union meant by "free" elections, in not providing some joint Allied machinery for guaranteeing that the agreements would be carried out fairly, and in not protecting the coalition government at Warsaw from being dominated by, instead of shared with, the Communists.

The Red Army was, nevertheless, standing guard over eastern Europe and could not easily have been dislodged short of a new war. There was no Western power on the spot to force the Soviet Union to carry out its Yalta promises.

It has been argued that, for its part, the Soviet Union had not been allowed any direct influence in determining the postwar political status of France and Italy, which were occupied by Western troops. Finally, the British and Americans were anxious to keep relations with the Russians mutually agreeable so that Soviet forces could be brought into the war against Japan, which the Allies then believed would continue for a year or more.

At Yalta, as an inducement to help hasten the victory over Japan, the Soviet Union was offered territories in the Far East, including the Kuril Islands, southern Sakhalin Island, and a naval base at Port Arthur. American military advisers insisted that Soviet participation in the Japanese war would save the United States a large number of men and perhaps avoid the necessity for actually invading the Japanese islands. Some State Department advisers, however, cautioned against bringing the U.S.S.R. into the war in the Pacific because of the Soviet expansionism it would encourage. The advice of the military men prevailed.

In 1945 the Soviets signed a treaty with the Chinese Nationalist government of Chiang Kai-shek, which it recognized as the legitimate government of China. However, when the Soviet Union did enter the Pacific war, it violated part of this Sino-Soviet agreement by turning over the war booty it captured in Manchuria, not to the Chiang Kai-shek government, but to the Chinese Communists. But at the same time, Stalin did warn the Chinese Communists not to break with Chiang.

Again Stalin showed his opposition to the emergence of a powerful local Communist regime which had won its power independently of Soviet aid. Greater frictions than these between Moscow and Peiping developed later.

CREATION OF SATELLITE GOVERNMENTS

After the Yalta agreements, the Soviet Union went its own way in imposing regimes of its choice on eastern Europe. The Soviet

216

Union insisted that whatever the outcome of the elections (some were rigged, others were not) local Communists were to be members of the first postwar coalition governments.

The pattern of imposing a Communist dictatorship was somewhat as follows: Generally, the Communists gained control of one or more of three key posts—foreign affairs, interior (police), or defense (army). They immediately purged these ministries of non-Communists and used their power to cripple all opposition and spread their influence. With the ever-present Red Army to back them up, the local Communists swallowed up the Socialist parties (their main rivals), took control of the trade unions, pushed through nationalization of heavy industry, and sponsored land reform to win peasant support.

When persuasion failed, ruthless and violent methods were used to fulfill these goals. Leaders of the opposition parties often were kidnaped, beaten up, or blackmailed. Communist toughs smashed the presses of opposition newspapers and beat their newsboys. Communist gangs broke up public meetings. All this occurred while the Communist-controlled police or army stood aside or looked the other way.

The final stage in establishing these eastern European puppet regimes was to outlaw the opposition parties, set up a dictatorship, and begin to follow the Soviet program of industrialization and collectivization.

THE GERMAN PROBLEM
AND THE END OF THE ALLIANCE

The defeat and occupation of Germany by the Big Three in May 1945 brought to a head the most important postwar problem: the future of Germany. According to previous agreements, the three powers (now joined by France) took up their positions in zones of military occupation. It had been decided that these zones were to be purely military and that Germany was to be treated as an economic unity.

The drawing of zonal boundaries left the city of Berlin deep inside the Soviet zone, occupied by the four powers. The United States Department of State had proposed creating a corridor from the city through Soviet-occupied territory to the Western zones which would guarantee free Western access to the city. However,

Soviet diplomacy in the early history of the United Nations was characterized by dramatic and repeated walkouts of the U.S.S.R. delegation. This famous walkout of Ambassador Andrei Gromyko followed the Security Council's rejection of his plea to postpone hearings of the Iranian question. Gromyko can be seen at the left as he turns and strides away from the council table.

the U.S. War Department preferred to handle the matter in its own way, through a verbal agreement between the U.S. and Soviet commanders in Berlin. Once again military calculations were allowed to overshadow political factors. An opportunity was lost to obtain the security of Berlin, a failure which was to precipitate the Berlin crises of 1958 and 1961.

Soon, East and West were in a stalemate over the future of Germany. The Soviet Union wanted four-power control of the key industrial area of western Germany, the Ruhr. If given a veto over the industrial production of this area, the U.S.S.R. could easily have blackmailed Western Europe into accepting its wishes on many problems, since the Ruhr mines and factories were necessary for postwar reconstruction.

The Soviet Union also demanded that the Germans immediately turn over to them large amounts of equipment and supplies as reparations for war damages done to the U.S.S.R. by the Nazis.

The Western powers were sympathetic to Soviet demands for reparations, but insisted that the powers had to agree first on the minimum standard of living for the German people. Otherwise, reparations of German industrial and agricultural goods would mean either starvation and chaos for the Germans or large American expenditures to support the German people, deprived of their means of support by the Soviet Union. Soviet Union officials refused to coöperate. They stripped eastern Germany of as much as they could. American General Lucius Clay then cut off reparations from the Western zones, and the economic unity of Germany was destroyed.

The Soviet Union also took action in the Eastern Zone to carry out the same policies of sovietization as in Poland and Romania. It accused the Western powers of failing to carry out agreements to democratize the Western zones and then defined that democratization in Communist terms.

In the Eastern Zone industry was nationalized, the Socialist and Communist parties were fused, and a political dictatorship was established. Land was redistributed to those who might prove useful allies. Gradually Communist domination spread across East Germany. The military zones had become political frontiers.

III. THE COLD WAR

As it became clear to the Western powers that the Soviet Union was determined to extend its influence by setting up a Soviet bloc in eastern Europe, the Western powers tried to insist that these moves be negotiated, rather than arbitrarily launched by Moscow whenever it alone decided to seize territory. Western diplomats hoped that recollections of the give-and-take of the wartime alliance and Soviet membership in the United Nations would soothe Soviet suspicions about the capitalist West and blunt the revolutionary zeal of Moscow.

The last of these hopes was dashed by Stalin himself in early 1946 when he declared that so long as capitalism survived, the world was not safe from war. Here was a clear-cut reaffirmation of the old Leninist-Stalinist doctrine. Stalin's declaration was ample evidence that he had no intention of modifying the long-range goals of Soviet policy. The prospects of any fruitful coöperation between the U.S.S.R. and the West had become virtually nil.

Stalin turned away from trying to work out problems with the West for several reasons. One of his main fears was that increased contact with the West during the war and growing good relations after the war would weaken his dictatorial hold over the Russian people. In 1947, when the United States had offered economic aid to the Soviet Union as part of its projected Marshall Plan, the Soviet representative walked out of the conference, calling the American proposal an unwarranted interference in Soviet domestic affairs. Stalin did not want the Soviet Union to depend upon outside help for economic reconstruction. Such aid, he feared, would mean the restoration of capitalism in the U.S.S.R. and the end of Communist rule.

Furthermore, Stalin intended to consolidate his hold over the eastern European satellites, where strong but disorganized resistance to sovietization persisted. Under these circumstances, good relations with the West would undermine the minority position of the Communists in the satellites by allowing increased contact between Westerners and non-Communist elements.

To keep his state power and his ideological monopoly intact, Stalin drew a cloak of fear tightly around his growing empire.

THE COMINFORM, MOSCOW'S NEW "FORWARD" POLICY

In the fall of 1947, at a secret meeting in Poland under Stalin's orders, the Cominform, or Communist Information Bureau, was created. Its purpose was to coördinate the activities and propaganda of the Communist bloc under the supreme command, of course, of the Soviet Union.

Under the Cominform, foreign Communists were now obliged to reject coöperation with democratic political parties, join in a chorus of denunciation of the West, and demand revolutionary policies abroad. These tactics were supplemented by outbreaks of political strikes and demonstrations in Western Europe and by belligerent Soviet diplomatic gambits.

The aggressive tactical assaults of the Cominform proved effective. In February 1948, with the Soviet Army standing ready on three frontiers, the strong Czechoslovak Communist party seized power in Prague.

Shortly afterwards, Greek Communists stepped up their antigovernment agitations during a civil war. In Turkey, Soviet diplomats badgered the government. In Asia, Moscow began openly to support the growing successes of the Chinese Communist revolution and the development of Communist activities against the French in Indochina.

WARSAW PACT NATIONS

Warsaw Pact nations   Other nations

ATLANTIC OCEAN

NORWAY
SWEDEN
FINLAND

IRELAND GREAT BRITAIN DENMARK

Baltic Sea

U.S.S.R.

EAST GERMANY POLAND

NETH.
BELG.

WEST GERMANY CZECHOSLOVAKIA

FRANCE

SWITZ. AUSTRIA HUNGARY

ROMANIA

Black Sea

PORTUGAL SPAIN ITALY YUGOSLAVIA BULGARIA

ALBAN. GREECE

TURKEY

0   200   400   600
MILES

In 1955 the Warsaw Pact was signed by eight nations: Albania, Bulgaria, Czechoslovakia, East Germany, Hungary, Poland, Romania, and the Soviet Union. This pact is a mutual defense agreement corresponding to the NATO Treaty which was signed by the United States and various Western powers.

MOSCOW'S "FORWARD" POLICY CHECKED

In 1948 Stalin closed the ground access routes to the Western zones of isolated Berlin. He tried first to starve the city into submission and then to exchange a lifting of the blockade for assurances that the Western powers would not unify their zones and create a West German government.

The Western powers organized an airlift to bring much-needed food and supplies to Berlin.

The Western World came suddenly awake to the necessity of stronger countermeasures against Communist boldness. Within six months the North Atlantic Treaty Organization (NATO) of the United States, Canada, and ten European nations had been formed to answer the stepped-up Soviet threat. Stalin's "forward" policy in Europe had failed.

"FORWARD" POLICY ADVANCES IN ASIA

The Soviet Union also pressed forward with its revolutionary policy in Asia, where, as Lenin had forecast, the opportunities for revolutionary action in the undeveloped countries appeared much riper than in Western Europe's advanced nations.

The Communist approach was to support a policy of national liberation from colonial rule. This policy masked long-range goals of Communist rule and often succeeded in winning the support of large sections of the population genuinely desirous of shaking off foreign controls but unaware of the true intention of the Communists.

In order to develop this policy, the party disguised itself by organizing "front movements" of the masses in which the Communists controlled key posts. The party was most successful in those areas where the Western powers opposed national independence for their colonies, as in French Indochina. They were least successful in places like the Philippines, Burma, Malaya, and India, which were given their freedom.

TENSIONS IN THE SOVIET BLOC

At the same time and for many of the same reasons that his policies were faltering in Asia, Stalin was running into trouble within the Communist bloc in the west. His insistence upon everyone following Moscow's orders led to a series of mistakes.

Soon after World War II, Stalin began to suspect that a number of local Communist leaders, including some of the more independent-minded "Spanish veterans," as well as those who had risked staying in their countries during the occupation to fight against the Nazis, were unwilling to accept Soviet domination of the bloc. Part of the purpose of the new Cominform was to control these men.

By far the most troublesome Communist leader in eastern Europe was Josip Broz, the Yugoslav known as Tito. He was one of the few Communist leaders who had not been under direct Soviet supervision during the war. His power, therefore, was self-made, and he owed less to the Soviet Union than did any of the other eastern European Communist leaders.

After the war, Tito held and openly expressed views on eastern European affairs which infuriated Stalin. In 1948 Stalin denounced Tito, demanded his replacement, and expelled Yugoslavia from the Cominform. But Tito's grip on his party was much too strong to be shaken by Stalin's angry attack.

Following his break with Tito, Stalin purged numerous other eastern European Communists who had not hurried to Moscow during the war and whom he suspected of independent leanings. Wladyslaw Gomulka in Poland was arrested. Traicho Kostov in Bulgaria, Rudolf Slansky in Czechoslovakia, and László Rajk in Hungary were executed. Actual and potential resistance to Stalin's control over eastern Europe was steam-rollered.

The Cominform became a lifeless organ, subject to the discipline of the various Soviet ambassadors and Soviet secret police.

STALIN'S KOREAN RISK

Stalin's last gamble for revolutionary success came in 1950 when the North Korean Army attacked the Republic of South Korea in an attempt to bring the entire country under Communist rule. Korea, which had been part of the Japanese Empire of 1945, had been divided at the 38th parallel into two zones of occupation (similar to Germany). The northern part of the country was Soviet controlled; the southern part was occupied by the United States. By 1950 the two zones had become two separate governments, and most of the Soviet and American troops had been withdrawn. The Communist attack brought U.S. forces back at once, and they, together with forces drawn from the armies of other United Nations members, hurled back the invaders and their spearhead of 100 Russian-built tanks and crossed into North Korea.

As they approached the Chinese frontier, 200,000 Communist Chinese troops counterattacked, driving the UN forces south in a dramatic forced evacuation of troops and civilians during the fall of 1950. In early 1951, as the United Nations General Assembly was

A typical disturbance by Communist demonstrators. This riot staged outside the parliament building in Rome protested Italian participation in the North Atlantic Pact.

naming Communist China the aggressor in Korea, UN forces repulsed the Communists. A truce line was established along the 38th parallel. Stalin's bid to expand Communist power by force had failed again.

Checked in 1949 at Berlin and in 1950-1952 in Korea, Stalin's "forward" policy had reached an impasse. Only in areas where he had had little influence (China and southeast Asia) did the Communists continue to advance.

IV. SOVIET FOREIGN POLICY AFTER STALIN'S DEATH

After Stalin's death (March 1953) his successors tried to eliminate the major liabilities of the late dictator's foreign policy. Soviet demands that Turkey surrender large strategic territories were dropped. The U.S.S.R. returned to Finland a naval base taken at the end of World War II.

After lengthy negotiations the U.S.S.R. agreed to the unification of Austria as a neutral and independent state. Yugoslavia was assured that the Soviet Union did not intend to threaten its national independence or Marshal Tito. Most important of all, armistices were signed ending wars in Korea and Indochina, but leaving the northern parts of those countries under Communist control. Thus did the new Soviet leaders seek to free their hands from embarrassing commitments of the Stalin era.

At the same time the new Moscow leaders were open to developing new policies aimed at shattering the Western alliances, renewing the Communist "forward" thrust in Asia, and welding the Communist bloc into a more cohesive and potent instrument of policy.

KHRUSHCHEV'S DOCTRINE
OF PEACEFUL COEXISTENCE

The Communist party was told that this new turn of Soviet foreign policy, in the direction of modified antagonism toward the West, came about as a result of the great strength of the Communist bloc.

Nikita S. Khrushchev, the Soviet leader, declared that the capitalists were now afraid to launch a war against the powerful Communist forces. Thus, since war was no longer inevitable, he continued, the two systems could live together in peaceful coexistence until the Communist system proved its superiority and conquered the world. The methods of conquest in each country would differ, but the end result—a Communist dictatorship—would remain the same. Some places would experience violence; elsewhere the change would be peaceful. Ultimately, however, Khrushchev announced, communism would triumph everywhere.

REASSURING THE RUSSIAN PEOPLE

By deëmphasizing the possibility of war, Khrushchev carried out the first important aim of his foreign policy: to reassure the Russian people that the new leadership of their country was dedicated to peace. He indicated that the Soviet Union could begin to build communism without having first conquered the world. Like Stalin's doctrine of "socialism in one country," Khrushchev's interpretation placed greater emphasis on the contribution of the U.S.S.R. than on the world revolution for the victory of communism.

Khrushchev's policy had the added effect of separating domestic from foreign policy to a greater degree than Stalin had ever done, thus permitting a policy of relaxation at home to exist side by side with an aggressive foreign policy. Khrushchev did not invoke the threat of war to urge the Soviet people to work harder. He believed that this kind of coarse, Stalinist tactic was no longer necessary.

DIVIDE THE WEST

Deëmphasizing the possibility of war was also part of Khrushchev's attempt to lull the Western powers into the belief that the U.S.S.R. was considering giving up its long-range goal of world conquest.

Local Communist parties in Europe also were "zagged" back to peaceful policies. The aim was to slow down and disrupt the consolidation of the Free World.

At the Geneva conferences of 1955 (heads of state from the U.S., Britain, France, and the U.S.S.R. at one conference, their foreign ministers at the other), the Soviet leaders proposed a pact between NATO and the Warsaw Pact (1955 alliance of eastern European Communist countries). Such a step would have destroyed the effectiveness of NATO as a defensive rampart against the Communists. The Russians appeared to be encouraging the feeling that a long period of stability in Europe had opened and that it would be safe to reduce military vigilance in the area.

At the same time the Western Allies of the United States were subjected to threats of nuclear attack to frighten them into parting company with the U.S. and abandoning a common Western defense alliance.

During the Suez crisis of 1956 (armed conflict which involved Britain, France, Israel and Egypt), Khrushchev sent notes to Western capitals ominously informing them that the Soviet Union had the power to destroy them.

In 1957 the Russians launched their Sputnik I (the first man-made satellite to be rocketed into orbit around the earth), and this served to underline Soviet threats.

In 1958 Khrushchev decided to put NATO to the supreme test by raising again the tension-laden Berlin question. He brashly proposed to liquidate what he called an "artificial situation" in Berlin by bringing to an end the four-power occupation of the city and setting up a "free city," which would actually be at the economic and political mercy of Communist East Germany. Khrushchev served up this proposal with a generous helping of Soviet bluster, all intended to bully and divide the West on a crucial issue. Clearly Khrushchev hoped for sufficiently serious disagreement between the United States, Great Britain, and West Germany to undermine the willingness of the German people to continue their close relationship with the West.

The U.S.S.R., of course, was prepared to offer the West Germans reunification. But the Communist price was high: a coalition government with the Communist East Germans in a neutral and disarmed Germany. In such a state, at least one key ministry (for example, interior, with its police authority) would undoubtedly be in the hands of a Communist, and the tightly knit Communist party organization would form the nucleus of an underground force capable eventually of overthrowing the coalition.

Therefore, following Stalin's death, the world began to view the zigs and zags of Soviet foreign policy in the Khrushchev manner: now peaceful coexistence, now the rattling of nuclear rockets. It was the old carrot-and-stick tactic which has long served Communist leaders in their struggle to divide and overwhelm the West.

The short-run target was NATO, the protective screen that stands between Moscow and its political, economic, and territorial goals in Western Europe.

THE RENEWED COMMUNIST DRIVE
IN ASIA AND AFRICA

Underdeveloped countries of the world are the most tempting object of Khrushchev's new tactics. Soon after Stalin's death the new Soviet regime took steps to end the fighting in both Korea and Indochina. In the case of the latter, the Soviet Union preferred to see the country partitioned into North Viet-Nam (Communist) and South Viet-Nam, Cambodia, and Laos, rather than risk intervention by United States forces to repulse a victorious Communist drive to the south.

Since that time Soviet tactics have concentrated on wooing the neutral countries through a policy of peaceful coexistence, and at the same time encouraging a more aggressive local Communist policy toward unstable regimes in southeast Asia. This tactic is another manifestation of the Soviet goals of undermining Free World resistance to Soviet encroachments and of isolating the United States.

At the Twentieth Congress of the Communist party of the Soviet Union in 1956 and again at the Twenty-second Congress of the CPSU in 1961, Premier Khrushchev appealed to the uncommitted countries, making up what he termed the "peace bloc," to work with the Soviet Union to avoid war.

His program was as follows: seat Communist China at the United Nations; condemn the United States for supporting the Nationalist Chinese regime of Chiang Kai-shek on Formosa; condemn the United States for supporting embattled regimes in southeast Asia and in Africa against Communist subversion; deny the U.S. the use of important military bases throughout the world.

Often, these appeals to the uncommitted nations are sweetened with Soviet economic-aid offers, designed always to have the maximum political effect; for example, funds for the Aswan Dam in Egypt, a giant steel mill in India, the purchase of Burma's rice surplus, building roads in Afghanistan. This aid-plus-trade routine is not likely to lead these countries into a Soviet harness — with the possible exception of Afghanistan. But it will play a definite role in weakening the ties these countries maintain with the West, as they become more and more dependent upon the Soviet Union for spare parts, technical assistance, and markets for food surpluses.

At the same time, Khrushchev has given greater opportunity to local Communist parties to carry on the struggle to establish their power without the direct intervention of Soviet troops. The most successful drive thus far has been in southeast Asia. Communist guerrillas in South Viet-Nam and northern Laos, following the pattern set down by Mao Tse-tung and later by the Indochinese Communist leader, Ho Chi Minh, threaten to take over vast new areas. While the challenge is not an easy one to meet, the Soviet Union has not always been successful.

For example, the Soviet attempt to develop a territorial base for a Communist sympathizer in the Congo, Antoine Gizenga, failed because the conservative government of the province of Katanga was brought under the control of the liberal central government. Civil war and chaos were avoided, and the Communists lost a target against which to mobilize public opinion.

On the other hand, in Cuba the unpopularity of the abusive, dictatorial Batista regime gave Fidel Castro much against which to rally the Cuban population, despite the fact that many of his early followers were not Communist sympathizers.

V. KHRUSHCHEV AND THE COMMUNIST BLOC

After Stalin's death, Soviet leaders sought to strengthen the unity of the eastern European Communist bloc, but at less economic and political cost to themselves. That is, Khrushchev moved to control the satellites in much the same way he envisaged the CPSU controlling the Soviet Union: without terror, yet without democracy.

The necessity for this was underscored by the economic difficulties in eastern Europe at the time of Stalin's death, troubles that

UNITED PRESS INTERNATIONAL

Freedom fighters head for Budapest during the 1956 Hungarian uprising which was ruthlessly suppressed by the Soviet Army.

were packed with potential revolt. In East Germany, in fact, serious riots did take place in 1953.

One of the first steps toward this moderate relaxation of Moscow's rein on the east European satellites was taken by Khrushchev in his secret speech to the Twentieth Party Congress in 1956 when he condemned Stalin for his brutal methods. Though he did not discuss problems of foreign policy, the implication was clear that Stalinist methods in the satellite countries were to be abolished. The de-Stalinization campaign raced throughout the Communist bloc almost out of control. Some of Khrushchev's remarks were even taken to mean that each country could by itself determine which path to socialism was most correct. In the fall of 1956, discontent in Poland and Hungary—both of which had suffered greatly from Stalinist terror and Soviet economic exploitation— boiled over in violent defiance of the Soviet Union.

In Hungary defiance slipped quickly into an anti-Communist revolution, spearheaded by student freedom fighters who fought barehanded with rocks and shouts against the tanks and machine guns of the Red Army, which was called in to crush the rebellion.

In Poland, Wladyslaw Gomulka, who had been imprisoned for years by Stalin, returned to head the Polish Communist party. Though he promised to keep a Communist dictatorship and maintain ties with Moscow, he introduced changes in the administrative, economic, and intellectual life of Poland to alleviate the burdens on the Polish people.

Staggered by these disturbances, the Kremlin declared that de-Stalinization was not the equivalent of revisionism; that under no conditions should the example of Yugoslavia be taken as a model for changes within the Soviet bloc.

CHINA'S ROLE IN SOVIET POLICY

The years since World War II have seen the emergence of a curious Chinese role in the evolution of Soviet policy. The revolutionaries from Peiping supported both the increased exchange of views in the Communist bloc and the continuation of Soviet leadership of the bloc. However, pointing to Soviet military might, as exemplified by the sputnik launchings, they called for it to be used in an all-out campaign of pressure against the West. This hardly jibed with Premier Khrushchev's peaceful coexistence, and was to become one of the factors in the Moscow-Peiping rift of the 1960's.

During the late 1950's and early 1960's, the Soviet leaders worked hard to hammer out a new personality for the Soviet bloc which would reflect a cross between Stalinism and Titoism. As you remember from the preceding chapter, this same tortuous process was being ground out in the field of intellectual and cultural life. The results of this effort have been unsatisfactory. The debate persists, especially as to the differences between Moscow and Peiping in their views of communism.

Leading the list of difficulties which have disturbed relations between the U.S.S.R. and Communist China is the fact that the countries find themselves in different stages of development. The Chinese are striving to overcome the most fundamental problems of guaranteeing a steady food supply for a population of 600,000,000 and maintaining political control over the countryside. The Soviet Union had solved that problem by the 1930's.

The Communist Chinese are faced with what they regard as a dangerous counterrevolutionary force in the form of Chiang Kai-shek and his bastion on Formosa. Anti-Soviet armies controlling Russian territory were destroyed by 1921.

Apparently the Chinese are still short of Communist-trained technicians and specialists. Again, this problem was resolved in the Soviet Union by the 1930's.

For these reasons, the Chinese Communists feel that their position is less secure than that of the Soviet Communists. The Chinese fear foreign intervention and they exploit this fear in driving their people to work harder for the Communist state. They favor a more aggressive foreign policy to drive United States and SEATO forces from countries along the Chinese frontier: South Korea, Formosa, and Indochina. The Chinese Communists believe that the Soviet Union has not brought enough pressure to bear on the West to force such withdrawals.

On the other hand, the Soviet leaders have become increasingly wary of becoming involved in tests of strength with the United States. They prefer to use their power as an umbrella over local revolutionary movements rather than as a direct challenge to the U.S. China counters this by being cool to the Soviet policy of peaceful coexistence. Open adoption of peaceful coexistence, the Chinese contend, will weaken the revolutionary thrust of Asian and African Communists and delay the final world victory of communism.

For these reasons, Peiping is also eager to secure control of Communist parties in neighboring countries where problems are similar or even more serious. These parties can be used to advance the revolution along the Chinese frontiers and to lend their support to China within the Communist world.

The Chinese Communist leadership is opposed to Soviet *dictation,* but endorses Soviet *leadership* as necessary within the bloc.

Clearly, China aims for a strong role in Communist world policy-making so as to guarantee satisfaction of its particular interests. These conclusions tend to be confirmed by the violent differences between the Soviet and Chinese delegates at the Twenty-second Party Congress. Chinese Communist support of Stalinist Albania in the face of Premier Khrushchev's attacks seems to indicate that China opposes Soviet dictation to one member of the bloc without Chinese consultation. Also, China is disturbed by Soviet reluctance to realize that the needs of local Communists may differ from those of the Soviet Union.

However dramatic the disagreement may seem to observers, there is little proof that it will lead to a major break in the Moscow-Peiping front. The two powers have too much in common for a major break to happen soon. Both adhere to the same version of Marxism-Leninism as a guide to action and a means of organizing and directing their resources toward the goal of world domination.

Geographically placed back to back, they offer the outside world a formidable land mass with enormous populations (more than 800,000,000 together) and great potential economic power. At present the Communist Chinese rely heavily on Soviet economic and technical assistance; in the future, China may serve as an untapped market for Soviet industrial products.

China is also dependent on the Soviet Union for military support in an armed showdown with the Western powers over crises such as those brewing in southeast Asia. In return the Soviet Union relies on Communist China to serve as a staging area for further Communist penetration of Asia.

The Chinese example of revolution and industrialization serves as a powerful attraction for many underdeveloped areas, as Moscow views its Asian ally. As an Asian power, China is better suited than the Soviet Union to represent Asian interests at international conferences.

To a continent long dominated by and hostile to the white man, the Chinese Communists pose as the champions of anticolonial forces. As long as Japan remains largely uncommitted politically, the U.S. has no comparable counterweight in the Far East.

These common ties are likely to withstand the strains and tensions of the foreseeable future. It is undeniable, however, that the Soviet bloc has become more diversified than ever before. Differences of opinion between Gomulka of Poland and Ulbricht in East Germany, or between the Chinese and the Russians, are almost certain to continue. But compromise, rather than disintegration, is more likely to resolve them.

Communist China is a primitive nation industrially. Man power is cheap and readily available.

While Soviet power is the mightiest in the Communist bloc and continues unchallenged, it has seen fit to diminish its hegemony over the bloc. The relationship between the Soviet Communist party and the local Communist parties of the bloc has changed from the Stalinist model. Moscow now realizes that its domination of the bloc is guaranteed by the bipolar world in which it lives.

At the beginning of the 1960's, the local Communist parties, including the Chinese, depended upon the Soviet Union for protection — witness the Hungarian revolution of 1956. Therefore, these parties lean toward the Soviet political-ideological line without the old cudgel of Stalinist terror being held over them. The slight degree of maneuverability which they gain relieves the Soviet Union of a large measure of political attention and strain and may even help woo emerging nations of Asia and Africa into the bloc. It is important here to note that representatives of Ghana, Mali, and Guinea were present at the Twenty-second Party Congress, though none of these countries is run by Communists.

SUMMARY

The Soviet Union conducts its foreign policy both through traditional diplomacy in political, economic, and military affairs and through millions of people in many countries who belong to the local Communist parties.

Soviet leaders have won many successes in eastern Europe and southeast Asia by a combination of tough and varied tactics. But

The production of iron and steel is a critical problem in Communist China. This blast furnace, the first ever to be put into operation in Shanghai, is expected to produce 125,000 tons of pig iron annually. By comparison, an average-size blast furnace in the United States has a capacity three times as great. Total annual capacity of the 263 blast furnaces in the United States is 96.5 million tons.

rigid thinking and serious miscalculations have led also to numerous and noteworthy failures of Soviet policy in western Europe, Africa, and the Middle East.

Abroad, as at home, Soviet leaders have often been forced to improvise and learn through trial and error. Their overall plan for world conquest does not provide them with a ready-made answer to every international problem.

Today the Stalinist technique of spreading revolution primarily by means of the Red Army has given way to a more flexible program. Moscow is now capable of inciting and manipulating several crises simultaneously. These tactics seem designed to avoid all-out war while attempting to win the world by a combination of military bluff and internal subversion aimed at breaking up the Western alliance.

UNITED PRESS INTERNATIONAL

TERMS TO KNOW

Yalta Conference	*Kuomintang*	Cominform
Treaty of Brest Litovsk	peaceful coexistence	Kellogg-Briand Pact
Comintern	Popular Front	Warsaw Pact

QUESTIONS ON THE CHAPTER

1. For what reasons did Lenin seek peace with Germany in 1918?
2. What were the chief purposes of the Third (Communist) International?
3. When it became clear in 1921 that a general Communist revolution was unlikely to break out in the Western nations, what policy did Lenin adopt?
4. Between 1921 and 1924, Soviet diplomatic tactics aimed at three goals. What were these goals?

5. Briefly explain how Stalin's policy toward the German Socialists aided the rise of Hitler and the Nazi party in Germany.

6. What were the aims of the Popular Front?

7. Describe briefly the general pattern followed by Communists in their attempts to seize power in eastern European countries after World War II.

8. In a few words, tell what steps were taken by the Soviet Union, after Stalin's death, to improve relations with certain countries such as Turkey, Finland, and Yugoslavia.

9. The program suggested to neutral nations by Premier Khrushchev in 1956 and 1961 consisted of what major proposals?

10. Give some results of Khrushchev's de-Stalinization campaign.

11. What are some of the differences of opinion which have disturbed relations between the Soviet Union and Communist China?

QUESTIONS FOR DISCUSSION

1. Communist tactics in foreign affairs have shifted many times, although their final goals have remained the same. Give some examples which show how Soviet foreign policy has changed from time to time without altering its ultimate aim of achieving world communism.

2. Both Lenin and Khrushchev at one time or another advocated a policy of peaceful coexistence. Briefly compare both Lenin's and Khrushchev's views on this policy. For example, did either or both leaders indicate whether peaceful coexistence among Communist and non-Communist nations could be permanent?

3. The Chinese Communist leaders oppose Soviet dictation, but they approve of Soviet leadership among Communist nations. In what way does this attitude agree with or differ from that of Marshal Tito and the Yugoslav Communists?

4. Soviet Communists sacrificed Communist parties in Germany, Spain, and China, to further their own ends. They allowed the Nazis, the fascist-backed Spanish revolutionaries under General Franco, and the Chinese *Kuomintang* to gain power at the expense of the local Communist parties. Discuss some of the reasons why they did this.

BIBLIOGRAPHY

For Reference: □ Adams, Arthur E., *Readings in Soviet Foreign Policy: Theory and Practice.* D. C. Heath & Company, 1961. □ Kennan, George F., *Russia and the West Under Lenin and Stalin.* Little, Brown & Company, 1961. □ Kulski, W. W., *Peaceful Co-existence: An Analysis of Soviet Foreign Policy.* Henry Regnery Company, 1959. □ Mosely, Philip E., *The Kremlin and World Politics: Studies in Soviet Policy and Action.* Vintage Books, 1960. For Further Reading: Cole, Allan B., *Forty Years of Chinese Communism.* American Historical Association, Service Center for Teachers of History, 1962. □ Jackson, W. A. Douglas, *Russo-Chinese Borderlands: Zone of Peaceful Contact or Potential Conflict?* Searchlight Books, 1962. □ Maclean, Sir Fitzroy, *Heretic. The Life and Times of Josip Broz-Tito.* Harper and Brothers, 1957. □ Salisbury, Harrison E., *Khrushchev's "Mein Kampf".* Belmont Books, 1961.

CHAPTER 8

BLACK STAR

THE WORLD'S RESPONSE TO COMMUNISM

Since the end of World War II,
the United States has adopted
a variety of policies—containment,
massive retaliation, economic warfare—
to meet the threat of Soviet power.

Until the United States became involved in World War II, its relations with the Soviet Union had been either distant or non-existent. During the early days of the revolution, the United States reluctantly participated in the intervention on Russian soil, but soon withdrew its troops.

Only in 1933 did this country officially recognize the Soviet Union. Then the Soviet Union promised to refrain from Communist propaganda in this country and to pay on the debt owed to the United States by the old Russian monarchy. These promises were never carried out. The hope of the first American ambassador to Moscow that arrangements could be reached by mutual trust was doomed to frustration.

Winston Churchill: "From what I have seen of our Russian friends and allies during the war, I am convinced that there is nothing they admire so much as strength, and there is nothing for which they have less respect than weakness. For that reason the old doctrine of a balance of power is unsound. We cannot afford, if we can help it, to work on narrow margins, offering temptations to a trial of strength. If the Western democracies stand together in strict adherence to the principles of the United Nations Charter, their influence for furthering those principles will be immense and no one will be likely to molest them."

I. THE WARTIME COALITION

When the Soviet Union was attacked by Nazi Germany in 1941, the United States extended lend-lease aid to Moscow. After the United States entered the war, a slow process of building up military and economic coöperation with the anti-Hitler coalition began. The war itself served to chasten the strong group of isolationists in the U.S. Congress. After being informed of the Japanese attack on Pearl Harbor, Republican Senator Arthur Vandenberg, one of the leading advocates of isolationism, stated: "In my own mind, my convictions regarding international coöperation and collective security for peace took form on the afternoon of the Pearl Harbor attack. That day ended isolationism for any realist."

But most Americans were not prepared to go much further at

this time than supporting a vigorous war effort. At Yalta in 1945, President Franklin D. Roosevelt told Stalin and Great Britain's Winston Churchill that he doubted the willingness of the American people after the war to agree to stationing American forces in foreign countries. In certain branches of the U.S. government, especially the War Department, there was strong sentiment against committing the United States to occupying parts of Germany and, more particularly, Austria after the war.

In dealing with Soviet leaders during the war, Roosevelt attempted to do two things: first, to convince Stalin that cordial and fruitful relations between the two countries were possible, and second, to bring the Soviet Union into a new international organization to keep the peace. Roosevelt tended, as his words reveal, to keep discussions with Stalin and Churchill confined to generalizations, at least up to the conference at Yalta in 1945. Reporting on the previous conference at Teheran in 1943, for example, Roosevelt stated: "We did discuss international relationships from the point of view of the big, broad objectives, rather than details. But on the basis of what we did discuss, I can say even today that I do not think any insoluble differences will arise among Russia, Great Britain, and the United States. In these conferences we were concerned with basic principles—principles which involve the security and welfare and the standards of living of human beings in countries large and small."

Specialists in Soviet affairs in the State Department warned against taking seriously Soviet adherence to declarations of principle. Soviet affairs specialist Philip E. Mosely stated that the failure at Yalta to propose practical means of enforcing principles meant that "The opportunity, perhaps the last during the war, to assure a more active and perhaps more effective participation by the United States in the wartime and postwar reshaping of East Central Europe was lost."

But the winning of the war and the formation of the United Nations appeared in those years to overshadow long-range political problems involving the Soviet Union and its Communist designs.

After the Yalta Conference and President Roosevelt's death (April 12, 1945) the outlines of the Soviet threat to the independence of the eastern European countries became unmistakably clear. The United States ambassador to Russia, W. Averill Harriman, told President Harry S. Truman that the United States was faced with a "barbarian invasion of Europe."

AMERICAN POLICY IN FLUX

Soon after the war Churchill argued that American and British troops should not withdraw from their advanced positions in Germany to the lines of military occupation already agreed upon until "the settlement of many things which would be the true foundation of world peace."

President Truman was reluctant to delay withdrawal, believing that the Soviet leaders would look upon this violation of an agreement as a breakdown of relations, thus making impossible any further negotiation between the U.S. and the U.S.S.R. He counted heavily on the United Nations to provide the framework in which negotiations could be carried on without recourse to arms. The successful testing of the atom bomb in the summer of 1945 contributed to Truman's belief that the United States would have sufficient power to defend its interests in the postwar world. He also believed that Soviet Russia would be too weakened by war to threaten the peace. As Soviet pressures increased, the U.S. government slowly adopted the position that these threats had to be resisted with force. As early as January 1946, Truman reacted strongly against Soviet belligerence toward Turkey and the presence of Soviet forces in Iran.

"Unless Russia is faced with an iron fist and strong language, another war is in the making," said Truman. "Only one language do they understand—'how many divisions have you' . . . I'm tired of babying the Soviets." The American people, however, were as reluctant to accept this view as they had been in the 1930's to accept Roosevelt's warnings about Nazi Germany. Furthermore, no group in the United States was at this time prepared to put forward any clear-cut plan to counter Soviet influence.

In fact, when Winston Churchill visited this country in 1946 and offered a powerful Anglo-American alliance because "there is nothing they [the Russians] admire so much as strength, and there is nothing for which they have less respect than for military weakness," he was criticized by many of the same people who were urging in Congress that the United States get tough. Even though they had no other policy to offer in its place, these critics scorned Churchill for dragging the U.S. into Europe's quarrels.

By this time, Republican leadership in Congress was vigorously criticizing the U.S. policy. In late 1945, a joint Senate-House committee of Republicans stated: "We believe in fulfilling to the

UNITED PRESS INTERNATIONAL

Former President Harry S. Truman: "We seek to use our military strength solely to preserve the peace of the world. For we now know that that is the only sure way to make our own freedom secure. That is the basis of the foreign policy of the United States. . . ."

George C. Marshall, former U.S. Secretary of State: "Our policy is directed not against any country or doctrine but against hunger, poverty, desperation and chaos. Its purpose should be the revival of a working economy in the world so as to permit the emergence of political and social conditions in which free institutions can exist."

Former President Dwight D. Eisenhower: "If we are going to continue to be proud that we are Americans there must be no weakening of the codes by which we have lived; by the right to meet your accuser face to face, if you have one; by your right to go to the church or the synagogue or even the mosque of your own choosing; by your right to speak your mind and be protected in it."

greatest possible degree our war pledges to small nations that they shall have the right to choose the form of government under which they will live, and that sovereign rights, and self-government shall be restored to those who have been forcibly deprived of them." Senator Vandenberg added: "The situation calls for patience and good will; it does not call for vacillation." However, the Republican leadership still had not put forward any clear-cut plan for fulfilling these war pledges in the face of Soviet pressure.

Meanwhile, the U.S. State Department continued to encourage President Truman to get tougher with the Russians. But from no quarter, did any detailed program emerge.

AMERICAN BIPARTISAN FOREIGN POLICY

After 1946 Republican congressmen began to back the administration in its increasingly firm stand. At this time the bipartisan foreign policy worked out between Republican and Democratic leaders (largely forged by Senator Vandenberg) was sharply attacked by Secretary of Commerce Henry Wallace, the former vice-president under Roosevelt, who called for peaceful competition with the U.S.S.R. "On our part," he said, "we should recognize that we have no more business in the political affairs of Eastern Europe than Russia has in the political affairs of Latin America, Western Europe, and the United States."

Thus, by 1947, American leaders of both political parties were moving toward defensive resistance. But Henry Wallace and the small group of Democrats following him still wanted to work harder for a compromise with the U.S.S.R. on the basis of recognizing Soviet power where it stood and assuming it would go no farther. Senator Robert Taft and Republicans loyal to him united to denounce the Soviet Union for violating the Yalta agreements, but they opposed military or economic programs which would involve the United States in European affairs. Most political leaders were hesitant to take too strong a stand because they were far from certain about the sentiments of the U.S. public.

II. THE TRUMAN DOCTRINE, THE MARSHALL PLAN, AND CONTAINMENT

The first attempt by the United States to apply a consistent policy toward the Soviet Union was called the policy of containment. It came in the wake of the Truman Doctrine and the Marshall Plan.

In 1947 the United States government decided to extend economic aid to Greece and Turkey, both strategically important because of their position on the southern flank of Europe and both under heavy pressure from the Soviet Union or from local Communists. President Truman supported this aid by stating: "I believe that it must be the policy of the United States to support free peoples who are resisting attempted subjugation by armed minorities or by outside pressures. I believe that our help should be primarily through economic and financial aid which is essential to economic stability and orderly political processes."

It soon became clear to American leaders that the economic destruction wrought by the war in Europe had been so great that individual European countries could not rebuild without some outside help. Secretary of State George C. Marshall urged that "the United States should do whatever it is able to do to assist in the return of normal economic health in the world, without which there can be no political stability and no assured peace." He then called for "some agreement among the countries of Europe as to the requirements of the situation and the part those countries themselves will play in order to give proper effect to whatever action might be undertaken by this [the United States] government." In a spirit of mutual coöperation, the United States launched the Marshall Plan to help economic rehabilitation in Europe.

At the same time George F. Kennan, Soviet affairs expert, set down the theoretical basis for the emerging American policy. After pointing out the fundamental antagonism between the Soviet Union and the United States and the aggressive nature of Soviet communism, he stated: "Under these circumstances, it is clear that the main element of any United States policy toward the Soviet Union must be that of a long-term, patient, but firm and vigilant containment of Russian expansive tendencies." Kennan hoped that in the long run the superiority of the American economic system would prove itself and that Soviet power would slowly erode until its challenge to the Free World would diminish.

The U.S. decision to contain communism applied at first largely to the European continent, for the dividing line between East and West was clear. In Asia, however, the situation was in flux.

THE CHINA PROBLEM

U.S. policy toward China during the Chinese Civil War illustrates the challenge of policy-making in the face of sharply conflicting opinions of U.S. leaders as to how far the United States could go in its policy of containment.

The long-smoldering Civil War in China, between the Chinese Nationalists under Chiang Kai-shek and the Chinese Communists under Mao Tse-tung, broke out again in 1945. The United States was immediately confronted with three possible courses of action. First, it could keep hands off the Chinese war, leaving the participants to fight it out alone. Second, it could try to bring about a peaceful settlement of the war through negotiation. Third, it could commit itself to all-out support of the Chinese Nationalists against the Communists. The official attitude of the government shifted between positions two and three.

In the four postwar years 1945-1949, the United States sent Chiang $2 billion in aid and helped airlift Chinese forces to reoccupy areas under Japanese control before the Chinese Communists could move in. At the same time the United States urged Chiang to end the Chinese Civil War by forming a coalition government with the Communists. The U.S. reasoned that Chiang might not be strong enough to crush the Chinese Communists (he had been fighting them off and on since 1927) without massive U.S. aid. The U.S. argued that for the United States to help Chiang crush the Communists would require billions more dollars and a large investment of U.S. troops and weapons at a time when the U.S. public already was urging rapid demobilization of the armed forces, and the government was reluctant to resist these grass-roots pressures. In addition, the U.S. considered Europe its first, and most important, line of defense. The fate of China was of secondary importance.

Most of all, the U.S. felt that Chiang's government was so corrupt and unpopular in China that it was defeating itself despite its superiority in weapons and military forces.

In 1946 and 1947 the Marshall and Wedemeyer missions were sent to China to survey the situation. Efforts to bring the warring factions together proved futile. General Albert Wedemeyer recommended continued support to Chiang but admitted that the Chinese Nationalists had little chance of success. The American policy then became one of limited support. After the collapse of the Nationalist forces in 1949, Secretary of State Dean Acheson gave a concise definition of the government's position during the conflict: "Nothing that this country did or could have done within the reasonable limits of its capabilities would have changed the result; nothing that was left undone by this country has contributed to it."

Critics of the China policy—especially after 1947—maintained that the United States had not done enough to save Chiang's government and his forces. More seriously, they charged that the U.S. State Department personnel were sympathetic to the Chinese Communist cause. In 1951 Senator Joseph R. McCarthy of Wisconsin charged that the State Department "was infested by Communists," and this, he said, explained the fall of China. Those strongly supporting Chiang after 1950, including Senator William Knowland of California and former President Herbert Hoover, urged that the United States help Chiang return to the Asian mainland in a campaign to liberate China.

President Truman replied: "The United States government will not pursue a course which will lead to involvement in the civil conflict in China." Subsequently U.S. aid to Chiang was scaled down substantially.

MILITARY CONTAINMENT

The Soviet advance in Europe continued. In 1948, the democratic republic of Czechoslovakia was overthrown by a combination of internal subversion and outside pressure from the Soviet Army poised along the Czech frontiers. In the same year, the Soviet Union blockaded Berlin.

United States response to the Berlin blockade was swift. It was not ready to see the defeat of democracy, as in Czechoslovakia, repeated. Support from political leaders and the public was almost unanimous. A massive airlift of more than 2 million tons of food and coal continued for six months, sustaining beleaguered Berlin.

President Truman decided to support a military alliance of western European countries against continued Soviet pressure. Congress backed him. In 1949 the United States, Canada, and ten European nations joined in forming the North Atlantic Treaty Organization (NATO). This alliance held that "an armed attack against one or more of them in Europe or North America shall be considered an attack against them all." This was the concept of military containment.

NATO relied on the idea of the sword and shield, that is, a combination of massive air power backed by U.S. atomic weapons and ground forces capable of resisting an initial attack by the Soviet Army from the east. New U.S. bases were built overseas to bring air and land forces within striking distance of the Soviet Union. However, the United States did not at once extend this concept of military containment beyond Europe to other areas of the world.

Under Soviet pressure, the United States had shifted from economic aid in Europe (Marshall Plan and Truman Doctrine) and a combination of economic and military aid in Asia to actual participation in a military alliance against Soviet expansion. Although this alliance was not a complete solution to the problem of Soviet expansion, it marked an important stage in the history of the United States and its efforts to counter the Soviet challenge.

III. THE KOREAN WAR

The invasion of South Korea by Communist North Koreans in 1950 brought home to the United States government the further need for military defenses in the Far East. It also raised the stubborn question of what kind of war should be fought against local Communist forces operating under Moscow's orders but without the participation of Soviet troops.

The initial attack by the North Koreans made it clear that the South Koreans were not going to be able to hold their own. The United Nations condemned North Korea as an aggressor and called upon all nations to render aid to South Korea.

President Truman acknowledged that "The attack upon Korea makes it plain beyond all doubt that communism has passed beyond the use of subversion to conquer independent nations, and will now use armed invasion and force." He then, without asking Congress to declare war, ordered U.S. air and naval forces to support the South Koreans. Troops were sent later. The U.S. fleet was also sent to protect Formosa, the new bastion of the Chinese Nationalists. As in the case of Berlin, support from the U.S. public and Congress was vigorous.

However, the problem of checking the Communist advance became acute when the successful United Nations counterattack was met by a massive intervention of Communist Chinese forces flooding into North Korea. General Douglas MacArthur, United Nations commander on the scene, maintained that this was an entirely new war. To meet this threat he advocated a four-point program: (1) the intensification of American economic sanctions against China; (2) the imposition of a naval blockade against the China coast; (3) the removal of restrictions on air reconnaissance of China's coastal areas and of Manchuria; (4) the removal of restrictions on the forces of the Republic of China, in Formosa, with logistic support, to contribute to their effective operation against the Chinese mainland. He opposed sending ground troops into China.

MacArthur further argued: "Once war is forced upon us, there is no other alternative than to apply every available means to bring it to a swift end. War's very object is victory, not prolonged indecision."

President Truman saw things differently. In a message to General MacArthur he outlined the official U.S. position: "Our course of action at this time should be such as to consolidate the great majority of the United Nations. This majority is not merely part of the organization but is also the nations whom we would desperately need to count on as allies in the event that the Soviet Union moves against us. Further, pending the buildup of our national strength, we must act with great prudence insofar as extending the area of hostilities is concerned. Steps which might in themselves be fully justified and which might lend some assistance to the war in Korea would not be beneficial if they thereby involved Japan or Western Europe in large-scale hostilities."

General Omar Bradley supported the President by maintaining that a conflict with China would be "the wrong war, at the wrong time, and with the wrong enemy."

What was at issue, therefore, was not whether to contain communism, but how best to do it. General MacArthur and his supporters stood for a strong military effort to defeat and roll back the Chinese, fully understanding the risk, but doubting the possibility of a general war with China and the Soviet Union.

President Truman and his advisers stood for a limited war to contain Communist aggression without committing the United States to a war effort which might lead to World War III or pin American forces down in Asia while the Soviet Union mounted some new attack in Europe.

One of the major factors in this dispute was the relative strength of the United States and the Soviet Union. By 1949 the Soviet Union had the atom bomb. It was never certain to either MacArthur or Truman whether the Soviet Union was prepared to support China and thus touch off an atomic war. Each was convinced that his way of checking communism was ultimately the most effective. The debate in the United States over the means to do this continued even after the dramatic dismissal of MacArthur by the President for disregarding orders from the White House.

IV. LIBERATION AND MASSIVE RETALIATION

As the Korean war dragged on inconclusively, some members of the Republican party urged the replacement of the policy of containment with what they called a combination of liberation and massive retaliation. The spokesman for this view, John Foster Dulles, became Secretary of State in 1953 under the first postwar

Republican government, led by Dwight D. Eisenhower. Secretary Dulles maintained that the U.S. should develop a program that would "mark the end of the negative, futile, and immoral policy of 'containment' which abandons countless human beings to a despotism and Godless terrorism which in turn enables the rulers to forge their captives into a weapon for our destruction." In contrast, Dulles promised a policy to liberate peoples from the Soviet system. His most precise statement on this matter declared: "Liberation normally comes from within. But it is more apt to come from within if hope is constantly sustained from without. This is what we are doing in many ways."

To bolster this policy, Secretary Dulles urged that the United States rely upon its newly developed hydrogen weapons as a means of forcing the Soviet Union to back down in crises. The policy of limited wars was to be discarded for a policy resting upon "the deterrent of massive retaliatory power . . . a great capacity to retaliate instantly, by means and at times of our own choosing."

Massive retaliation met its supreme policy test in the Indochina crisis of 1954. The French Army was on the brink of military disaster in the French colony, and without U.S. aid there was little doubt that much of this southeast Asian territory would fall to communism. Secretary Dulles did not urge using massive retaliation against the Communist Chinese who were helping the local Communists. His attempt to obtain approval of United States allies for air strikes against the Communist forces failed. Congressional leaders of both parties were unwilling to go into a limited campaign on the order of the Korean war. As a result northern Indochina fell to the Communists.

The problem in the case of Indochina seems to be that there was no overt evidence of outside aid to the Indochinese Communist rebels. Aid probably did arrive from Communist China and the Soviet Union, but it came in clandestinely to bolster the internal subversion of local Communists. The problem, therefore, appeared to be a domestic one. And neither containment nor massive retaliation was designed to counter this tactic.

ANTI-COMMUNIST PACTS

One way to meet such subversive challenges, Secretary Dulles reasoned, was to strengthen and increase the anti-Communist military pacts around the world. In 1954 the Southeast Asia Treaty Organization (SEATO) was formed. Differing from NATO, its European counterpart, SEATO included only a few of the countries in the area.

The members of SEATO were Pakistan, Thailand, the Philippines, the United States, Great Britain, France, Australia, and New Zealand. The states newly carved out of Indochina (Laos, Cambodia, and Viet-Nam, the latter soon to split into northern and southern territories with the northern Viet Minh district under a Communist constitution) were not members. Nor were India, Burma, Ceylon, and Indonesia.

In 1955 West Germany was brought into NATO, and a new regional defense organization, the Baghdad Pact, later (1959) to be designated the Central Treaty Organization for the Middle East (CENTO), came into being. But with CENTO, as with SEATO, its membership did not include many of the countries in the area. Officially not even the United States was a member except indirectly through bilateral treaties with CENTO members—Iran, Pakistan, Turkey, and Great Britain. Iraq dropped its membership in 1958.

Following the Korean war, both Democratic and Republican administrations placed increased emphasis on such alliances to expedite the military containment of communism. This policy had succeeded in checking Soviet advances in some instances. However, new tactics devised by the Soviet Union after Stalin's death and its development of nuclear strength equal to that of the United States forced the policy makers of the Free World to revise their strategy.

THE SEARCH FOR A NEW POLICY

Between 1956 and 1958 three critical events occurred which pressed the United States to forge a new, more flexible foreign policy. First, in October 1956, was the anti-Communist democratic uprising of the Hungarian people. Second, in early 1957, was a period of crisis in the Middle East. Third, in July 1958, was an alleged Soviet-United Arab Republic effort to engineer the overthrow of the government of Lebanon.

The Hungarian uprising appeared to be succeeding until the Soviet Army entered Hungary to crush the uprising. Although

Earl Warren, Chief Justice of the U.S. Supreme Court: "Our Bill of Rights, the most precious part of our legal heritage, is under subtile and pervasive attacks. . . .In the struggle between our world and Communism, the temptation to initiate totalitarian security methods must be resisted day by day. . . .When the rights of any individual or group are chipped away, the freedom of all erodes."

John Foster Dulles, former U.S. Secretary of State: "It is our own policy to check the Communist use of threat of force by having retaliatory power and the will to use it, so that the Communist use of force would obviously be unprofitable to them."

Dean Rusk, U.S. Secretary of State: ". . . the Western world must recapture the leadership of its own revolution of political freedom. It is a revolution which the West itself has taken into every continent and which continues to stir men to action. This struggle for freedom in the West itself was not painless, nor will it be in other places in our own time. But we dare not yield its leadership to those who would seize it, subvert it and use it to destroy us."

the United States was at this time committed to the policy of liberation, it made no active move to support the Hungarians. The U.S. condemned the Soviet Union for its aggression in the conflict, but this was no more than it had done in 1945 and 1946, when the Soviet Union first asserted its postwar control over Hungary and the other countries of eastern Europe. Had the United States intervened in Hungary, there is little doubt that war with the Soviet Union would have occurred. The U.S. was not prepared to carry its policy of liberation to that extreme.

In 1957, the mood of the Middle East was troubled. The American Sixth Fleet was shifted to the eastern Mediterranean to show its force in the face of revolts such as that which tried to topple young King Hussein of Jordan. In response to the unstable situation, President Eisenhower enunciated the Eisenhower Doctrine to give economic aid to those nations in the Middle East "desiring

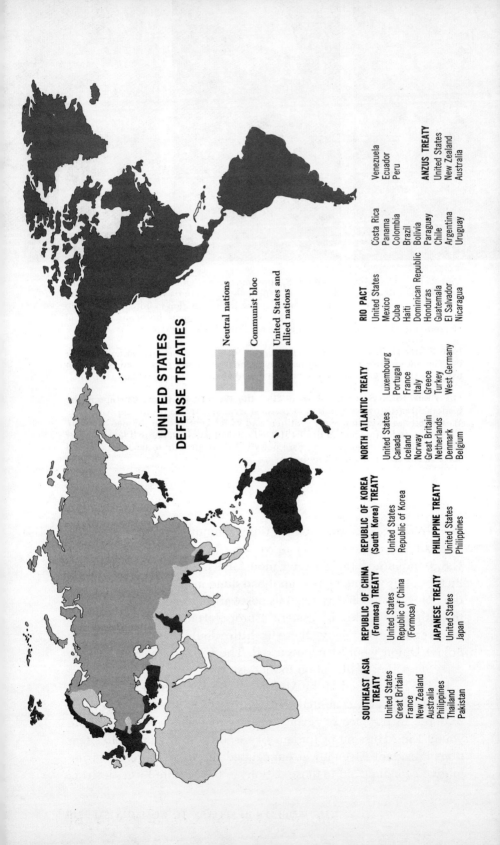

UNITED STATES
DEFENSE TREATIES

Neutral nations

Communist bloc

United States and
allied nations

**SOUTHEAST ASIA
TREATY**

United States
Great Britain
France
New Zealand
Australia
Philippines
Thailand
Pakistan

**REPUBLIC OF CHINA
(Formosa) TREATY**

United States
Republic of China
(Formosa)

JAPANESE TREATY

United States
Japan

**REPUBLIC OF KOREA
(South Korea) TREATY**

United States
Republic of Korea

PHILIPPINE TREATY

United States
Philippines

NORTH ATLANTIC TREATY

United States
Canada
Iceland
Norway
Great Britain
Netherlands
Denmark
Belgium

Luxembourg
Portugal
France
Italy
Greece
Turkey
West Germany

RIO PACT

United States
Mexico
Cuba
Haiti
Dominican Republic
Honduras
Guatemala
El Salvador
Nicaragua

Costa Rica
Panama
Colombia
Brazil
Bolivia
Paraguay
Chile
Argentina
Uruguay

Venezuela
Ecuador
Peru

ANZUS TREATY

United States
New Zealand
Australia

such assistance in the development of economic strength dedicated to the maintenance of national independence."

The doctrine added that "if the President determines the necessity thereof, the United States is prepared to use armed forces to assist any such nation or group of such nations requesting assistance against armed aggression from any country controlled by international communism."

In 1958 an appeal by the president of Lebanon for just such assistance was answered by the dispatch of American troops to Lebanon to save the government.

Almost simultaneously, half a world away, Communist rebels in Laos began to move into action against the U.S.-supported government there.

The problem raised by the Middle Eastern crises was, as in Indochina, one of surprisingly active local Communists. Much more active than in Stalin's time, they were threatening to overthrow existing anti-Communist governments primarily through internal subversion.

While these local Communist operations moved into action, Soviet diplomacy went to work on splitting the Western Free World alliance. In 1958 Premier Khrushchev demanded that the Western powers leave Berlin and create a united free city, which would have been at the mercy of East Germany. At the same time he put increased pressure on the United States to meet at a summit conference to settle the world's outstanding problems.

In 1959 President Eisenhower invited Premier Khrushchev to the United States. While on his visit, the Soviet leader tried to present an image of sweet reasonableness, urging a summit conference for 1960. Since there was disagreement among the Western Allies as to the usefulness of such a meeting, Premier Khrushchev found Western policies highly vulnerable to his propaganda and policy gambits.

In May 1960, an American high-altitude reconnaissance aircraft, the U-2, was shot down over the Soviet Union. Premier Khrushchev stormily demanded a U.S. apology, wrecked the proposed Paris summit conference, and generally made certain that circumstances continued sufficiently troubled to block a good-will visit by President Eisenhower to the Soviet Union.

At the end of his second term, in 1960, the President was striving for all possible ways "to search out methods by which peace in the world can be assured with justice for everybody." The policies of liberation and massive retaliation had been set aside. Soviet nuclear power was growing, and local Communists were stepping up their subversive maneuvers, taking power in Cuba without any form of external attack. American leaders of both political parties tried a variety of approaches to the vexations of the international Communist challenge, while the threat of catastrophic nuclear war loomed ever more darkly.

THE "NEW FRONTIER"

When the Kennedy administration took office in 1961, it immediately faced the full catalogue of Communist problems: Cuba, Laos, the Congo, Berlin, and nuclear disarmament, which reflected the growing ability of the Soviet Union to drive multi-pronged threats deep into the Free World.

In response the new U.S. administration feebly supported the abortive invasion of Cuba in the spring of 1961. It refused to recognize the Soviet right to turn over control of access routes to Berlin to the East Germans and reinforced the Western garrison in the city. It tried to bring about an end to fighting in southeast Asia by encouraging the formation of a coalition government in Laos. It supported and trained South Viet-Nam non-Communist troops to fight the guerrilla threat against the government. It supported the United Nations policy in the Congo of attempting to hold the new Congo nation together and preventing Communists from taking advantage of a civil war to plunge the whole area into chaos.

In the early days of the administration, a pattern was difficult to discern in these scattered actions, but in the second year (1962) a world policy was definitely taking shape.

V. PRAGMATISM AND FLEXIBILITY

United States policy in 1962 was summed up in a *New York Times* report: "We will prepare for the worst; we will not be misled by our opponents or misdirected by our allies; we will not be soft toward the nonaligned. Yet, we will not be inflexible; we will always be ready to negotiate when there is the faintest chance that negotiation will succeed."

The new administration viewed both the containment policy

(primarily defensive) and the massive retaliation policy (primarily offensive) as too inflexible to meet the global challenge of communism in the 1960's. The United States must draw on just as varied an arsenal of policy weapons as that of the Soviet Union, the strategists of the Kennedy administration declared. Each crisis was to be met in terms of its particular characteristics and at two levels: (1) the local, with all its prospects and dangers, and (2) the world—that is, the relationship of the local problem to international affairs, including Soviet strategy, the views of the Western Allies, and U.S. capabilities.

KENNEDY POLICIES IN PRACTICE

President Kennedy supported a policy of military preparedness to hold in check the growing military might of the Soviet Union. This policy has meant enormous defense expenditures (more than $45 billion in the fiscal year 1961) and a resumption of nuclear weapons testing in the spring of 1962 to keep pace with the Soviet Union, which initially violated the moratorium on atomic testing. The President stated that without such military preparedness, the United States would find itself vulnerable to Soviet political aggression that was backed with superior military power.

"The most novel and alarming aspect of Khrushchev's apparent view of nuclear strategy," Philip E. Mosely, the Russian scholar, notes "is his conviction that the Soviet leadership is now [the 1960's] in a stronger position than the democratic West to force a new crisis close to the brink of war and to compel the other side to flinch from this fateful decision. Instead of bringing to the Soviet leadership a greater sense of power and security, the achievement of nuclear parity—combined with some slight and uncertain margin of missile superiority—has raised the level of risks, stepped up the frequency of crises, and increased the danger of war."

President Kennedy reassured United States allies that they need not fear nuclear blackmail, that is, a Soviet threat to destroy a small Western Ally on the assumption that the United States will not retaliate in order to avoid unleashing a world nuclear war, thus sacrificing the ally to preserve peace.

Thus the leading U.S. strategists of the 1960's reasoned that the Soviet Union should never be permitted to gain such a military advantage. Continued U.S. experiments with military technology—

weapons delivery systems, and weapons detection systems—have been encouraged by the administration.

Another aspect of the Kennedy policy toward the Soviet Union was to develop a flexible striking force of conventional military capacities, to be ready to counter any limited or local Communist thrust anywhere in the world. Planners were determined to keep the United States from being caught between the choice of having to start a nuclear war to halt a Communist raid or sit helplessly by while that raid was carried out.

Meeting strength with strength was but one phase of current policy. Another was to make every effort to settle the recurring problems between the Soviet Union and the United States so that small crises would not spawn major ones. Therefore, negotiations proceeded on disarmament, on limiting arms, on Berlin and Laos, on cultural and scientific exchanges, on joint exploration of space.

Negotiators for the West found that it is important to let the other side know what it stands for, in order to prevent miscalculations such as that which led to the Communist invasion of South Korea. By engaging in constant exchanges of opinion, Western negotiators argued that Soviet leaders might be drawn into discussions which would help correct many of Moscow's misconceptions about the hostility of the so-called capitalist world.

Exchange of cultural, scientific, and educational people, for example, gives the Soviet elite a chance to see for themselves the strength of American resolve and the dynamic character of American society. Americans in the Soviet Union are beginning to break down the barrier of misinformation there.

Consequently, Soviet policy makers are no longer relying exclusively on reports from their representatives abroad, which often were designed to include what would please the Kremlin.

The Kennedy administration has sought to avoid much-ballyhooed summit meetings, preferring instead to work more quietly in diplomacy at lower levels. Washington has become increasingly wary of being forced to the conference table to rehash old problems with Soviet leaders unless settlement of at least one of them is highly probable.

Thus U.S. policy on negotiation has two sides: (1) negotiations are in order where power is balanced, and (2) intensive competition is in order where power is not balanced.

The United States concludes that NATO presently stands as its most reliable and necessary alliance. With its large population, great resources, tradition of democratic practices, widespread influence in Asia and Africa, and advanced bases, and even with its nationalistic frictions, Europe remains a bulwark thwarting Communist ambitions.

The loss or neutralization of Europe would isolate the United States militarily and economically, foreshadowing almost certain Free World decline and defeat. The Kennedy administration is committed wholeheartedly to defending every inch of free territory in Europe, including West Berlin. The shield of United States power is still Europe's main guarantee of freedom.

Yet, this close relationship with Europe does not mean, according to Washington's policy makers, the automatic acceptance by Europe of American ideas. The alliance must be one of sovereign states sharing common interests and responsibilities.

VI. U.S. POLICY AND THE UNDERDEVELOPED WORLD

Until 1960 the United States had borne the bulk of the burden of economic aid to unstable countries and new nations. Since then the U.S. has called on the prosperous nations of Europe (helped to their prosperity by the Marshall Plan) to do for others what was done for them.

Soviet-U.S. competition in foreign aid has grown increasingly intense and significant. In searching for effective techniques in this field, both sides have committed ludicrous blunders: complex U.S. farm equipment has gone to areas where only the most primitive of plows are in use; the Russians have sent snowplows to tropical Guinea in Africa. As one U.S. Department of State official

BLACK STAR

Economic and technical aid to needy countries has been a significant weapon in the efforts of the United States to combat world-wide communism. These U.S. cattle are being shipped to Iran as a part of a program to improve livestock in that country.

said in 1962: "They're no better than we are, and no worse. They're having their successes, and they're having their setbacks."

The government calculates that since 1955, when Communist aid programs were launched in earnest, the Communist bloc has committed $4.5 billion in economic aid and $2.1 billion in military aid to 28 so-called underdeveloped nations. Of this, the U.S.S.R. has spent $3.2 billion in economic aid; Communist eastern European satellites, about $950 million and Communist China, about $390 million. Communist help has flowed primarily (80 per cent of it) to eight countries: India, Indonesia, Egypt, Cuba, Afghanistan, Iraq, Ghana, and Syria.

Because terms, values, and project appraisals differ, comparisons with Free-World aid to underdeveloped nations can hardly be precise. However, since 1948 the United States has diverted almost $17 billion to military and economic aid *to the same 28 countries* and some $12.2 billion since the Communists began economic aid on a large scale in 1955. This $12.2 billion is almost twice the Soviet investment during that period.

As of mid-1962, the Communist bloc had nearly 8500 technicians busy on economic aid projects in underdeveloped lands — more, according to Washington figures, than the United States has in all the 80 countries it is helping.

The political problems of the newly emerging nations often tend to be even more difficult than the economic problems. In some cases the interests of America's European Allies clash with the interests of non-Communist peoples in Africa and Asia.

United States policy has been to strengthen those countries which seem ready and able to resist any international threat to their independence. For example, the Kennedy administration supported the regime of Cyrille Adoula in the Congo (1961) instead of the secessionist movement of Moishe Tshombe, despite the fact that Tshombe was the more outspoken anti-Communist. The administration stated that the Adoula regime had the best chance of holding the Congo together as a single non-Communist state. Support of Tshombe would undoubtedly have led to civil war, it reasoned, and dissolution of the young Congo state.

Had this occurred, the pro-Communist forces under Antoine Gizenga, in a northern province, would have been able to take control of a territory which would have served for later attacks on the balance of the Congo and other African territories to the south, very much on the model of Mao Tse-tung in China.

In Laos, the United States supported a coalition government under a neutralist, with the participation of Communists. But this situation was in a serious state of flux and tension, underscored in mid-1962 by the swift movement into Thailand of 5000 U.S. marines and soldiers to bolster the Thailand border against Communist incursions from Laos.

Along with military aid to governments under Communist pressure, the United States has revived the policy of stepping up economic and technical aid, believing that the will and spirit of the men fighting is just as important as the quality of the weapons with which they are fighting. It believes that successes of Communists in Asia and elsewhere hinge to a large extent on the unwillingness of the mass of the population to support their governments. This reluctance was due to miserable social and economic conditions prevailing in these countries. Thus the Free World has awakened also to the fact that military aid alone cannot block the inroads of communism.

The President has indicated his view of a long and difficult test of strength between the Soviet Union and the United States, with neither one able to destroy the other. He is confident, however, that the United States will succeed in defending the Free World from Soviet aggression and subversion without recourse to nuclear war.

VII. THE U.S. AND COMMUNISM AT HOME

The Communist party of the U.S. was formed in 1921, joined the Comintern and, despite many quarrels and splits in its ranks, has remained subservient to Moscow. Its organization and purpose are the same as the Communist party of the Soviet Union.

At the end of World War II the Communist party of the United States was at the peak of its power and influence, with 85,000 openly registered members and perhaps many more secret members throughout the nation. Some of these full-fledged party members and sympathizers infiltrated government offices, trade unions, and schools. Often they spread their influence by means of "front organizations." Secretly controlled by Communists, these "fronts" claimed to be working for worthy purposes while in fact they were advancing the interests of the Soviet Union. Eventually the FBI and rigid government loyalty programs weeded them out of their influential posts, not always, however, without harm to innocent people in the process.

In 1962 Arvo Gust Halberg (Gus Hall), general secretary of the CPUSA, counted membership at approximately 10,000, concentrated mostly in such major cities as New York, Boston, Philadelphia, Chicago, Detroit, Cleveland, Seattle, and San Francisco.

Reflecting the weak state into which the party has fallen is the party newspaper, the *Daily Worker*. From a daily circulation of 100,000 in 1945, it has become a twice-a-week publication of 20,000 copies in 1962.

Legal action against Communists in the United States has involved a long and complicated legal campaign. In October 1949, eleven leaders of the U.S. Communist party (including Hall) were convicted of advocating the violent overthrow of the United States government. Three years later, in March of 1952, after much additional appeal litigation, the United States Supreme Court upheld the sentences.

In 1954 the Communist party in the U.S. was outlawed by an act signed by President Eisenhower.

In the Immigration Act of 1957, amending the McCarran-Walter Act of 1952, "Persons who seek to enter [the United States] to engage in activities against the public interest and likely to endanger the welfare, safety, and security of the country" were excluded from the United States under the "subversive activities" provisions of the law.

In June 1961 the Supreme Court upheld the constitutionality of the registration provisions of the 1950 Internal Security Act, which required the Communist party to register as a Communist-action organization, to divulge its membership lists and the sources of its income. But the party did not register. Pressure mounted to force the Justice Department and Attorney General Robert Kennedy to act against the defiant Communists. On March 15, 1962, two party officers (Hall and Benjamin J. Davis, the party's national secretary) were indicted by a federal grand jury in Washington, arrested and freed on bond awaiting trial.

More dangerous than party members are the professional Soviet espionage agents such as Colonel Rudolf Abel who was caught in 1957 and identified as the highest-ranking Communist spy ever apprehended in the U.S. Abel was sent to the Soviet Union, after his conviction and imprisonment, in exchange for U-2 pilot, Francis Gary Powers.

Thus communism in the U.S. is manifest in the activities of the local Communist party and in the clandestine work of professional Soviet spies. The Federal Bureau of Investigation through open and covert activities, keeps watch over the conduct of both.

In general, the Kennedy administration has continued the vigilance of its predecessors in subduing the domestic menace of communism.

VIII. THE CRITICS

Criticism of present administration policies has been generally of two varieties: (1) calling for tougher measures against the Communists, and (2) calling for military disengagement in sensitive areas.

THE "GET TOUGH" CRITICS

A leading advocate of position one is Arizona Republican Senator Barry Goldwater, who contends: "Our strategy must be primarily offensive in nature." American economics must remain strong and we must "strive to achieve and maintain military superiority. We should adopt a discriminating foreign-aid policy. American aid should be furnished only to friendly, anti-Communist nations that are willing to join with us in the struggle for freedom."

Senator Goldwater maintains that "the world Communist movement is an outlaw in the community of civilized nations," and recommends withdrawing "diplomatic recognition from all Communist governments, including that of the Soviet Union."

Offensive tactics, according to the "get tough" critics of the administration's policies, should include an underground resistance movement in all Communist countries behind the Iron Curtain, "furnishing them with printing presses, radios, weapons, instructors." These critics call for a cautious, prudent, but courageous policy of encouraging captive peoples under communism to revolt.

Senator Goldwater supports the argument that the United States should rush mobile nuclear forces to crisis areas—such as Budapest in 1956. "An actual clash between American and Soviet armies," he reasons, "would be unlikely; the mere threat of American action, coupled with the Kremlin's knowledge that the fighting would occur amid a hostile population and could easily spread to other areas, would probably result in Soviet acceptance of the ultimatum [to withdraw]."

Such a policy, he goes on, would risk war, "but any policy short of a surrender does that. The risks I speak of are risks on our terms instead of Communist terms."

Supporters of this position see only two alternatives in the bipolar world of today. In the senator's words, either the Communists "will invite us in local crisis after local crisis to choose between all-out war and limited retreat, and will force us, ultimately, to surrender or accept war under the most disadvantageous circumstances. Or we will summon the will and the means for taking the initiative, and wage a war of attrition against them—and hope, thereby to bring down the internal disintegration of the Communist empire."

THE "DISENGAGE" CRITICS

Those who advocate disengagement believe that greater efforts toward negotiation with the Soviet Union can result in lessening the danger of war at a time when the confrontation of Soviet and American forces throughout the world threatens at any moment to unleash a nuclear war. They argue that, while the Soviet Union has not given up its doctrine of world revolution, it now believes that the best means toward that end is economic and social competition with the United States. The main purpose of this policy would be to disengage the opposing forces by negotiating joint withdrawals from areas of friction and contact.

The chief supporter of this view is George F. Kennan, author of the policy of containment, who was named Ambassador to Yugoslavia in 1961.

With his policy of containment made obsolete by weapons developments and internal changes within the Soviet Union, Kennan has suggested the mutual withdrawal of U.S., British, and Canadian, as well as Soviet troops, from central Europe; the unification and neutralization of Germany; the creation of a nuclear-free zone in Europe, perhaps all of Europe; a relaxed attitude toward the future of underdeveloped countries.

Kennan sees little hope of a middle road between disengagement and atomic war. As for limited wars, he regards these as no longer feasible with the development of tactical atomic weapons. Infantrymen armed with atomic bazookas, for example, might use this weapon in a limited war. The enemy might counterattack with larger atomic weapons, and so the process would grow until an all-out war was fought.

The withdrawal of U.S. forces from Europe, Kennan maintains, will not mean the collapse of Western Europe. The main Soviet threat, he says, will not come from conventional Soviet forces, but from internal political threats. This threat can be met best by strengthening "the internal health and discipline of the respective national societies . . . to prevent conquest by unscrupulous and foreign-inspired minorities."

Kennan concludes that disengagement in central Europe would permit the freer development, for example, of the Polish and Hungarian peoples, who are now occupied or surrounded by Soviet troops. This in turn would reduce the likelihood of another uprising such as that of 1956 in Hungary, which threatened to spread beyond the Hungarian frontiers.

There are many variations on these three main bodies of opinion and policy: (1) the pragmatic policy of the administration, (2) the "get tough" approach, (3) the disengagement approach. Each position poses serious problems and dangers. Disengagement, for example, might cause NATO's collapse, the gradual subversion of a united, neutral, disarmed Germany by a highly organized conspiratorial German Communist party. The "get tough" approach risks heightening tensions and the possibility of nuclear war, and the prospect of uncommitted nations leaning toward communism. The flexible and pragmatic approach of the administration requires enormous expenditures and risks losing those areas where local U.S. power is inferior to local Communist power.

These views reflect the great complexity of the problems that arise from the challenge of communism and the Soviet Union. Discussion of such opinions helps develop our understanding of these problems and underscores the vitality of the Free World in its search for peace with liberty.

CONCLUSION

Drawing lessons from history is an elusive and dangerous game. The Soviet Union today is a product of Russian history. But it is different in many ways from old Russia.

George F. Kennan, U.S. ambassador to Yugoslavia: "Let us by all means remain militarily strong and alert. . . .Relying for defense on our strength, let us . . . recover our composure and turn resolutely . . . to the doing of those things — both within our country and with relation to the outside world — that we ought to do, and ought to have been doing, even if Communist power had never reared its menacing head above the horizon of our world."

Milovan Djilas, Yugoslav author: "Every revolution and even every war, creates illusions and is conducted in the name of unrealizable ideals. . . .Contemporary Communism is that type of totalitarianism which consists of three basic factors for controlling the people. The first is power; the second is ownership; the third is ideology. They are monopolized by the one and only party, or — according to my previous explanation and terminology — by a new class; and at present, by the oligarchy of that party or of that class."

Senator Barry Goldwater: ". . . the affairs of nations are not determined by good-will tours, alms-giving, gestures of self-denial, rehabilitation projects, and discussion programs. The affairs of nations are determined — for good or evil — by power."

The tsar was an autocrat relying on the traditional institutions of the army, police, bureacracy, and church to maintain order. The Soviet system today is totalitarian. By totalitarian methods it seeks not only to maintain order, but to create a new kind of society. It relies on more subtle and powerful means than its tsarist predecessor to achieve these ends.

The key to the stability of the Soviet system has been the ability of the Communist party to manipulate the people under its control. It is very important to understand the word *manipulate.*

Lenin and Stalin believed that they could not do what they wanted to do if they permitted the Russian people the right to take part in the government. They also realized that they could not take power and hold it without some kind of support from the people. Therefore, they relied on a small group, the Communist

UNITED PRESS INTERNATIONAL

President John F. Kennedy, in 1961: "So let us begin anew — remembering on both sides that civility is not a sign of weakness, and sincerity is always subject to proof. . . . Let us never negotiate out of fear but let us never fear to negotiate . . . .Let both sides explore what problems unite us instead of belaboring those problems which divide us."

party, to make policy and to impose that policy on the people by manipulating them.

There were many ways of doing this. Terror was one way of getting things done, especially during the early Soviet period. Today the threat of terror is still used by the leaders. Propaganda is another way and economic reward still another. These and other methods of influencing people without their approval have been blended and alternated skillfully by the party to achieve its ends.

At the same time the control of the party over political life, the economy, and the cultural and educational institutions is so great that organized resistance to this manipulation is extremely difficult.

This method of ruling has not been entirely successful. It has cost a great deal of suffering. But the Soviet leaders have built a powerful military and industrial state without losing control of the Russian people. This system survived the test of World War II.

THE WORLD'S RESPONSE TO COMMUNISM 263

It now poses a real challenge to the free nations of the world. The tsarist government was never able to accomplish so much.

The authors urge strongly that you do not lay this subject aside as if it were finished, understood. They suggest that you make vigorous and honest efforts to learn more about the Soviet Union and communism. Your understanding will be a vital asset to free nations.

TERMS TO KNOW

Eisenhower Doctrine	Yalta Conference	CPUSA
CENTO	NATO	Truman Doctrine
Marshall Plan	policy of massive retaliation	SEATO

QUESTIONS ON THE CHAPTER

1. What principle of American foreign policy was established by the Truman Doctrine?

2. Why was it thought necessary for the United States to institute the Marshall Plan?

3. In what ways did the United States aid China during the years 1945-1949?

4. Briefly describe the policy of President Truman and his advisors with regard to the Korean war.

5. Between 1956 and 1958 three critical events took place, which caused the United States to form a new foreign policy. What were these three events, and what is the name of this foreign policy?

6. The meeting of strength with strength (the building up of our armed forces and weapons) is but one phase of the Kennedy administration policy. What is the other phase?

7. List some of the ways in which the United States has moved against the Communist party in the United States to counteract its subversive activities.

8. Name a leading advocate of the "get tough" policy and a leading advocate of the "disengage" policy. Briefly describe the major points of each policy.

QUESTIONS FOR DISCUSSION

1. In your own words, briefly explain the basis and purpose of the United States policy of containment.

2. During and since World War II, the United States has maintained a massive foreign aid program. The Soviet Union also has a program of aid to other countries. Compare these two programs in terms of (a) money (b) technical personnel (c) number of countries helped.

3. Methods used by the United States to assist underdeveloped countries to maintain their independence have varied from place to place. Compare the different moves made by the United States to assist the new Congo Republic, Laos, and Thailand.

4. United States policy on negotiation has two sides: (1) negotiations where power is balanced, and (2) intensive competition where power is not balanced. Explain briefly what, in your opinion, is meant by each of these aspects of our policy on negotiations with Communist powers.

BIBLIOGRAPHY

For Reference: □ Draper, Theodore, *American Communism and Soviet Russia.* The Viking Press, 1960. □ Kissinger, Henry A., *The Necessity for Choice: Prospects of American Foreign Policy.* Harper & Brothers, 1961. □ United States Senate, Committee on the Judiciary. *Exposé of Soviet Espionage.* U.S. Government Printing Office, 1960. □ United States Senate, Committee on the Judiciary. *Khrushchev's Strategy and Its Meaning for Americans.* U.S. Government Printing Office, 1960. □ United States Senate, Committee on the Judiciary. *The Technique of Soviet Propaganda.* U.S. Government Printing Office, 1960. □ Whitney, Thomas P., ed., *The Communist Blueprint for the Future.* E. P. Dutton & Company, Inc., 1962. **For Further Reading:** □ American Bar Association, *Peaceful Co-Existence: A Blueprint for Disruption.* The Association, 1962. □ Dulles, Foster Rhea, *America's Rise to World Power: 1898-1954.* Chapters 12, 13, 14. Harper & Brothers, 1955. □ Dunham, Donald, *Kremlin Target: USA.* Ives Washburn, Inc., 1961. □ Roberts, Henry L., *Russia and America: Dangers and Prospects.* New American Library, 1959. □ Stebbins, Richard P., *The United States in World Affairs, 1961.* Harper & Brothers, 1962.

INDEX

A

Abel, Rudolf, Colonel: Communist spy caught in U.S., 258

Acheson, Dean: U.S. secretary of state, U.S. government's position during Chinese conflict, 243

Adoula, Cyrille: regime in Congo supported by Kennedy administration, 256

Agriculture: Leftists advise wholesale reconstruction of, 131; Lysenko offered quick and easy way to improve, 176; never flourished in northern Russia, 14; Seven-Year Plan includes reorganization of, 140; widespread purges of personnel, 159

Alexander I (1777-1825), tsar: called the "enigmatic tsar," 45, concerned with foreign policy, 45

Alexander II (1818-1881), tsar: assassinated by Populists, 48, 66, illus., 49 reforms of, 47-48

Alexander III (1845-1894), tsar: crushed revolutionary organizations, 48; wiped out remnants of terrorist group, 66

Alexei I (1629-1676), tsar, 39

Alphabet: Russian alphabet based on Greek, 34

Anti-Communist pacts: Dulles advocates, 247-248

Anti-Semitism: mounting wave of, 183

Architecture: constructivist style, 169; functional form of American skyscraper captivates Soviet architects, 170; waiting room in Kiev, illus., 193

Armistice: signed ending wars in Korea and Indochina, 224

Arts: limited freedom in, 169

Asia: forward policy advances in, Communist approach, 222

Atheistic indoctrination: youth of Russia prime targets for, 108

Atomic bomb: Soviet Union has in 1949, 246

Atomic development: secret police control over, 101

Austria-Hungary: greatest rival of Russia in Balkan area, 51

"Autocracy, orthodoxy, and nationality": slogan to arouse loyalty of people, 46

Automobiles: 155; exhibit of Soviet-made, illus., 159

B

Baghdad Pact: regional defense organization later designated Central Treaty Organization, 248

Bakunin, Mikhail: Populists inspired by, 66

Baltic Sea: overall access to, 19

Beria, Lavrenti P.: head of secret police, 101

Berlin: failure to obtain security of precipitates crises, 218; Khrushchev demands that Western powers leave, 251; Khrushchev proposes setting up free city, 226; occupied by four powers, 217; Soviet Union blockades, 244; Stalin closed ground access routes to Western zone; 221; U.S. Dept. of State proposes creating corridor, 217

Bill of Rights: 1918 Constitution provides, 108

Bi-partisan foreign policy of U.S.: worked out between Republican and Democratic leaders, 240-241

Black-earth region: most fertile soil in USSR, 15; map, 13

Blok, Alexander, 169

Bolsheviks: choose dictatorial rather than democratic means of control, 93; key positions held by committeemen, 94; later became the Communist party, 106; Lenin's group split from Russian Social Democratic party, 69; seize power in November 1917, 92; volunteers for Red Army, illus., 92

Boundaries: western boundaries of U.S.S.R., 1914 to the present, map, 204

Boyars: upper nobility, 33

Bronstein, Lev Davidovich, see Leon Trotsky

Broz, Josip: see Marshal Tito

Building materials: of poor quality in U.S.S.R., 154

Bukharin, Nikolai Ivanovich: leader of group of rightists, 128, 129

Bureaucracy: of Communist party, control of by Stalin, 94

C

Canals: major canals in waterways system, 17; map, 19

Capitalism: Communist ideology designates as source of world's troubles, 55; labor as just another commodity under, 60; some restored during NEP, 127; theories of Marx regarding, 61

Capitalists: Communist strength strikes balance of power with, 79

Castro, Fidel: dictatorship in Cuba, 80; illus., 86

Catherine II, called the Great, (1729-1796), tsarina: agreement with Prussia and Austria to partition Poland, 45; illus., 44; traditionally grouped with enlightened despots, 44

Central executive committee: empowered to appoint Council of People's Commissars, 107; power to act when Congress of Soviets not in session, 107

Chiang Kai-shek: Chinese Communists regard as dangerous counterrevolutionary force, 230; Chinese Nationalists under, 242; Chinese Communists ordered to coöperate with, 207; studied military tactics in Soviet Union, 207; U.S. policy of limited support to, 243; U.S. sent aid to, 243

China: communism in, 83-85; Moscow-Peiping rift, 230; primitive labor, illus., 232; role in Soviet policy, 230 ff.; problems of food supply, 230

Chinese Civil War: broke out again in 1945, 242; U.S. policy during, 242

Chinese Communists: aim for strong role in Communist world policy-making, 231; dependent on Soviet Union for military support, 232; fear foreign intervention,

267